For Emma!

Sorry to [illegible]

a second time, but maybe it will feel different now we're getting to know each other (no doubt not for the first time!).

Love & blessings,

[illegible]

28/09/22

KARMIC RELEASE

Journeying Back to the Self

ANN MERIVALE

KARMIC RELEASE

First Edition, June 2006
ISBN 81-86822-66-6

Cover Illustration by Christine Shirley

Co-Published by
Message Publications
23/1142, V L Colony, Kadugodi,
Bangalore 560 067, India
www.saitowers.com

A catalogue record for this book is available from the British Library.

Typeset in Baker Signet, 11 pt.
Printed and bound in India by Vishruti Prints

DEDICATION

To

Paul, Alice

and Christopher

Ultimately it is not even the love of this Name and Form that you long for. Your deepest innermost urge is to return to yourself – to love yourself – to become the Being, the Awareness and the Bliss which is all you ever were and all you ever will be.

Inner message from Sai Baba to Joy Thomas, quoted in Life is a Dream – Realise It, Sri Sathya Sai Publications Trust, Prashanti Nilayam, Andhra Pradesh, India.

ACKNOWLEDGEMENTS

I am indebted firstly to Aron Abrahamsen, an "Edgar Cayce successor", whose past-life reading received in 1992 gave me the idea for this book, and to the well-known English clairvoyant Edwin Courtenay, who gave me both additional information about my previous lives and the conviction that I had a book worth publishing. Without David's, John's and Lawrence's constant encouragement, I would probably have given up whenever the going got tough. David, my husband of more than one lifetime, has always been ready to make useful stylistic comments, and Lawrence has very kindly read through many sections of the book and made invaluable suggestions for improvements. My former wife Maria (described by Edwin Courtenay as a woman of letters with long red hair and dressed in purple) is apparently my writing guide in this lifetime. Last but by no means least comes my beloved Lord, Bhagawan Sri Sathya Sai Baba, who finally led me to the right publisher, and at whose lotus feet I offer my entire life and work.

ABOUT THE AUTHOR

Ann Merivale was born in England in 1940, grew up in Oxford and Bristol, and graduated in French and Spanish from the University of Bristol. She worked for many years for organisations supporting the Third World. In Geneva she made use of her expertise in languages working with Catholic Relief Services and later as an editor with the World Council of Churches. There she met her husband, David Pearson, who is now Emeritus Professor of Mathematics of the University of Hull. After bringing up three children, Ann gave up language teaching in order to devote herself full time to research in spiritual matters, and writing and healing. In 1997 her first book, *CORDS THAT CANNOT BE BROKEN – A Study of Twin Souls*, was published under the pseudonym of Judith Merville. In 1998 she gained a diploma from the London College of Past Life Regression Studies under Dr. Keith Hearne. After further training with Dr. Roger Woolger, she was awarded his Diploma in Integral Regression Therapy in 2001. When they are not travelling to other parts of the world in pursuit of mathematics and/or spirituality, Ann and her husband live in Shropshire, England, where she runs a healing and counselling practice. She is also currently studying shamanic practices and working on a book about the Life Plan.

CONTENTS

INTRODUCTION

Although healing therapies, as well as healing therapists and their books on the subject, abound these days, it is often difficult to see the wood for the trees, and there is always a demand for more information. My own expertise is in regression, the aim of which is to uncover the root of a problem – be it physical, mental or emotional – to allow the client to work through it, and to encourage him or her to let go of it. More often than not the origins of everything that we experience can be traced to previous lives, although we do not need to believe in reincarnation for regression therapy to be effective. Immense relief can come – often extraordinarily quickly - through what Jungian therapists such as Dr. Roger Woolger call "psychodrama"[1]. Whether this transformation is experienced through reliving a past life, or whether it seems to the client more like a story they have made up, or the equivalent of a dream, may be immaterial.

Of the books already written on regression therapy, those of respected authors such as Woolger, Brian Weiss and Michael Newton do report on their clients' progress following regression, but I feel nevertheless that there is still a certain *lacuna* in the form of personal witness, which is partly what has prompted me to recount my own story. Even the late Joan Grant's beautiful books about her previous lives[2] do not aim to demonstrate how they affected her current one. A notable exception is the French regression therapist Denise Desjardins, whose compelling book *De Naissance en Naissance*[3] (*From Birth to Birth)* tells the story of her very

---

1. *Other Lives, Other Selves,* Roger J. Woolger, Thorsons, London 1999 & Doubleday, NY 1987.

2. All Joan Grant's books are published by Ariel Press, USA.

3. *De Naissance en Naissance – Le témoignage essentiel d'une vie antérieure,* Denise Desjardins, Editions de la Table Ronde, Paris, 1977.

tragic past life as an Indian orphan. Denise and her husband Arnaud Desjardins, who is also an author, travelled widely in India and Asia studying under spiritual masters, and – perhaps surprisingly for those who regard regression therapy as having originated in the West – she learnt the trade from Swami Prajnanpad, who took her in numerous lengthy and fascinating sessions back through the entire life of the orphan Sariputra.

For the regression therapist the only worth while purpose of recalling one's past is to benefit the present, and so I have endeavoured to show how working on my past has improved life for me now. But, since there are already numerous good books which explain the theory of regression, my aim also is to demonstrate the practice of the therapy.

Autobiographies may be of lesser interest if the author concerned is neither remarkable nor famous, and so I have made the sections about my present life brief. I am telling my story not because there is anything particularly exceptional about it, but as a graphic illustration of the workings of karma – a concept not yet fully understood in the West. The word *karma* is a Sanskrit one which literally means *action*, and it is commonly used to denote the law of cause and effect. The basic idea is very simple: if I throw a pebble into a pond there will be ripples. But the intricacies of the ripples are endless, as my own past life stories demonstrate.

Although belief in reincarnation is currently spreading rapidly in the West, alongside it often go a number of misconceptions. Typical of the remarks sometimes made to the regression therapist are: "I suppose you get people coming along who want to confirm that they were, for instance, Cleopatra"; "I certainly wouldn't like to go into any of my past lives. I'm sure it would be much too traumatic!"; "Of course in places like India people make excuses for not helping others on the grounds that their difficulties are their *karma*".

Well firstly, what purpose would it serve to find out that one had once been a famous historical figure? For a start, you could well meet half a dozen other people who also believed themselves to have been Cleopatra or whoever it was. I myself have not to date ever regressed anyone to the life of someone famous, and asking for regression merely out of curiosity is always to be discouraged.

Secondly - and this ties in with saying that undertaking regression from curiosity is not a good idea - it is quite true that it can be traumatic, but that is because it is the residues of trauma rather than the peaceful contented lives that we may still need to deal with. The great American Christian prophet Edgar Cayce, who died in 1945, was probably the first Westerner to be famous for his ability to read people's

Akashic[4] *Records*, but nowadays there is an abundance of clairvoyants who offer to read past lives. A good clairvoyant will in a past life reading give only those lives from which you at present need to learn – those of which the knowledge can be beneficial to your spiritual development. Similarly, in regression the subconscious will bring up what you need to know at that precise moment. Traumatic though it may be, a qualified regression therapist will never leave you embroiled in the trauma. Rather, I repeat, he or she will help you to work through it and then allow you to let go. Hence the dramatic "instantaneous cures" that are so often witnessed in this therapy.

Thirdly, anyone who studies spiritual matters in depth will soon learn that failure to give help where one could will only accrue bad karma for oneself. Even if it is true that some people do show a lack of caring for others on the grounds of their misfortune being their karma, this is very far from being the essence of either Hindu or Buddhist teaching. The great Paramahansa Yogananda, for instance, who first brought Indian spirituality to the West, says

I want to ply my boat, many times,
Across the gulf-after-death,
And return to Earth's shores from my home in Heaven.
I want to load my boat with those waiting,
thirsty ones who are left behind,
And carry them by the opal pool of iridescent joy,
Where my Father distributes,
His all-desire-quenching liquid peace.[5]

By this he means – just like the Buddhists who vow to keep returning to Earth even after they no longer need to for their own development - that he wants to go on and on indefinitely helping to bring to God those who are suffering.

Since everyone is unique, people vary immensely in their experiences of regression. Some go much deeper than others, some are very visual, while others get only feelings, sounds and/or smells. What really matters is to learn to trust whatever comes, however far fetched or "irrelevant" it may seem. The subconscious is in charge, and the subconscious knows best what one needs to deal with. I myself usually find that the images I get during regression are somewhat jumbled and by no means totally clear. Only when I sit down afterwards to write up the life does it all get sorted. For that reason I often advise my clients to write down their experiences

---

4. *Akash* means "ether". All that has ever happened since the beginning of time is recorded etherically.
5. This comes from Yogananda's *Man's Eternal Quest* and is quoted in the *Spiritual Diary – An Inspirational Thought for Each Day*, published by the Self-Realization Fellowship, California, 1996.

following a session. Though hypnotherapy is used widely for regression, it is not necessary, and even those who are regressed under hypnosis do not normally lose awareness of what is going on around them at the time.

Some of the most important healing work that we do in regression therapy is in what we call the *Bardo*, which is the state immediately after death. The word is a Tibetan one and it means "in an intermediate state" (literally *between islands*). The famous *Tibetan Book of the Dead* is actually a mistranslation of *Bardo Thodol.* It is the custom in Tibet to read the text of the *Bardo Thodol* to a person who is dying, to guide them on their way, and the word *Thodol* has to do with liberation through listening.

It is after a life is over that we can review it, see what its main lessons were (lessons that we can carry back into the present), find out what had been our chief purpose in that life and whether we had fulfilled it, confront those who hurt us and be reconciled with them and – most importantly of all – forgive ourselves for any wrongs committed. A regression session, therefore, will not normally end with the death of the past life character.

I actually started writing about my previous lives some time before I decided to train as a regression therapist - partly because I was so fascinated by the previous links with the members of my family and my friends that clairvoyants had told me about. Before writing up each lifetime I took vast numbers of books out of the library, and was looking forward to impressing readers with my erudition about the historical periods I was dealing with. But nothing can beat personal experience in all aspects of life. Once I had started working as a regression therapist, and consequently ceased to rely upon clairvoyants, I decided to rewrite this book more or less from scratch, using only the information that I had discovered myself. It has not been easy ditching the chapters I worked so hard on and always enjoyed re-reading, but, as I was so happy to learn at the end of my life as an astronomer (see pg. 197), no work that we do is ever completely wasted. I see this all now as part of my own healing process. Along the way also, I have relinquished the need to prove myself. A need given me by my father, who had condemned me as "no good for anything", and which was cured partly through regression therapy, partly thanks to my two good friends and therapists, Lawrence and John, each of whom appear in at least one of my past life stories.

Although the stories are personal, their themes are all universal ones which crop up over and over again in past life work. For that reason I have given each section of the book a generalised title in order to provide examples of typical issues that can be worked on in this therapy. To most sections also I have appended some simple exercises that anyone feeling so inclined can do on their own. The therapist can only really be a catalyst for self healing, and if we want to heal the world, we all need to begin by healing ourselves. These exercises contain elements which should be of use to most people, but if you find a blockage somewhere, or have a problem which you feel could really do with some professional help, you may wish to embark on some regression therapy yourself. Dr. Roger Woolger does many workshops in America and in Europe, and you can consult his web page (www.woolger.com) for the programme. To obtain a list of Woolger-trained therapists practising in Britain, you can either consult the Integral Regression Network (www.integralregression.org.uk) or get in touch with Jane May, Woolger Training International, Briarwood, Long Wittenham, Oxon. OX14 4QW, Tel. 01865 407996, email woolger.uk@talk21.com Jane can also send you a copy of Dr. Woolger's programme of introductory weekends and workshops. You do not need to be a Regression Therapy trainee in order to attend a one-week workshop, and many people have found them to be invaluable for their own healing.

I was born into a Christian family, but brought up by parents who found it difficult to show love, and it was the discovery of the Indian avatar Sathya Sai Baba that gave me firstly a belief in the love of God from personal experience, and secondly a desire to serve Him to the best of my ability. This book is therefore now offered primarily to Him, in the hope that it will help others on their own spiritual journeys.

I
A DIFFICULT BEGINNING

PART ONE
BIRTH - 9 FEBRUARY 1940

Some of you feel neglected by Me, when disappointment or trouble comes upon you. But such difficulties alone can toughen your character and make your faith firm. When you hang a picture on the wall, you shake the nail and find out whether it is firm enough to bear the weight of the picture. So, too, in order to prevent the picture of God (His image in your m ind and heart) from falling and being shattered to bits, the NAIL (i.e. God's name) driven in to the wall of the heart has to be tested by shaking it, to ascertain whether it is firm and steady.

Sathya Sai Baba

"A girl ?" Was that my father's horrified voice the other side of the bedroom door in my grandparents' house?

"Yes, a healthy girl. Congratulations! Come and have a look." That was certainly the midwife's voice. "Of course your poor wife's exhausted now after such a long and painful labour, but come in for five minutes. She'll be anxious to see you."

The door opened, but then there was total silence. Eventually I heard the man's voice again and became sure that it was my father's. "So it's a girl, is it?"

"Yes." A pause. "I'm sorry!" Another pause. "But she's rather lovely, don't you think?", pleaded my mother. Another silence.

"Looks like a drowned rat to me!"

"I'm sure all new-born babies look something like that."

"Do they? Well, at least it's all over. You'll be needing some sleep now. It's been a long time."

"Yes, I am very tired. But they say they'll have to wake me up every four hours to feed her."

"Every four hours? That won't give you much chance for a good rest."

"Never mind. I'm sure I'll survive. But I'm worried about you, who have had to stay up so late waiting. Are you going straight to bed now?"

"Yes, I'll get off to bed because, as you know, my train to London is quite early."

"Well, have a good day at work if I don't see you before you leave. Good night."

I lay in the crib and before long my msother's breathing changed. She had obviously fallen into the much needed sleep. So was this the new life on Earth I had chosen to enter? A father whose work seemed to be more important than his new family, and who didn't even like the look of a new-born baby. Worse still, who thought that a girl was of no value! Well, I had been warned, hadn't I? I had been told another soul would volunteer for this life if I didn't want to, but I had insisted. But then, when I had been up there a few months ago discussing the decision, a lot of my soul group had been around; and of course my guardian angel had reminded me just before I left that other world that he had been with me right through all my previous incarnations and would never leave my side. But where, oh where were they all now? There seemed to be no-one here at all. Only my mother, whom I didn't know very well, and who was sound asleep anyway. When I had been fighting my way out through that dreadfully narrow canal an hour or two ago, my aunt and my grandmother and several other women had been around too, but now they had all disappeared. Ah well, perhaps it was time for me to have some sleep too.

******

I was still tired from the effort of the birth, and yet here I was being woken up even before I had left my body! Someone dressed in white was putting me into my mother's arms, and now they were forcing something into my mouth and telling me to suck. Suck? What did that mean? I turned my head away, but the big brown thing was immediately thrust back into my mouth.

"Don't worry if she isn't very hungry yet. Sometimes they take a while to learn to suck, but we must just keep trying." Now the thing was being pushed still further into my mouth and suddenly some liquid came out of it. It trickled down my throat, and automatically I made a little movement with my lips and then some more of the liquid came.

"That's a clever girl," said the woman in white. "Keep it up."

Keep it up? Keep what up? The liquid trickling down my throat was not unpleasant, but it seemed a rather useless occupation when all I really wanted was sleep. Eventually I was put back into the crib, and quickly I was back where I belonged[1]. And there, thank goodness, were my friends!

"I don't know what's going on," I said to them. "I've been having a terrible time. I'd completely forgotten how awful it was being born! In fact this may have been the worst birth I've ever been through. You can't imagine the feeling of utter powerlessness when you're stuck for ages and ages with no-one giving you any help at all. I was really torn because on the one hand I knew I had to fight my way through that narrow passage, but on the other hand I really didn't want to get out at all. When it was finally over I understood why, because I obviously wasn't welcome in the world. I felt completely unloved and abandoned, even though there were a couple of women in uniform seeing to me. Then, to make matters worse, I wasn't even allowed to sleep when I needed it, my father made rude remarks about my appearance, and a big brown thing was thrust into my mouth...."

"That's because you're back on Earth now," said one of my best friends. "Remember that you volunteered to be born as a girl to people who were hoping for a son? You knew that, although your mother was a very sweet and loving person, she wouldn't be able to stand up to your father's criticism, and that you weren't going to be given the love that a baby needs. Remember how you said you were ready to take on a pretty tough incarnation this time because you felt you were strong enough and still had certain lessons to learn such as patience and perseverance?"

"Yes, that's true, it's all coming back now. I said I'd like to help people through therapy and writing, and that having first to work through certain difficulties would be good preparation for that.... Oh, but look. Here comes Sai Baba!"

"Sai Ram[2], dear friend! I'm appearing to you to you now in the form in which

1. We always leave our bodies during sleep. The soul is attached to the body by a silver cord, which enables speedy return upon waking. This cord is severed only on death.

2. *Sai Ram* means "The God in me salutes the God in you". It is the normal phrase used for greeting in Sai Baba's ashram.

you knew me during one of your most recent lives on Earth, but in fact I've now returned there in a different body – one which will never grow as tall as this one that I had in Shirdi. I am now Sathya Narayana Raju and am only fourteen years of age, but very soon I shall be leaving school and declaring myself as Sathya Sai Baba. Some of my former devotees will come to recognise me as the reincarnation I foretold shortly before my death in 1918. You did well to choose to be reborn during the year in which I shall begin my mission, because I shall be calling you back to me later on."

"Later on? Are you in Bharat[3] again? Why couldn't I have been born there so that I could be close to you all the time?"

"Of course I understand your love for Bharat, which has been your homeland many times, but this time your work is to be in the less spiritual West, where many people still need educating in some of the things most dear to your heart. I will put you through some tests before I eventually call you, later on in your life. This will be to make you stronger, and I assure you that you will be rewarded for it in due course. But now you must return to that little baby's body, which will shortly be woken up for another attempt at teaching you to feed at your mother's breast. Try to remember how strong you are, that you belong to me, and that you can always call on your friends for assistance and advice. If you take up meditation again when you are older, that will help you to be in tune with your spiritual helpers."

PART TWO - 1997

I had been studying the question of reincarnation in depth for a good five years now, my book on twin souls was soon to be published, and I had developed a strong desire to train in regression therapy. A desire which was reinforced when I attended one of Dr. Roger Woolger's introductory weekends in London. When I talked to him at the end of the weekend, however, he said that I was too much "in my head" and that he would not train me until I had done some body work. (I later came to learn that focus on the body was the cornerstone of Woolger therapy, since we store all our *samskaras* (karmic residues) in our etheric bodies and they get re-imprinted on to our new physical bodies when we reincarnate. But people who have a traumatic childhood tend to flee the body in order to escape the pain, which makes starting regression from sensations in the body difficult.) In the meantime I firstly enrolled for a course with the London College of Regression Studies, and secondly took Roger's advice and had some sessions with one of his graduates who specialised in body work.

3. *Bharat* is the Indian name for India.

It was this therapist who regressed me to my birth in this lifetime, and what a powerful experience it was! I had already tried hypnotherapy for my backache but had proved to be one of the ten per cent of the population who are "unhypnotisable". I had made repeated efforts with a "regression tape" that my clairvoyant friend Edwin Courtenay had made for me, had even travelled a hundred miles to visit a therapist who did regression without hypnosis, and had come to the conclusion that I was "unregressable" as well as "unhypnotisable". In fact this complex I developed was reinforced when the latter therapist wrote me off because I was the first client she had ever had who had not gone "straight to the root of the problem". She made me feel that I was "unregressable" despite the fact that I had got a very clear picture of a town on fire and walking away from it into a drab and dreary existence with an old man who did not speak to me! (I hasten to add that she was not trained by Roger Woolger. In fact I do not think she was trained at all – a thing I would not recommend to anyone interested in performing regressions.)

However, the regression to my birth, done with the aid of cushions held tightly around me to simulate being inside the womb, brought back extraordinarily clear memories of what I had suffered at that time. A few more sessions, combined with a lot of "inner child" work done on my own, subsequently helped me to release the pain that lack of love inevitably gives to a child. Reliving the pain does not erase the memory, but with time and effort one can reach the point where it no longer affects us. According to Buddhism, total acceptance of what is is vital for our spiritual development; only when we stop saying "No" can we escape rebirth.

As for the dialogue with my soul group on the other side, and with Sai Baba of Shirdi, whom I would come to know later on in this life as Sathya Sai Baba, the Indian avatar[4] of our age, that came to me later in meditation. Finding my path in this life has been a gradual process. A Plan for each of our lifetimes is made in advance, and some discover it quickly and easily while others have much more difficulty, but that is the subject of a future book.

---

4. *Avatar*, which literally means *descent* in Sanskrit, is the word used for "divine incarnation". In contrast to Christianity, which maintains that Jesus is the only divine incarnation ever, in India it is widely believed that the Lord incarnates on Earth whenever we have gone so far astray for it to be necessary. It is claimed not only that Sathya Sai Baba was previously the well known saint Sai Baba of Shirdi, but that He also incarnated as Rama and then as Krishna.

EXERCISES

I. Did you have parents/a parent who did not appreciate you for exactly who you were, and with whom you consider your relationship to be not entirely as you would desire? If so – and this applies equally whether they are alive or dead – you could try the following:-

a) Write a letter to him/her (if it is both parents, do the exercise first for one and then for the other) expressing all your feelings of anger, resentment, bitterness, etc. When you have said everything that you have been wanting to say for years and years, make up your mind that it is now time to let go of it all and burn the letter (making sure that you are either over a sink or out of doors!).

(b) Give some thought to what you know about the relationship that your parent(s) had with their parents and do your best to imagine the sort of difficulties that they must have been through on account of it. You may well find parallels with your own relationship(s), and this should help you firstly to appreciate that their actions were based on what they knew, and secondly to forgive them for having been unable to give you what you feel you needed.

(c) Imagine yourself as a young child and remember the feelings caused by the difficult relationship with your mother/father. Now imagine your mother/father as the same age and make a playmate of her/him. Then visualise the grandparent who gave your parent a difficult time and feel the two of you protecting each other from him/her. Repeat the exercise until you find that you can both stand up to the grandparent, but try to argue your case politely and don't get aggressive.

(d) Ask yourself what you learnt from the difficulties that you went through. Have they made you stronger? More independent? Did it make you resolve to have a better relationship with your own children? There is a reason for everything that happens to us in life, so resolve to view all your past experiences as positive learning ones.

2. Even if you had no big problems in relating to your parents, was your childhood in any way less happy/good than you would have liked? Jung said that we need to experience all four stages of life – childhood, adolescence, maturity and old age – but that it does not matter in which order we do them. If you feel that you missed out on, say, childhood, why not make up your mind to enjoy it now? Buy yourself some huge pieces of paper and some paints and have fun messing about with them. Do something "naughty" like climbing over a forbidden fence (so long as there is no risk involved!) or eating far too much ice-cream. Go to the seaside and make a

huge sand castle. Put yourself before everyone else and do just what <u>you</u> want for a few hours.... (N.B. This exercise also applies to those who need to work through No. 1.)

3. When you get up in the morning, ask your inner child (we all have one!) what he/she would like to do today, then send him/her off to do it (finding him/her an accompanying spirit guide if necessary) while you get on with your work.

4. If you have a relationship with, for instance, a parent (alive or dead) that you feel to be really detrimental to your well being, you might like to consider performing a tie-cutting exercise with them. You could use Phyllis Krystal's book *Cutting the Ties that Bind*[5], or find a therapist to help you with it. (I for many years had scary dreams about my father, and they stopped instantly as soon as I had performed a tie-cutting exercise under the guidance of a friend.)

---

5. Published by Sai Towers Publishing, Bangalore, India.

II
SHEDDING OUTDATED LABELS

PART ONE - HOSPITAL 1945

How horrid it was being in here, and how sore my throat was after the operation! Eating was difficult, except for the ice-cream which was quite soothing, but I had to be a good girl and make an effort. Of course being a good girl seemed to be impossible for me – that was what Daddy always said anyway – but at least people would be less cross with me if I ate up most of my dinner. Yesterday that had been particularly difficult. They had brought me a plate full of different bits and pieces, but the only thing on it that appealed to me at all was the tomato. So I decided to leave that till last, as a little treat for myself at the end. Swallowing was really painful, and the canned meat seemed to stick in my throat however much I chewed it. Why did God make people with tonsils if they had to be taken out? It didn't make any sense!

"I see you're not hungry," the nurse had said as she swept my plate away still adorned with the appealing slices of tomato. Why had I been too shy to protest? How silly I am! Surely she would have understood if I had explained, but talking to grownups was so difficult. Ah well, perhaps there will be tomato again today, in which case I shall make sure to eat it straight away. But there's no sign of lunch yet and I'm sleepy. Then even after lunch it will be a long, long time till Mummy comes to see me. Of course it's not her fault that the days here are so long and boring. She can't come till after she's put Sandra and Christian to bed. I wonder what Mummy would have said last night if I had told her about losing my tomato? I expect she would have thought me terribly silly. No, I'd never dare tell her... Oh, how sore my throat is, and how sleepy I feel.

BANG! What happened? Oh, I must have fallen out of bed while I was asleep. I'd better get back in quickly, or they'll be cross.

"What are you doing you stupid girl? Don't you remember I said you shouldn't get out of bed?"

I hadn't been quite quick enough. It was difficult when I was in a bit of a daze after landing on the floor with such a bump. Then Sister tucked me in so fiercely and ticked me off so severely for getting out of bed that I was too scared to explain that I had fallen out in my sleep. "Stupid," she said I was. That's just what Daddy always said too. They must be right! After all, if I weren't stupid I wouldn't have been too shy to say that I'd fallen out, or that I wanted the tomato yesterday.... Yes, that's what I am – just stupid. STUPID!

PART TWO - THE VILLAGE IDIOT

"STUPID! He's stupid. Come on, let's get him. He's no good. He made a right mess of those bricks he was supposed to be sorting yesterday."

"That's right. He put the rejects in the pile with the good ones, and even started breaking up some of the good ones for rubble. Lucky I noticed before too much damage had been done!"

"Our nice new church won't be much good if we have people like <u>him</u> helping to build it!"

"Helping? You can't call what he does helping. He's just an idiot!"

"Look at that. Thinks he can run faster than us. Come on, let's show him!"

They were drawing closer and closer. A whole huge crowd of them. Why can't they just leave me alone? I'm too weak to run much faster now. I've hardly had a thing to eat all day – only those crusts that kind Patricia managed to salvage for me. But I'd better keep on running or they'll catch up, and then I dread to think what they might do to me. They could bash my brains out. They nearly did the other day, when they made me fall on to that rock I'd had to carry up the hill. Brains? Have I actually got any brains? Well, probably I haven't. That's why they all say I'm so stupid. All except Patricia, that is. But she's much too good for me. I could never tell her how much I love her even if I were good at talking. Which I'm not. That's another reason they all laugh at me. Oh, they've just about caught up now and I can't run any more. I'm going to fall. I know I'm going to fall...

"Doppit! L-l-l-leaf me... leaf me..."

"What does that mean?" jeered Wilfred. "Doppit, leaf – those aren't words at all. You can't even talk proper. You're just a stupid idiot!"

"That's right, an idiot," joined in Charlie, kicking me hard on the shin. "Why don't you just stay put in your little hovel and leave us who know how to build get on with the work?"

"N-need work.... Ungry..."

"You'll be ungrier still when we've finished with you," said Jack, kicking me on the other shin. And so they carried on relentlessly, a dozen of them or more, till I was black and blue all over and it was almost nightfall. I couldn't move from pain and exhaustion, and I was scared I would die of cold if I spent the night out there, near the cliff edge. I didn't know what to do. Then suddenly I remembered how Louisa had taught me to pray years ago, when I was a little boy. I couldn't remember the words of the prayers she'd taught me, but I did remember her faith that they would be answered. So under my breath I murmured "God, if you exist, please help me. PLEASE!" Then I fell asleep.

What's that nice soft thing on top of me? I opened my eyes. Oh, it's a quilt!

"I guessed I'd find you somewhere around here." It was Patricia's gentle voice. "I heard them bragging about how they'd left you to die. I had to be careful, though, getting out of the house with these, because my parents won't let me go out after dark. I didn't dare light the torch till I was right away from the village, but I know the path pretty well. Look, I've smuggled you a morsel of duck and a few bits of vegetable in this kerchief. Mother says we can't afford to feed the poor because we've barely enough for ourselves, but I wasn't very hungry this evening anyway. We don't have duck very often, but Father got this one off the pond this afternoon.

Suddenly I realised how hungry I was. I struggled to sit up, but Patricia had to help me. I wondered whether I would ever walk again.

"Oh, you poor thing! They really have hurt you badly this time. I'm going to tell my father what swines they are, but I'm afraid he'll say he can't do anything. Who was your father, by the way? They say Louisa never married."

"Lou-Lou-Louisa not my mudder. She died."

"Your mother died, did she? So is that why no-one ever explains how Louisa came to have you? But she cared for you well, didn't she? You must miss her now."

How I yearned to tell kind Patricia the whole story. If only it weren't so difficult for me putting things into words! She might understand what it had felt like being brought up just by an old woman, feeling different from everyone else who had families to live with. Louisa sometimes used to talk to me about my mother. Said she was a real beauty and so young to die. It was really sad. She died giving birth to me. In fact I nearly died too, she said. Such a difficult birth, and when I was finally out I didn't breathe for what seemed like ages. I was all blue and they didn't know what to do. In the end it was Louisa herself who shook me and got me to yell. After that she felt she had no choice but to take me in. Well, there wasn't anyone else to do it. My grandparents were both dead, and my mother would never say who my father was. Just that he wasn't from our village and that she hated him anyway.

Yes, it would have been nice to be able to explain all that to Patricia, but she had to hurry home anyway before anyone noticed her absence. She wanted me to walk home, but she realised that I wasn't up to it, so she just put her shawl under my head for a pillow and said she hoped I would be all right in the morning. Yes, I would be all right with this nice thick quilt over me, and I could just lie there and daydream about what it would be like to be handsome and able to talk well and have the courage to propose to Patricia.

A few days went by. I was still aching and sore, but I had managed to struggle home while no-one was looking. If you could call Louisa's little hovel home, that is. Well, it was the only home I had ever known, and Louisa had done her best to keep it spick and span right up until the last weeks of her illness. How hard, though, those last weeks had been! Louisa was handy with a needle, and right through the time I was growing up she had managed to get enough odd jobs here and there to keep us both from starvation. But when her eyesight started going it got more and more difficult. Sometimes I went out and begged, but I could never go into the village without someone shouting names at me or even throwing stones. It made sense of course that they should treat me like that since I was so stupid, but it didn't seem fair when I was trying to help Louisa. When she started coughing so badly and couldn't get out of bed, I just had to do something. That's when I persuaded the master builder to take me on, though it was difficult convincing him that I would be of any use.

Patricia used to visit Louisa. Sometimes she brought her herbs for the cough, but in the end of course nothing could save her. She was really old by then. She probably only lived as long as she did because of me. She always worried about what would happen to me when she'd gone. I worried about it too, but I tried not to show it. The day she died I just wanted to die too. When Patricia came she felt so sorry for me. It was her parents who got the priest to do the funeral for free. They were quite kind too really in some ways.

But that was the past. Now I had to find a way of living on my own without being dependent on food from Patricia's house. Building the church was the only work there was at the moment in our little village. So as soon as my bruises had more or less healed, I showed up again.

"Where have you been the last few days?" asked the master builder. "I can't afford to have people slacking."

"Sick," I pleaded.

"Sick? We need strong young men on this job. Well, I'll just give you one more chance. Go fill that barrow over there with some of the best bricks and take it to where they're just starting on the first pillar."

How hard I worked all day! It was exhausting, but at least I got a meal at the end of it. And Wilfred and his pals left me alone too. Perhaps I would be able to carry on like this for a few weeks. A few months? A few years? Well, it would take years to build this beautiful church. Perhaps none of us would live to see it completed. But what would happen to me before that, when I was too old to work? Patricia would surely have a family of her own by then. She wouldn't want to bother with me any more.

I set off for a walk. There was no point in worrying now about the future. I had enough to worry about just getting through each day. I wandered away from the village along the path leading to the cliff edge. My life might be full of sorrow, but it was a beautiful place to spend it, that had to be admitted. I sat down near to where I had been left lying in such pain a few days previously, gazing out to sea. It was very peaceful. The sun was setting on the Moors behind me, throwing its last rays on to the sea below. Those Moors which I had never really explored, but which, Louisa used to tell me, stretched for miles and miles with hardly any dwellings. The North Sea so cold and hostile.... Hostile, yes, in some ways, but yet it was also my friend. My friend because it was always there; because it never called me names.

"There he is, the idiot Julius!" It was Wilfred's voice behind me.

"Aha, you thought you'd escaped us today, but we saw you currying favour with the master."

"Yes, we did," added Jack, "and we thought we'd have a little game this evening. How about a little game, folks?"

"What would you like to do with him?" asked Justin.

"Well look, I've got a good strong rope here. Why don't we tie him up into a ball and then play catch?"

"Yeah, that sounds good fun!"

I screamed as the rope dug through my clothes right into my flesh, but that only made them pull it even tighter. There was no way I could fight to get free amongst all of them, and in no time I was hurtling through the air. First Charlie caught me, then Wilfred.... Then Justin yelled "Oh God, I've missed!" Flying through the air was the most terrifying experience of my life, and now the flight was lasting longer. The next thing I felt was the massive pain of my head striking a rock, and then straight away there I was looking down at my body stretched out on the beach, with blood spurting from my forehead.

PART THREE
MICKLETON HALL – OCTOBER 2000

Gosh, that was scary, when Roger picked me up and dropped me on to the mattress! It was the first time that he had chosen me to demonstrate on at a workshop, and I was surprised at the extent to which I had got into the life of a village idiot. Next he made me go through parts of the life again and look for the origin of that notion of being stupid.

"You had a speech impediment?" he asked.

"Yes, I seemed to have."

"Right, let's try and see where that came from. On the count of three you're to go back to your birth."

And what a traumatic birth it was! When it was all over, Roger applied his logic again. "When you were first born, you didn't breathe for a bit. That meant a lack of oxygen to the brain, so is it surprising that you had a speech impediment?".... "And so were you really stupid?".... "And what about Ann? Is she stupid?"

"Well, my father certainly thought so."

"Whatever grounds did your father have for thinking that? You're a good linguist, you've got a degree, you've written a book..."

"And perhaps one day," I laughed, "most difficult of all, I might manage to get a Woolger diploma!"

"Aha," Roger smiled, "you will. Maybe sooner than you think."

My fellow trainees were laughing too now, and when they had put their questions to either Roger or myself, we went back into our pairs.

"Yes, I suppose it is about time," I said to my partner, "that I let go of the notion of being stupid.... But no wonder it was so deeply ingrained!"

"These things always are, but can you let go now of that nonsensical idea about being stupid?"

"I can certainly keep working on it," I laughed. Later I thought about going to nursery school in Oxford when I was four and how I could already read and so had rapidly exhausted all the books they had on the shelf. Yet despite that, when I was at the primary school in Bristol and helped the other children in the class with their reading, I wasn't allowed to move up into the next class at the end of the year. No-one asked the reason. My mother didn't know whether it was because they had made a mistake about my age – everyone in our family grew late – or whether it was because they had found me useful helping the others with their reading. Many years later she told me secretly that she suspected the latter, but at the time my father had thought it was because I was so stupid.

Then I remembered the agonies of learning to ride a bicycle. It was scary and I always fell off as soon as Mummy let go of the saddle. Night after night I would dream that I had learnt to ride. It was a wonderful feeling, and the disappointment when I woke up and realised it was only a dream never got any better. But of course I did master the bicycle eventually, and now, following the regression, I could at last finally let go completely of that idea of being stupid!

Then Suzanne asked me whether any of the characters I had seen in the regression were familiar to me now. I thought deeply and suddenly it dawned: Patricia was my current friend Patrick. "I really don't know how I know," I said to her, "but it's a really strong feeling. And helping someone that no-one else would help is exactly the sort of thing he would do now."

"How interesting! I agree, it is strange when you recognise someone from a previous life even when they look completely different. I suppose it's something about their soul quality that you can just feel."

EXERCISE

Think about any labels that you have given yourself over the years, or that other people have given you. Write them down in two lists, putting the negative ones on the left hand side, the positive ones on the right. Which list is longer? Now look carefully through the negative ones and see whether there are any that you can cross off immediately because they are no longer appropriate. Have you got any left now? If you have, get some sticky labels. Now write the first of the negative adjectives on to one of your labels and stick it on to your forehead. Leave it there for not more than a minute, saying to yourself "This label belongs to the past. I don't need it any more." Now remove it, look at it again and think of a positive adjective with which to replace it (e.g. stupid – intelligent, plain – attractive). Write your new adjective on to another label and put the negative one into the bin. Repeat the process until all your outdated labels are in the bin. Now, one by one, put your new labels on your forehead and leave them there for as long as you like/can. (You can take days or weeks over this bit of the exercise; it doesn't matter.) While the new label is on your forehead, say to yourself over and over "I am intelligent/attractive/ resourceful/ patient...." – whatever it is, letting the meaning of the word really sink in to the depths of your being. When you have reached the point of truly believing it, give yourself a pat on the back.

III
SPIRIT RELEASEMENT

PART ONE
THE SECOND WORLD WAR

It was 1945. Following my grandfather's retirement, my grandparents had just moved to a huge house they had bought in Somerset. My aunt who was a primary school teacher lived with them, and I was taken there from hospital to convalesce after having had my tonsils and adenoids out. It was my fifth birthday, and my kind aunt, who had taught me to read before I went to nursery school, made a chocolate cake, but I didn't have any fun in that big, cold house, where my grandmother always told me that I wasn't a good girl and didn't do enough to help my mother. At night I was kept awake by the owls hooting outside. I knew they were only birds, yet the noise they made was <u>so</u> scary – even more scary than the sound of the sirens at night in Oxford. To this day (2004) the sound of sirens sends shivers down my spine, yet during the war I never really gave them any thought. I had just got used to them, I suppose, whereas the sound of the owls was something quite new and different, and it made it hard to sleep in the big bedroom all by myself when I was used to sharing a room with my sister.

Not long after I got home again, Mummy kept turning on the radio and saying that we might hear any moment that the war had ended. I have no recollection of getting the news that it had ended, but I have a very clear memory of being given my first banana to eat, and a really vivid memory of our first ice-cream. That impressed me a great deal more than the banana did, and is still a huge weakness of mine, but the thing I remember most about it was Sandra putting hers by the fire because it was too cold. I can still see the saucer of milk and my poor little sister's astonished face!

So no, I do not remember hearing that the war had ended.....

PART TWO
A SPIRIT RELEASEMENT, MAY 2003

For the third year in succession I was in the south of France with a small group of fellow Woolger graduates. Our good friend Kris and his partner ran a guest house not far from the Pyrenees, which was a perfect setting for workshops, and Kris himself had achieved a real mastery of combining participation with very efficient organisation. It is important for therapists not to give up working on themselves as well, and the bonds of friendship and trust that we had built up between us facilitated work of the most profound nature and enabled deep transformation to take place.

On the first day my friends gave me the opportunity to talk at some length about the difficulties I was experiencing in being unable to help my sister in her present troubles, and after a while I slipped into a lifetime in which I was being pinned down by a very brutal man whose job was keeping me prisoner in a castle. I felt that I had been tightly bound in a sort of bandage made from rough sackcloth and was fighting furiously to break free. The story, however, was not completed in that session, and somehow, under Grace's skilled hands, I went back to the womb in my present life, and there it was found that a part of my soul had split off before my birth[1] on account of the difficulties that I knew this life would bring to me. Before helping me to reintegrate that split off part, Grace suggested that I compare my own envy of that part of me that was still "free up there" with the envy that my sister feels of my life, which obviously looks to her freer and easier than her own.

The next morning I noticed that a rash had appeared on my neck, and over the next couple of days it spread to other parts of my body and became increasingly

1. See *SOUL RETRIEVAL: Mending the Fragmented Self,* Sandra Ingerman, Harper SanFrancisco, 1991.

itchy. So on the morning before we were due to go off to Rocamadour for a two-day holiday, everyone agreed that another regression was called for....

The Soldier Who Never Found Out That The War Had Ended

They had taken our castle – those wretched invaders! How dare they? I would go on fighting until we got it back. I was young, my horse and I were both strong, my sword was sharp, and I knew we could defeat them in the end despite the numbers of my companions who were falling to the ground around me. Yelling, blood, the clashing of sword against sword, the noise of sword being broken on armour, the deafening neighing of frightened horses, and cries of revenge or despair, surrounded me, yet nothing would deter me from doing my bit for my country and fellow countrymen. I had already killed several enemy soldiers and now I was plunging my sword into the little gap between helmet and armour of yet another of those treacherous cowards. You had to aim very carefully and it was not easy, but how good it felt when you hit the right spot and the blood came spurting out as the villain fell to the ground! But then suddenly I lost my balance too. My dear horse reared as an enemy horse came too near to him, and I was thrown to the ground, where I was kicked and trampled on. I tried to get up (I said I wasn't going to be defeated and I meant it), but I got kicked again, and my armour dug into my flesh until I was bleeding almost as much as I had seen those dying around me. My next attempt to get up was thwarted by a riderless horse running directly towards me, and then I suddenly realised with horror that in falling to the ground I had lost my own horse.

Before I had had time to decide on my next move, I found myself being picked up and carried off the field by a couple of burly men. They tore off my armour brutally and when I protested, they bound me up in sackcloth so that I could barely move. The next thing to happen was that I was carted up some stairs in one of the towers of the castle and hurled to the floor of a room right at the top of it. I struggled and struggled to get free, which made the horrid sackcloth chafe even more against my skin, and then I was made to sit up and drink some water and eat a piece of bread. Thirsty though I was, it was almost impossible to swallow, and one of the men pushed the cup against my lip until he had drawn blood. I choked on the bread which they forced into my mouth, and then started coughing up a mixture of crumbs, blood and water. What a nightmare, but I was going to show them that they could not get the better of me. Soon they left me lying there alone, locking the door behind them. My body was sore and aching, but I thought much less about that than about how to escape. I was strong and so it should not be too difficult to break free from these wretched bandagey things and then attack my captors.

I did not have to wait too long. After struggling desperately for several more minutes, suddenly I found myself free, and at that very moment in came the most vicious looking of the men who had been forcing me to eat and drink. He left the door unlocked, so I got up, gave him an almighty kick, which must surely have thrown him to the ground, and fled down the stairs as fast as my now weak legs would carry me. I then crossed the courtyard to a little iron gate, which fortunately proved also to be unlocked, and made my way to a wood that I could see in the distance. I thought that if I stayed there till nightfall, then slept till the morning, I would have a good chance of getting back to my own army without being seen. The wood was quiet and peaceful, and I made myself quite a comfortable bed of leaves. I tried to sleep, but the toowit-toowooing of owls made that impossible. As night drew in I started to feel cold and, though one bit of my mind knew quite well that the noise was only birds, I became terrified. Images of witches and monsters came into my head, and I just lay shivering with fear until dawn...

******

"Now go back to the castle, have a look at that bruised, bandaged body, and see whether it's alive or dead." It was Nicholas' firm voice, and Grace was reiterating what he was saying. They were my friends, Ann's good, intelligent, highly trained friends, yet the Ann who was reliving her life as a soldier wanted to say to them "Don't be silly. What's the point in going back to the castle? I've escaped. It's dawn now and I'm walking towards a little cottage I can see in the wood. There might be a kind woman there who will dress my wounds and give me some food and drink." But they were becoming more and more insistent. "Think about what happened. You fell off your horse. You got kicked and trampled on. Your body is bruised and sore, you've probably got some broken bones.... Now go back to the castle. Have a good look at that body and just see whether it's alive or dead."

Of course I didn't want to go back to the castle, our castle, which those accursed invaders had wrongfully taken over, but the whole little group around me were so insistent that I felt I had no choice. It took me no time at all to get there, and as soon as I entered the room I had to admit that the body lying on the floor, which looked like mine, was not breathing. Then Esmeralda made me see that I and my companions – for there was now a big group of us who were trying to rejoin our own army –

really had nothing at all to do with Ann's body and had never belonged there. She talked to us telepathically, telling us that the war was over and encouraging us to call on deceased relatives or friends who could escort us to the light. So they came, and they led us away from that woman's body and from Earth, and lo and behold there was light, peace and beauty on the other side....

And while all this was going on, I as Ann was working hard at distinguishing myself from that soldier's life that I had just relived. I knew that it was not uncommon for people not to realise that they had died, and I knew all about the theory of spirit attachment[2] - had even passed an examination in it - yet it was hard to believe that I had been experiencing it myself. I had by now done many past life regressions and this one had felt no different from any other, but I knew that my friends were expert at detecting and releasing attached spirits. Esmeralda had already noticed "a little something" at table the previous day, when the three of us who were old enough to remember the war had been discussing our scanty memories. This made me realise the extent to which the "alien's" feelings and emotions became intertwined with one's own – even to the extent of manifesting physically in such a thing as this rash, which was to carry on causing me discomfort for several days to come - and after all, it seemed that I had been carrying this poor chap and his fellow soldiers for a very long time now. "He could have attached himself because you were waiting to hear that the war had ended, or because you were scared of the owls, and his companions would have just come along with him naturally" said Grace. "It doesn't matter why or when. The only thing that matters for all of you is that they're now freed."

And now the whole atmosphere in the room had changed. When I opened my eyes everyone looked lighter, but my back was aching badly. The chronic backache that I had suffered for years was my best friend in a way, since it was the search for a cure for it that had first led me into alternative therapies, and it was that path which had later led me on to my present spiritual one and into writing. But was it now time finally to let go of the backache? My friends certainly thought so, and to end the session I turned on to my tummy and they gave my back some wonderful healing. As the healing energy passed through their hands into my heart chakra area, I visualised angels digging out the pain with little golden spades, and it occurred to me that this was an exercise I could do on my own at any time if the pain returned. When they had finished and I got up, I looked at my watch and realised

2. The pioneers of Spirit Releasement Therapy are the Baldwins. See *SPIRIT RELEASEMENT THERAPY: A Technique Manual*, William J. Baldwin, Headline Books, USA, 1995.

with a shock that the entire morning had gone and lunch would already be on the table. Everyone was more than ready for it, but they all denied that the session had seemed long, and as for my back, it felt very much lighter. (Well, so would *yours* if *you* had suddenly released part of an army that *you* had been carrying for well over fifty *years*!) This was the prelude to an even deeper healing that was to take place at the end of the week, but that is more relevant to a later chapter.

IV
THE COMPLEXITY OF SIBLING BONDS

PART ONE - COMPLETING THE FAMILY

I gave many of you an unhappy childhood... In doing this, I removed from you the temptation to become attached to human parents or a specific family situation. That left you with only one option – to attach yourself to Me......

Inner Message from Sai Baba to Joy Thomas[1]

I was very excited about the birth of my youngest brother. That made me the eldest of six now, which gave me a lot of responsibility – too much probably - but I quite enjoyed changing the baby's nappies. Philippa, however, my youngest sister who was born when I was nine, while I was in France, still seemed to be the favourite. The only good thing about those three months spent in France with my godfather's family, when I had been so homesick, shy and lonely, was that I had learnt French. I had forgotten a lot of it already, but at least I was still the best in the class at French. It meant that nowadays there was just one thing at which I wasn't regarded as stupid and useless.

1. *Life is a Dream – Realize It*, Joy Thomas, Sri Sathya Publications Trust, India.

Well, it wasn't surprising that Philippa was everyone's favourite, because she was so pretty. Self-confident too. In a few years' time, when I needed to make telephone calls and found it scary, I would get her to do them for me. Philippa seemed able to do anything, even though she was only four. No wonder Daddy thought the world of her! Just now she always got twice as many presents at Christmas as the rest of us. That was because so many people outside the family also thought she was wonderful. They were right of course, and I didn't begrudge it to her, but it did seem unfair of God to have made me so inferior.

PART TWO - PERU

CHAPTER ONE - FELIPA

It was cold and the sun was only just rising, but I simply had to get up now to fetch some more wood. Otherwise Mother would complain that she couldn't cook food for the baby, or that the baby might die of cold. Of course, once I was outside, it was awe-inspiring to watch the sun rising over our beautiful Andes mountains; it was just making the effort to get up that was so difficult.

How life had changed since the baby had arrived! I was thrilled about it of course. My parents had been wanting another child for such a long time now, and none of us would ever get over the death of my little brother. Pity in some ways that Felipa[1] hadn't been a boy, but she was beautiful. More beautiful than I had been at that age, Mother always said, but at least Father said that looks weren't the only thing that mattered. Poor Father, he had to work so hard to make a living for the four of us! It would have been good for him to have a son to help with the hard labour, but now that didn't look possible since Mother was getting old for child bearing. Perhaps I would have a son later on, Father said, but I didn't see how when all the boys my own age aspired to going off to the town. "There's nothing for us up here," they would say, and it was hard to deny that they were right really.

"Ana, have you got the fire going yet? Felipa's hungry and I'm cold. And once I've seen to her, it'll be time to get food cooked for Father for when he comes in from the fields."

"Yes, Mother. The flames are just getting a hold now, but I had to go quite a long way for the wood, you know. Everything within the confines of our compound seems to be used up now." At least winter would soon be over, and then we wouldn't need the wood so much for warmth and would be able to live partly on fresh fruit.

"It's those wretched colonials! Our life had been hard enough already before they

1. I have translated my own and Philippa's names into Spanish, since Peru was already under Spanish occupation at this time, but in reality we are much more likely to have had Quechua names.

arrived; now it's getting impossible." Perhaps she was right. I had no memory of life before the Spaniards. I did think they looked handsome, though, when they passed by on horses in their bright uniforms.

CHAPTER TWO - THE SPANIARD

"Where's Felipa, Ana?""I don't know," I replied, but in fact I strongly suspected that she had disappeared with that handsome Spaniard who had stopped to talk to us the other day when we were both working in the vegetable patch.

"Can't you go and find her? I think it's her turn to sweep the hut, and anyway she promised to bring me some potatoes in time to get Father's meal ready.'

"I don't know where to look."

"That's ridiculous! There's nowhere for her to go. Just go and find her quickly, please."

I did find her, walking up from the stream, her hair very disheveled. She was on her way back anyway. The same happened the next day, and the next.... "I'm allowed to go off for a walk!" she would say in response to my parents' questioning. As for me, well Felipa knew that I knew what was going on, but she counted on me to defend her. And defend her I would. She was my only sister, my best friend really, and if I got the chance to do what she was doing, I would probably take it too.

******

"I'm going off to the town to get married," Felipa announced one day to our astounded parents.

"Married?! But you don't know anyone in the town."

"Yes I do. He's handsome and he's rich. He says we can live in a mansion and I won't have to slave away any more growing vegetables. I've been seeing him most days for the past few weeks now."

"So that's....!" My mother was speechless, but Father said "Why not? There's no life for her here, and we'll still have Ana to care for us in our old age."

"Yes," continued Felipa. "You'll always be able to count on Ana."

And so off she went. I would have loved to be able to go to the wedding, but how could I? The handsome Spaniard came for her on horseback and there wasn't room for two of us. I didn't understand his tongue, but he gestured that it was too far to walk. Would I ever see Felipa again, I wondered?

******

Her husband did bring her to see us, a couple of years later, with the baby – a beautiful bouncing boy with skin a bit lighter than ours. How I envied her! It must be lovely to have a child, and a husband who adored you. "But I don't recommend childbirth," she said. "The pain was excruciating. Far worse than anything I could have imagined." Then we never saw her again. Occasionally she sent news with one of the young men from our compound who had gone to the town to seek work and then returned to see their family. At least the news was always good. It sounded as though she was really happy with her family of three children. I had to be glad for her.

CHAPTER THREE - OLD AGE

Father was dying and there was absolutely nothing that either Mother or I could do for him. How painful it was to see him suffering so! The medicine man's herbs no longer seemed to help. If only Felipa could come and see him before he left us, but there was no way of getting news to her. The men who had gone to the town had either returned home permanently because they were unhappy there or had no work, or else had disappeared to all intents and purposes. "Life is so full in the town," Felipa had explained the last time she had sent a message. "It's hard to get time to keep up with one's family."

******

Now there was only Mother and me to think about. She was getting old and frail and so I had to do all the work. It wasn't that hard really – I was used to it – but every day was the same and life had little meaning. The mountains were still beautiful of course, but I had exactly the same view all the time. It would have been nice to be able to explore them. Ah well, one had to accept one's fate. Before long Mother would be dead too probably. Then I'd be left on my own. All on my own. If only Felipa would come and take me to live with her, but maybe she'd forgotten all about me. Anyway, I didn't suppose I would like the town. It must be so different there, and I was used to these mountains....

PART THREE - MAY 1998

I was near St. David's, a beautiful spot in Wales, on my first full week with Roger Woolger. A Healing Retreat which included swapping regressions. The weather was unusually warm for May, and we did some of the exercises in the garden as well as being able to go for walks during the afternoon breaks. Best of all, Katarina drove us down to the beach to do Qui Gong before breakfast! Katarina was a T'ai Chi and Qui Gong teacher, and was thinking of training in regression too. She asked me about the course I had just completed. I was awaiting my exam and essay results and was confident of having passed, but less confident about my abilities as a regression therapist. I told her that the course was a very good introduction to the work and that I was glad to have done it, but that if she was wanting to get a lot of good practice, she would do better to train with Roger, "who wouldn't want to train me, because he thinks I wouldn't be any good at the body stuff."

"Yes, body work comes naturally to me," said Katarina, "but I'm sure you could learn too with more practice."

When we got to the first regression, Katarina and I paired up. She was an extremely good subject and went quickly into a life in which she fought against her twin soul, who was now her husband. I had brought a few copies of my book on twin souls, so she bought one. Roger had got us to draw pictures of a scene we had seen during a meditation, and mine was of myself "stuck up a mountain in Peru" – a place I was longing to visit. Thinking of myself as a "hopeless subject", I was surprised when it was my turn to lie down on the mat and the story about my pretty younger sister came through.

"But it makes sense, does it?" asked Katarina when we had been through the life.

"Yes, it does. It certainly explains why I always used to be so envious of my youngest sister. But I don't know whether it was the same sister."

"I feel sure it was." Katarina seemed to have a knack for this! I felt sure she would do well if she did decide to do Roger's training. "But you're not still envious of her now?"

"Well, there isn't so much to be envious of now, because she's had a really difficult life, even though she was always expected to be the one to succeed."

"That must have been a big burden to carry!"

"I suppose it was. I'd never really thought of that. But at least she's with her twin soul now. He's really nice – no comparison with the husband she finally managed to break with. And she's had a brilliant book about Aura Soma published by Element. She's a very gifted therapist."

"So you're on the same sort of path then?"

"Very much so! Actually she was the one who started me off on all this spiritual and healing stuff. The only thing I've done for her is to introduce her to Sai Baba."

"The <u>only</u> thing?"

"Well, I used to cook her breakfast when she was little, but that was only because I was nine years older. She can write much better than I can."

"There doesn't seem to be anything wrong with your writing! I was looking at your book before I went to sleep last night. Anyway, are you and Philippa good friends now?"

"Yes, we're extremely good friends. It's nice to have someone to talk to who really understands what I went through in my youth, and of course I've been able to be a listening ear in the recent trauma of her marriage break-up."

"So it's very different now from when you were young?"

"Oh yes, very different. For one thing we've both learnt about karma, and of course we find that explains so much. I'll tell you one interesting thing. I always used to hate Christmas, and one of my most vivid memories about our family Christmases is that Philippa seemed to get about twice as many presents as the rest of us. It wasn't my parents' fault - my mother was incredibly careful about fairness – but people outside the family used to give her "special treatment". For instance, I remember one woman who said "I was a fifth child too, so I know what's it like." Well, just recently Philippa was saying to me how she used to feel bad at Christmas because she always got more presents than the rest of us, but that Edwin, our clairvoyant friend, who gave me spiritual information for my twin soul book, had told her that there were a lot of people this lifetime who were paying karmic debts to her from a time when she was persecuted for following Jesus."

"How interesting! So what about the envy now? "

"Well, yes, I can see that it belongs more to that life in Peru than it does to our present one."

"So now you can let go of it?"

"Yes, that's right. I can let go of it! Anyway, as I told you, we're really good friends now, and I think we do support each other. Oh, and I've just thought of an interesting thing. I've been feeling such a strong yen recently to go to Peru. When we can afford it, I want to go on one of those tours that take you more or less everywhere, and do the Inca Trail. Maybe it's because in that life I've just looked at I never got away from my tiny village."

"Makes sense!"

EXERCISES

1. Have you got a sibling – or if not, perhaps a friend – to whom you have always tended to feel inferior? Make a list of the qualities you believe him/her to have that you particularly envy. Now make another list of the qualities you have which he/she has not got. Which list is longer? If the first is longer, keep working to expand the second until they are of equal length. Now have a good look at the two lists and realise that people are not inferior/superior to each other, but just different. Embrace your sibling in your mind and tell him/her that from now on you can both appreciate the other for who they are.

2. Have you got a sibling (or a friend) who is envious of you for any reason? Does this make your relationship difficult? Realise that the difficulty probably relates more to a previous life than to your present one. (You might care to seek out a regression therapist to help you to trace the root of the problem.) Try to visualise yourself in the other person's shoes in order to feel compassion, but DO NOT allow yourself to get sucked into his/her difficulties. Before any meeting or telephone call with him/her, protect yourself. This can be done in various ways: e.g. visualise a bubble of white light around you, or call on your guardian angel or a spirit guide to protect you from the other person's negative energy, and keep your own mood positive.

V
FINDING THE ROOT OF COMPLEXES

PART ONE - SEPTEMBER 1957

Ballroom dancing lessons with boys from Clifton College – one of the privileges of getting into the Sixth Form! Up until now, with us girls not being allowed to walk down the road our school was on and the boys not being allowed to walk up it, meetings between the sexes had been impossible. So it was exciting but scary. Goodness knows how, but a few of the girls in our class had managed to meet some of the boys, and an even smaller number had actually acquired boyfriends. I envied them. Perhaps I would meet someone I liked too, but it was hard to imagine how when I couldn't dance. They would think me such an idiot!

In preparation for the dancing classes Miss Seddon gave us a little talk on how we should behave and so on. She said we didn't have to wear school uniform that evening, and that we were even allowed to wear lipstick. My friends and I all had a good laugh about that. "Fancy wanting to wear lipstick!" we said to each other, but when I got home and told Mummy about it, she went straight out and bought me one. To make matters worse, she insisted that I put some on when I was getting ready to go off to the lesson. Maybe that's one of the reasons I was a wallflower almost the whole evening. There weren't enough boys to go round, even though the College is bigger than our school. It seemed a lot of them were less eager to come than we girls were to receive them, and of course the ones whose girlfriends were in the class wanted to dance with them as much as possible. So I only got a turn when the teacher ordered one of the boys to take me as a partner. I felt silly with the lipstick on, which probably showed, and anyway I already knew from when we'd had dancing lessons lower down in the school that I couldn't dance. When I did get a partner, we'd usually start by asking each other's names, but after that it would be difficult to think of anything else to say. Then I'd feel awkward and embarrassed about being so hopeless at learning the steps, and that would make conversation more difficult still. What agony it was! "Gradually over the weeks," I thought to myself as the teacher made us all change partners, "every single boy in the Sixth Form of Clifton College will get to know that I can't dance."

PART TWO - INDIAN DANCER

"Oh no, I can't dance any more! That humiliating fall has ruined my life for ever...." I was back in my home village now, lying on the bed that my youngest sister had taken over since I had left but had now had to give back to me. The pain in the area of my coccyx was excruciating, and everyone was quite sure that the bones were badly broken. I hadn't been paid for that last, shameful, performance, and no-one in my family could possibly afford to pay for a doctor. Even if they could, it's unlikely he would be able to do anything for me. "You might never even walk again," said my father grumpily. The family had got used to the little bit of money I had been able to give them at regular intervals, and now he was worried about how they were going to be able to manage.

As for Raju.... Would I ever see him again? Probably not. Oh, the thought was unbearable. My mind wandered back to the very first time we'd made love, in my tiny dwelling soon after the evening's performance. He didn't dare to take me to his own room in case his parents saw, and he said that even meeting me where I lived was extremely risky. It had undoubtedly been love at first sight. I had noticed him sitting near the back on the very first occasion that he came with his parents to watch me dance in our village. He looked so handsome in his nobleman's clothes, but at that point it never entered my head that he could ever take an interest in a peasant girl – someone of a much lower caste than him – however beautiful I was. For yes, I am still beautiful even now. This appalling pain in my lower back can't change my facial features!

Raju came with his family to watch the performance over the space of several months before his father offered me employment in his household. I was always aware of his presence, and each time he seemed to have made an effort to sit a little bit closer to where I was performing. I still didn't let myself think very much of it, but after the first time I had performed at a dinner in his home, he came back stage and thanked me in such a way that I began to form romantic notions. After that, I have to admit, I made efforts to dress and dance more seductively. Many of the men in those circles made propositions to me, but I could have eyes for no-one but Raju. They thought I was pure. How wrong they were! They would say "Bharat may well have a great reputation for being a spiritual land, but there's no reason for a beautiful young girl like you to be totally spiritual. In this great country we are known too for our expertise in matters sexual. I have just been studying the *Kama Sutra* and would love to try out some of what I have learnt with you. Isn't it time that you lost your virginity? Why do you dance so seductively if you don't really want a handsome man like myself to respond to it?" I had to pretend that I only did it because I thought it was what was expected of me, that I would really prefer to tend the temple, and that I only danced because my poor family were so greatly in need of financial support. The men who talked to me in this sort of way seemed old and unattractive compared with Raju.

Raju and I talked several times before he admitted to being in love with me. We both knew that what we felt was something much deeper than the idle pleasantries of the other men who made advances to me. But the relationship was painful from the start. Raju said that he could only ever be happy with me, but that his parents would never agree to him marrying a girl from a lower caste - one who was not of their own choosing. And so we always had to meet secretly and make love rather too hastily. He never dared to linger an entire night in my bed, much though he appreciated my reluctance to let him go. The most painful part of all was when he announced that his father had found a wife for him. I even had to dance at the wedding! He told me that he would never consummate the marriage, that he would pretend to be impotent, but in the end I think they forced him. A son and heir was of course of vital importance in a family of his standing.

Perhaps it was because I was thinking about Raju's relationship with his wife, and consequently not concentrating sufficiently, that I took the false step which caused my humiliating fall. I do not know. What I do know is that everyone in the audience except Raju boohed as though I was a total failure. No-one even asked whether I was in a lot of pain. They simply carted me off stage and called on the next performer. When she had finished her turn, they came back to see whether I could get up and dance again, and when I replied "No, I'll never be able to dance again" and they realised that I couldn't even walk, they sent for a cart to bring me back here to my family. For the first few days I just lay yearning for Raju to appear, thinking that he simply must make the effort to seek me out, but gradually it dawned on me that he would never be able to do such a thing without his wife learning of it.

******

It was time to die. I wasn't very old, but I had nothing left to live for and was a burden on my family. I had learnt to walk a bit with a stick, but as far as my parents were concerned I was simply another mouth to feed and they already had more than enough difficulty feeding themselves. A bout of pneumonia caught during one exceptionally cold spell was enough for that frail body of mine to give up the ghost, and I quickly found myself back with old friends on the astral planes. "What happened to Raju?" was the first question I had for my guide, and he replied that he was sorry to say that he had poisoned himself after only a few weeks of trying to live without me. "So you mean he's here too?" I asked excitedly, but the reply was that suicide was never an answer, and so Raju was now wandering alone in a dull grey place, feeling that he had nowhere to go and no-one to turn to for help.

"Can't I go and find him?" I asked. "You obviously know where he is."

"Yes, don't worry. I'm sure in due course you'll be able to help him, but you must be patient. First you need to review your own life and think about the lessons you have to learn from it. Your accident was certainly a great misfortune, but was it really sufficient excuse for giving up completely? Also, did not you and Raju put your love and your love-making before God?...."

I thought long and hard about what my dear guide was saying, then I commented "I suppose it's never a very good idea to have only one string to one's bow in any lifetime. I suppose it's too risky because accidents can always easily happen."

"That's right. And there are always ways to be found of being useful. Even someone who is completely paralysed can still meditate and pray for others. You just moped around the house, didn't you?...."

"Feeling sorry for myself! You're right. Of course there are useful things one can do even sitting down. I suppose I could have learnt to weave or something, and made beautiful textiles for saris...."

"You could indeed have done something like that. It could both have brought some income for your family and made you feel that your life wasn't completely wasted after all. But worse still, what about your attitude to yourself? Did you ever forgive yourself for making that one false step?"

"How could I possibly do that? The humiliation was unutterable! My family were so ashamed of me, and I was so ashamed of myself."

******

I had moved forward several centuries now and was lying on the mat in a Roger Woolger workshop. Katarina, now one of my fellow trainees, was guiding me. "So is that what makes you nervous about speaking in public?" Katarina asked. "Are you afraid of somehow humiliating yourself?"

"Yes, that does seem to ring true. I was a really skilled dancer and it was just so silly making one little mistake. Breaking my back was my own fault entirely!"

"But no-one is infallible. We all make mistakes from time to time. There's no point in blaming ourselves indefinitely for it."

"Carrying blame subconsciously for centuries – I suppose that's what I must have been doing. No wonder I've been feeling so nervous about presenting my case history to Roger at the graduate gathering next weekend. But I'll have to do it somehow. I do so want this diploma!"

"I'm sure you won't have any problem. Can you forgive that dancer now? She was very talented and she did give a lot of pleasure to many people before she had her fall. What's one little mistake to all those other evenings when she performed absolutely perfectly?"

"Yes," I laughed. "I suppose it's certainly time now to forgive her."

"Good! So now you can let go of all that fear. What about Raju? Is he someone you recognise as Ann? Have a good look at him."

"Gosh yes! I'm sure he's my lovely friend James. That must be why, when we first met not so long ago, I felt a little sad about not being young and beautiful."

"Well, do you want to go and find him now? Do you think you still have some important things to say to one another?"

"I'm sure we do. Oh, there he is looking lost and miserable. Raju dearest, look, it's me, Shanti!"

"Do you want to give him a hug?" asked Katarina, handing me a cushion. The hug was so comforting! "What does he say? Is he pleased to see you?"

"Oh yes, so pleased. He'd thought we'd lost one another for ever. He says he couldn't forgive himself for not going and finding me after the accident, but he didn't see how he could without his family finding out. He's begging my forgiveness."

"And do you forgive him?"

"Of course I do. It's wonderful to see him again. He says he realises now that it was cowardly to take his own life, but he just missed me so much.... His parents had consulted an astrologer, who had insisted that his wife and he were compatible, and he says he can see in a way why the man had thought that, but that it was impossible for him to love her as he had loved me.... But now he realises too that neither of us put God first. He wants to make it up both to God and to me, but doesn't know how."

"So is there anything you can do to help him?"

"Yes, I suppose I can tell him that he can have lots more chances to do better, and that there is always help available if he only asks for it.... Now I think I'll lead him towards the light and call for someone who can advise him on how best to prepare for his next incarnation."

PART THREE - APRIL 2001

It was still the same Woolger workshop – hopefully my last before getting his diploma.

"So someone has suggested that you do some shamanic training?" said Lama Ngawang, with whom I had paired up this time. "Well, let's just try and see where that idea takes you.... So you say you've still got that pain in your lower back which started before the workshop?

"Yes, that's right. It's interesting because you remember how Roger was saying the day we arrived that we might have been subconsciously preparing ourselves for regression a week or two before we got here? That we might have been suffering unaccustomed aches or pains somewhere? Well this ache, which isn't at all in the usual place where I get backache, started about ten days ago, I think, and in the regression I did the day before yesterday with Katarina I found myself as an Indian dancer who fell and broke her back just there and could never dance again."

"But the regression didn't improve it at all?"

"No, but at least I no longer feel quite so nervous about presenting my case history next weekend among all those graduates, and that's what prompted that regression."

"Good!" said Ngawang kindly. "And anyway it isn't only graduates who'll be there.

You'll be with friends.... Silvia and myself for a start! So now I'd like you to focus fully on that pain in your lower back. Describe it to me.... What exactly does it feel like?...."

PART FOUR - AMERICAN INDIAN SHAMAN

CHAPTER ONE - THE STAG

"Ouch! That stag, it's gored me. Gored me in the lower back. Oh, the pain!" It was ironic really, since I'd felt so reluctant to kill it in the first place, and then after my arrow had misfired, it had got its own back on me!

"Well Sitting Bull, you're a man now," my father had said earlier this morning. "You must come off with us today to the hunt. It will be your first real chance to show off your skills and make us all proud of you."

I knew it had to be done of course. That we needed meat to eat. But it grieved me more than I can say to slay those beautiful creatures – especially the deer, who was my totem animal. There was no getting out of it, however, now that my boyhood was over, and it was impossible to explain my feelings to my parents or any of the other men in our tribe. The hunters had welcomed me warmly as we set off, but after both the stag and I had got injured, they were much less enthusiastic about my efforts. "You must shoot cleanly," they said. "Aim straight for the heart. If you only get its head or its backside, it will obviously get angry and then you're bound to be the one to suffer."

"But the stag's bound to suffer when you kill it," I thought to myself, not daring to utter the thought out loud.

My mother was very upset when we got home. She had been expecting me to return in glory, not on an improvised stretcher! The wound was very deep and she was afraid I might even bleed to death. Laughing Cloud was among the first to notice my return, and she offered to fetch the medicine man quickly. "Yes please," said Mother. "You can run faster than I can. I'll start to bathe it while we're waiting."

Laughing Cloud hovered in the background as the medicine man prepared a poultice and gave his instructions. "You must change the herbs twice a day," he said firmly. Mother was already looking in danger of fainting, and she cringed visibly at the words. "I could do it," said Laughing Cloud. "You're so busy looking after your younger children, and I've seen exactly how he made the mixture." How I loved her!

"What do you think?" asked Mother tentatively.

"I can't see any reason why not," replied the kind medicine man. "The most important thing is to keep it clean, and if Laughing Cloud isn't too squeamish..."

"No, I've never been squeamish. My mother always gives me the rabbits to skin because she hates doing it."

And so Laughing Cloud came to my teepee twice a day over the next couple of weeks. She seemed to have healing hands, and her cheerful conversation always made me feel a lot better too. In her I felt able to confide my feelings about killing the animals. She understood completely. Gradually, too, I gained the courage to make hints about my feelings for her, and even to suggest that one day our parents might be agreeable to our getting married. My joy when she made it obvious that she liked the idea was indescribable. It compensated for the shame of the rueful day when I had failed to prove my manhood at the hunt.

CHAPTER TWO - MEDICINE MAN

Laughing Cloud and I had been married a couple of years now. We were so happy together! My lower back still troubled me at times, but she had learnt from the medicine man what herbs to give me and how to massage the painful area. My shooting had improved since that first occasion, but I still dreaded every expedition. "You shouldn't feel obliged to do it," Laughing Cloud would say. "We can always eat vegetables." But my father was getting older now and I would be expected to support my mother as well once he was no longer able to go hunting. Besides, our first child was on the way. If it was a boy I would in due course have to train him to be skilful with arrows.

But no, when the baby arrived she turned out to be a girl. A beautiful girl with bright brown eyes just like her mother's! We were overjoyed. We named her Running Water. Two more years passed and then Laughing Cloud gave birth again. We called our second daughter Babbling Brook. How proud we were of our little family! Two children seemed quite enough to cope with, and anyway Medicine Man advised us not to let Laughing Cloud get pregnant again because she was small and the births were very difficult.

Medicine Man was getting on in years now, and his only son had sadly died in infancy. One day he came and asked Laughing Cloud whether she would like to learn more of his skills, since she obviously had an aptitude for it. She replied that she would dearly love to, and asked whether I could join her. His answer was "Yes certainly, if he's not too busy with the hunting." So Laughing Cloud whispered in the kind man's ear that killing animals was not really my vocation, and he seemed to understand our sentiments.

I was thrilled when she gave me the news, as I had been very concerned about who could take over now that Medicine Man was getting older and obviously weaker. I hardly dared imagine that I could ever develop his immense skills, but on the other hand I felt that, with Laughing Cloud beside me, it could surely be possible to learn to move mountains. The very next day I made an effort to kill a couple of extra rabbits so that we wouldn't go short of food, and then we started eagerly on the lessons.

Medicine Man was pleased to find that I learnt fast. So did Laughing Cloud of course, but there were certain things that he said only I should master. It was not simple. There were so many things to study besides which herbs to use for what, but Medicine Man said that I had a natural aptitude for it all. He also said that journeying would come easily with practice, and of course he taught me his drumming skills as well. Laughing Cloud would always be a very good assistant for me, but just now the care of our growing daughters took up much of her time anyway.

A few months went by, and then Medicine Man announced to the whole tribe that he was training me as his successor. My parents were now really proud of me at last, and everyone felt relieved that they would not be left without a shaman to care for their ailments and give them advice on so many important matters. It was a somewhat daunting prospect, but at least I felt confident that I could count on Medicine Man's support for a few years yet.

In fact he lived another six years before peacefully leaving his body. Laughing Cloud and I were grieved to say "goodbye", but we knew that his spirit would continue to guide us. Some time before this sad day I had already been able to give up hunting completely, as the people whom Medicine Man referred to my care paid me with game sufficient for my family, and Laughing Cloud had always done well anyway with our little vegetable patch. By the time I was formally nominated as the new Medicine Man I had enough self assurance to believe that I could serve my people well.

******

"And so you did," commented Medicine Man as he greeted me in the Bardo at the end of a long, fulfilled life. "I am proud of you. And so are your parents who are also waiting here to greet you." I gave them all a hug. How good were such reunions! Laughing Cloud was still on Earth enjoying watching our grandchildren grow, but I knew that we could be together again at night, and anyway that her days were now numbered too.

"Is your wife someone you know now as Ann?" asked Ngawang. I thought hard for a moment and then said "Yes, I feel sure it's the same friend as the one who was my lover in India. Gosh, isn't that interesting? He must have felt he had a karmic debt to me after I'd fallen and broken my back and he never saw me again. The injury when I got gored by the stag was in just the same place. That must be why he wanted to tend it and then become my wife."

"And so?"

"And so that's the reason we can be such good friends now. It's a really comfortable relationship because there's obviously no outstanding karma between us."

"How nice! It was a good life, wasn't it? Usually in these regressions we look for trauma that still needs dealing with, but sometimes it's good to find a rewarding past life, to help us to see that it isn't all doom and gloom." Laughing, Ngawang made me sit up and gave me a hug. "So there is a latent shaman in there! Does that make you feel inclined to rush off for some training?"

"Well not rush probably, but it's certainly something to bear in mind for the future...."

By the following Saturday the pain in my lower back had gone and I had been awarded my Woolger diploma! And a bit over two years later I went on my first shamanic workshop with the Sacred Trust.

EXERCISES

1. Is there anything you are obliged to do sometimes that makes you very nervous?

(a) Lie down and visualise yourself doing it. Take a little time to complete the picture thoroughly and really feel yourself immersed in the scene.

(b) Keeping yourself firmly in the scene, scan your entire body, noticing any aches, pains, areas of tension, butterflies, etc.

(c) When you have picked out a part of your body where the sensation is particularly strong, focus your full attention on it and amplify it.

(d) Can you give the sensation a shape? A colour? Now give it a voice too. What are the words it would like to say?

(e) Encourage some dialogue. If you have found, for instance, a small black ball in your chest that is saying "Help me!", reply "OK. I'm here to help you. Just tell me what I can do for you." Let it have its full say and find in you a sympathetic listener.

(f) Ask your small black ball/ache in your lower back/lump in your throat/sore red splodge in your stomach (<u>whatever</u> it is) whether it would like some healing, and if so, in what form. It might request some golden light, some blue healing oil, a red rose.... Visualise whatever it asks for appearing and taking effect.

(g) Now return to (a) and tell yourself that you no longer need to feel nervous. Visualise yourself doing whatever it is with total confidence.

2. Is there anything you would like to achieve but that seems beyond your reach? The very fact that you are so keen probably indicates that it is a talent you have had in previous lives, in which case it will still be latent. So make up your mind that there is no real reason why you should not be able to achieve your ambition.

(a) Make a list of the apparent "obstacles" that lie between you and your goal.

(b) Now eliminate them one by one. For this you may take as many minutes, hours, days, months or years as are necessary. The methods you might use will vary according to what your ambition is, but here are a few suggestions:-

(i) The first most important thing to do is to ASK. State your request clearly and unequivocally, either naming the person you are asking (e.g. God, Jesus, etc.), or trusting that whoever is best equipped to help you is listening. You may ask for anything on condition that it will not be detrimental to anyone else.

(ii) The second most important thing is to TRUST THE OUTCOME, appreciating that those on the other side can get a broader picture, and that we ourselves are not always in the best position for seeing what is best for us.

(iii) Devote a little time every single day to practising/studying/learning something new – whatever it is. If you really want to do it, you must make it a priority however busy or tired you are.

(iv) Believe that money is never an obstacle. If you really need it, it will miraculously appear.

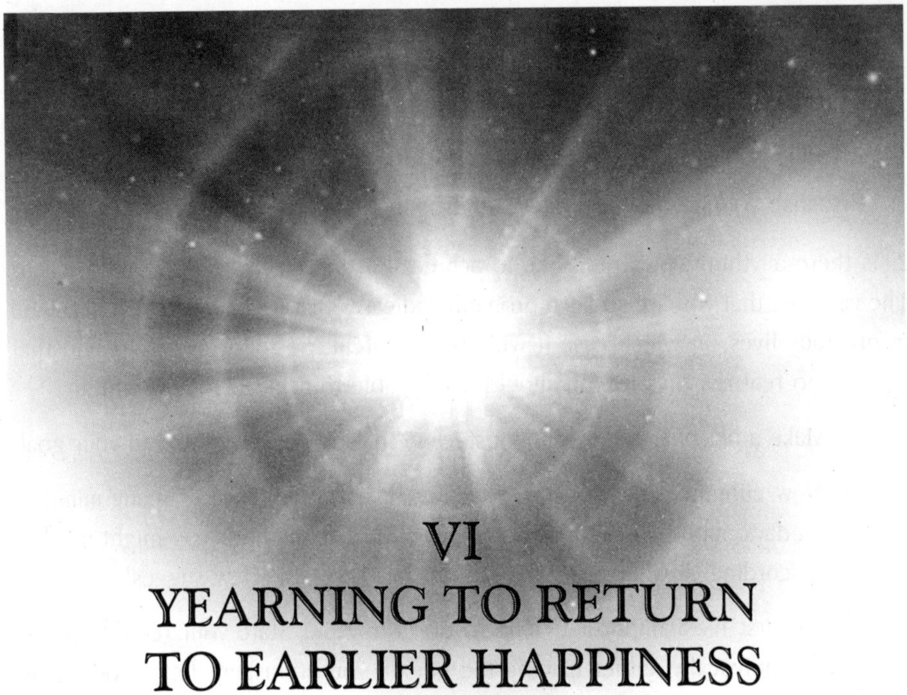

VI
YEARNING TO RETURN TO EARLIER HAPPINESS

PART ONE - 1960 UNIVERSITY

I had achieved what for so many years had seemed an impossible dream, yet I was still far from being happy. The five close friends that I had had all through secondary school had all always been expected to go to university, while I had been regarded as the "stupid one". Major change suddenly came with my first ever good school report at the end of my first term in the sixth form. I was doing 'A' Level French of course – the only subject I was considered any good at – but I had also started Spanish and was found to be good at that too. My father, who had a tendency to go from one extreme to the other, immediately contacted the headmistress and they agreed that, if I stayed on an extra year and did Spanish to 'A' Level, I might have a chance of getting into university. (Many years later I felt grateful to him for this because it was a private school and the fees were by no means small.)

I was incredulous but excited, and gradually the impossible dream turned into reality. The only possibilities were Bristol (my home town) or Hull, as at the time they were the only two universities in England which would accept 'O' Level Biology as my science rather than insisting on Mathematics, which I would clearly have no hope of passing. I had never been to the North of England and did not fancy the idea of Hull at all, and also my Spanish teacher was the wife of the Professor of Spanish at Bristol. (Perhaps the biggest irony of my life is that I ultimately became the wife of a Professor of Mathematics at Hull University, but at the time nothing could have been further from my imagination!)

I enjoyed most of the courses at the University, and made some good friends, particularly in the Catholic Society, but I did not enjoy still living at home when most of the other students were in halls of residence. I had been overweight ever since I was about seventeen, my father always criticised my appearance (comparing me to Philippa, the pretty one, who still lived at home too of course), and made me feel that I would never manage to acquire a boyfriend.

Eventually an engineering student started walking me home from "Cath Soc" meetings, and after a bit we plucked up the courage to hold hands and kiss each other goodnight. The sexual attraction was mutual, but really there was no more to it than that as we had nothing in common apart from our religion. I regarded him as my boyfriend, however, and was deeply hurt when I went off to Paris for a semester of study at the Sorbonne and he failed to keep his promise to write regularly. I wrote to him frequently and he replied once or twice, which allowed me to give myself the illusion that the relationship was still on. So the pain when I returned to Bristol and bumped into him one day hand in hand with another girl was intense.

I did not acquire another boyfriend during my remaining time as a student, which greatly disappointed my mother but did not at all surprise my father. While feeling hopeless and complexed about it, at the same time I always held an inner conviction that somewhere out there in the world was a man who would one day fall in love with me, someone who would understand me totally, someone with whom I could really communicate. To love and be loved seemed more important than either getting my degree or finding the right job afterwards, and deep down I always believed it to be possible despite all the contra indications surrounding me.

PART TWO - COMPANION SOUL MATES

CHAPTER ONE - GIUSEPPE

On Tuesdays the market was in our village and on Fridays it was in Giuseppe's. My family always had lovely fresh eggs to sell, while Giuseppe's had cheeses. Wonderful cheeses both hard and soft, some made from cow's milk, some from goat's and some from sheep's – such a variety! In fact the Giuseppe cheeses (his father's name was also Giuseppe) were known as the best in the whole of the Ticino. Perhaps our rich grass and the sun gave the milk a special quality; perhaps Giuseppe senior had a secret knack which he passed on only to his son. I did not know, nor did it concern me. The only thing that concerned me on market day was how close our egg stall would be to Giuseppe's cheese stall. I loved the smell of the cheese, and Mother often let me choose which sort to exchange for some of our eggs, but most of all I loved Giuseppe.

Giuseppe was two years older than me, as he had loved to boast when I was only eight and he was ten. Because of that he would never have wanted to play with me then, even if his father had given him time off from helping unload the cheeses and so on. But gradually, as we both got well into our teens, he started to notice me. So then on market days I would get up a little bit earlier and spend time doing my hair as prettily as possible in front of the mirror. It was difficult for Giuseppe and me to talk at the market when we were both always so busy, but sometimes he brought bunches of flowers, which he hid behind the stall and gave me when our parents weren't looking. How long all the other days of the week used to seem compared with Tuesday and Friday!

Then suddenly one summer evening I was outside seeing to the hens, when Giuseppe popped his head round the back of the hen house. What a lovely surprise! "How on Earth did you get here?" I asked, and he replied that he had walked, that it wasn't too far really now that he was big and strong, and then he took me in his arms and kissed me. I was absolutely thrilled, but afraid to tell my parents because I was only fourteen and anyway I didn't know whether they had a lad in our own village in mind for me. Though I never dared let him stay very long, Giuseppe came once a week throughout the rest of that summer. When winter came and it got too dark for him to do the walk, he decided one day to tell his parents that we wanted to start courting. His parents then spoke to mine on the next market day and, though they all approved of the match, they agreed that we were both a bit young to marry. But they decided to let us see each other regularly while they saved up for the wedding.

And what a lovely wedding it was! Lots of people from both our villages came, my mother made me the most beautiful dress, and Father Paolo was only too happy to perform the ceremony. My mother would miss me, she said, when I moved over to Giuseppe's village, but at least now my sister Giovanna was old enough to take over looking after the hens. I missed my family too at first, but we could still always meet on market days, and Giuseppe's folk welcomed me immediately as one of their own. We moved into a room at the back of his parents' house at first, but Giuseppe was good at much more than making cheeses, and gradually in his spare time he started to build us a little house of our own.

What a happy day that was when we finally moved into our very own abode! By this time both my mother and my mother-in-law kept asking me whether I was pregnant yet. They always looked disappointed each time I replied negatively, but it didn't bother me particularly. I was just so happy with Giuseppe, we felt no need for anyone else in our life, and anyway we were both always very busy. Besides helping with the family cheese business, Giuseppe cut down pine trees from the side of the mountain and made beautiful furniture for us. Also, we were both very interested in herbal medicine, and old Geronimo, to whom everyone used to go with their aches and pains, agreed to teach us all he knew. When Geronimo died we took over as the "village doctors", and we often said to each other that it was just as well that no babies ever came along as we would have had little time for them.

CHAPTER TWO - DEATH ON THE MOUNTAIN

We had had a long, rich, rewarding life, but Giuseppe was getting quite old now. I worried about him still working so hard, especially since I was getting old too and was fearful that I would not always be able to look after him properly. He kept telling me not to worry, that our love and God's love would see us through, but I was scared of widowhood for either of us. We both loved our mountains and our lake so much. Well, they weren't really ours of course, but we felt they belonged to us just as much as we belonged to them. But our legs no longer permitted us to walk as far as we used to. Giuseppe was stronger than I was, though, and I sometimes let him go off walking without me.

Then one dreadful day he did not return at the usual time. I tried not to worry, but after a couple of hours had passed and his evening meal had grown cold, I began to panic. It was nearly dusk, but I didn't want to disturb the neighbours, and I knew his favourite path like the back of my hand. So off I set up the mountain side. It was tough going for an old woman, but the gathering darkness made me ever more frightened and determined. "Perhaps he's had a fall," I said to myself, "or perhaps his heart has failed him. I really must hurry to find him." But the more I hurried, the weaker my legs got, and the weaker my legs got, the more I panicked. It was getting cold too, and eventually I could carry on no longer. "Perhaps he's dead. Oh, help me God!" I yelled before collapsing into a heap, and the next thing I knew....

There was Giuseppe smiling at me. "Thank goodness! You're not dead after all. I was beginning to be afraid you must be." Giuseppe laughed long and loud, took me by the hand and led me to the most beautiful garden I had ever seen. " Where on Earth are we?" I asked. " I thought I was on the mountain side and that it was dark and cold."

"If you want," he replied, "I can take you to see a beautiful mountain side, but it won't be dark because we're not on Earth any longer."

"So you mean we're <u>both</u> dead?"

"Yes Anna, my dear. Isn't that fun? Well, we'd had long enough lives, hadn't we? And aren't we lucky to have been spared lonely widowhood? Now, you see those beings of light at the other end of the garden? They're waiting to take you for your Life Review. Come..."

PART THREE - WHAT I NEEDED TO LEARN ABOUT LOVE

Although I always knew deep down that love was not something unattainable for me, many years were yet to pass before I learnt that loving oneself was the most important – and so often the most difficult – thing to be done. Once we love ourselves, other people will be drawn to us naturally. People born into a loving family have a big advantage, but those who are not always have something to learn from it. One major thing that I learnt was how important it would be to show love to my own children, and I firmly believe that it is partly thanks to that, and also thanks to having a wonderful father, that my children are much happier young adults than I ever was.

My weight continued to be a major problem right through my twenties. Every now and then I would go on a crash diet and lose a lot, but it never lasted because it only took a little bout of depression to start me off on the chocolate again. Once I reached about thirty and my life was turned around, I ceased to have any difficulty in remaining reasonably slim. Whatever we focus on grows. This is why (according to research carried out in the United States, which I heard mentioned in a lecture at Sai Baba's ashram in Puttaparthi) such things as slimming clubs rarely have a lasting effect.

In one Woolger workshop, when Roger played us a piece of music and had us draw a picture of the scene it depicted in our minds, I entitled my picture "Death on the Mountain". At that point, however, I got no further into that life in the Italian part of Switzerland, and it was later still that "Giuseppe" himself appeared in my life. By that time I was long married with three grownup children. In any case – before finding the man who was to be my partner for this life – I should have realised that marriage was not essential to leading a worth while life. We all have certain numbers of celibate lives as well as married ones. When I was young, my good mother did not help, since her only concern was whom I would marry, not what I would do for a career. Fortunately times have changed, and I learnt through my mother's attitude to try not to put pressure on my own daughter. And Alice? Well, I am glad to say that at twenty-eight she is happily absorbed in a successful career and not desperately seeking a partner at the moment.

EXERCISES

1. Do you have difficulty in loving yourself? If so, I strongly advise you to work through Louise Hay's books or go on a Louise Hay workshop (or something equivalent), or both. There is little point in my repeating here the ideas for which people such as Louise Hay are so renowned.

2. Are you seeking a relationship? Then stop looking! Focus instead on what you want to make of your life, what you can do for others, and so on. Any relationship you make before you have sorted yourself out is likely to prove disastrous. On the other hand, once you <u>have</u> got yourself sorted, Mr./Miss Right is likely to come along naturally.

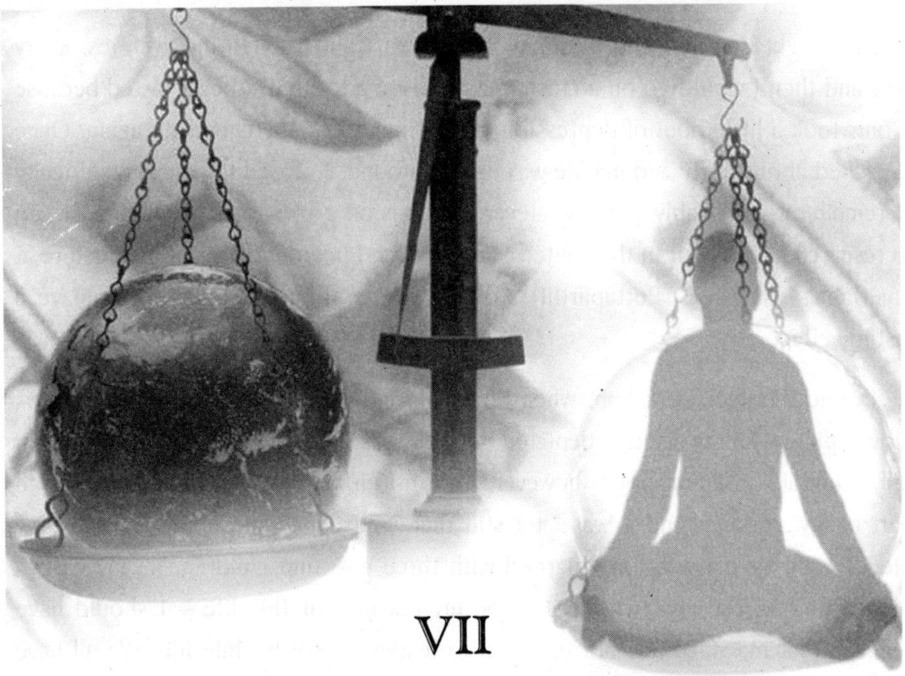

VII
PAYING KARMIC DEBTS

PART ONE - WORKING LIFE

When I started at university three years seemed like an eternity – plenty of time for choosing a career – but by the end I was no clearer about what I wanted to do. The only thing that was clear was that I did not feel cut out for teaching. "You want to use your languages, but you don't want to teach! What else can you do?" the woman in the University Careers Office had said unhelpfully. Anyway, one of the careers talks was given by someone from the Foreign Office, who assured us that, if we did a secretarial course when we had graduated, we could be guaranteed a job with them and would in due course be posted to a French or Spanish-speaking country. So I settled for that, staying on at home to do a brief Secretarial course.

The move to London was more scary than exciting, and I still dutifully went home for the weekend once a month as well as writing weekly letters to my parents. To start with I lived in the Foreign Office women's hostel, along with Jenny, the French graduate friend I had made on the secretarial course, but after a very few months we joined up with two other friends to share a flat in Lambeth. My net salary was £10 per week, which was meagre even in the 1960s. After paying for rent, food, and travel to work, there was nothing left for entertainment, so it was impossible to make the most of living in London. Worse still, I found the work at the Foreign Office unbelievably boring.

My only salvation was the *Ad Lucem* group. *Ad Lucem* was an international organisation founded by Cardinal Lienhart, whose aim was to train people both spiritually and culturally to work in the Third World. My friend Tim had founded a branch at Bristol University, and joining it had aroused my interest in the plight of the poor – a concern given much less publicity back in the early sixties. So on moving to London it seemed only natural for me to join the London *Ad Lucem* group, and in due course I was appointed as its leader and played a big role in organising national conferences and so on. It was extremely time consuming, but for a young woman who had little hope of acquiring a boyfriend and no money for concerts or the theatre it was a lifeline – something to make me feel useful.

Thanks to contacts made through *Ad Lucem*, I was soon offered a very much more interesting and rewarding job with Catholic Overseas Appointments, recruiting teachers for Africa. I had very much more responsibility than I had had at the Foreign Office, worked much longer hours as there was so much to do, and made great friends with many of the teachers and headmasters I met. But the salary was still the same, and only after a couple of years was I awarded a small increase. So yes, I seemed destined to be poor, yet – far from resenting it – I felt guilty about being "so rich" compared with the people in Africa I was trying to help.

PART TWO - CRUSADER

Treasures wickedly come by give no benefit, but right conduct brings delivery from death. Yahweh does not leave the virtuous man hungry, but he thwarts the greed of the wicked.

Proverbs 10: 2-3

CHAPTER ONE - THE MISSION

The sun was setting on my beloved Burgundian hills when I left the vineyard to return home for the evening meal lovingly prepared by my mother. It was going to be a real wrench leaving Cluny and setting off for war, but it made more sense than continuing in my present life of poverty. Apart from feeling ourselves to be an integral part of this beautiful rolling countryside and indispensable in the production of the world's very best wines, what did my family and the other workers like us really have to live for? It was the *propriétaires* of the châteaux who gained all the profit from the sale of the great Burgundies. We, who did all the hard work of picking the grapes under a sometimes relentless sun, treading them to extract the juice, hauling the heavy barrels, filling the vessels, we were hardly paid enough to survive on in return for our labours. There was no justice here. Christian though they might call themselves, the château owners showed no inclination to follow the Cluniac ideal of "holy poverty".

So, within the next few days, I would pack all my clothes on my back and set off for Vézelay to join the next band of pilgrims who were leaving for the Holy War. Mother would stitch a cross on to my tunic. She would miss me dreadfully, but she felt proud that her son was going to join the army of Christ. "I shall pray for you daily, *mon cher Jules,*" she said when the time came, "and I trust the good Lord to bring you safely back to us once you have done your bit in ridding His world of the dreadful threat of Islam. Remember to pray for all of us too, and take care not to catch cold. The weather will not be as clement all the way to the Middle East as it is here at present, during harvest time."

"Have no fear, Mother. I am old enough now to take care of myself. I shall return a wealthy man, and you and the rest of the family will come to live on the farm I shall buy, so that you will no longer be dependent upon your pittance from the care of the *vignoble.*"

For that was what I had been promised by the leader of the contingent I would be joining in Vézelay. In return for my pilgrim's service to Christ by killing as many as I could of the infidel, I would have the right to certain spoils, which I could then take home with me to Burgundy once my duties were done. No longer would I be the victim of a lowly birth. Already, in recognition of what we would be doing, several of the local nobility had contributed funds towards the necessary expenditure. I was given a horse of my very own, as well as a good sword, and bread for the initial part of the journey towards the Iberian peninsula. Much though I loved my homeland, I had often felt a yearning to travel, and no doubt there would be much excitement along the way.

******

The landscape had changed beyond recognition, and we were truly well on our way. Although the days were already growing shorter, the heat of the daylight hours was of greater intensity now that we were journeying southwards, but I had been warned that once we were climbing up through the Pyrenees we might find ourselves subject to bitter cold such as I had never previously experienced. Sometimes I thought nostalgically about my family, who would all be extremely busy now trampling on the grapes and relaxing of an evening over a jar or two of smuggled *vin nouveau.* Yes, I could just do with a spot of that right now; my leather bottle had long since been emptied, and there was not even a waterfall or a clear stream in sight. Certainly the hardships of long distance travel were immense.

******

At other times, however, I was so thrilled by the new sights that I completely forgot my homesickness. When suddenly one day we caught our first glimpse of the sea, I could hardly believe my eyes. So large an expanse of water I could never have imagined, and watching the white-topped waves breaking on the shore held me enthralled until some of my companions told me to make speed. This was the Camargue, I was told, and its flatness was a huge contrast to the rolling hills where I belonged, yet it had a very special beauty all its own. I did not feel like hastening towards the Pyrenees, especially if we were going to find them capped with snow.

******

Another thing that held me back mentally was the thought of killing. Of course I was quite used to killing birds and rabbits, but killing <u>people</u> – plunging my sword through a man's heart – that would surely be totally different. "You quickly get used to it," said François, who had already been on the great Crusade led by Bernard, "and when you reflect that every Moor you slay is to the greater glory of God, it gives true purpose to your action." Ah well, we would see, and in any case my own, Christian, purpose was to return with a cartload of spoils with which to care for my parents in their old age. The Pyrenees were breathtakingly beautiful in spite of the cold, and how exotic and varied were the different kingdoms of the Iberian Peninsula! "To liberate the glorious province of Granada" was one of our avowed aims. However, before we reached that city, I got practice at fighting the Moors in several smaller places, and it was here that I began my plundering. Some of my companions took me to task on it. "You are a disgrace to the great name of Cluny," they said. "Do you not remember that the Cluniac ideal is sharing, not stealing?"

"Yes, but was I not promised material gain before we set out on this pilgrimage, and have I not just earned these goods by slaying so many Moors in the name of Christ? Just look at these bodies I have laid low by the strength of my own arm!" For François was right: one did quickly become inured to the sight of blood. I almost began to enjoy the massacre for which my skill was rapidly developing.

Of course the first problem I had to solve was what to do with the goods to which I was so liberally helping myself. Obviously the amount that my horse could carry was strictly limited, and we still had much journeying to do. So I decided that the only sensible course of action was to bury it, marking the spot carefully in a way recognisable only to myself, and dig it up again on my way home. This could only be done at night when my companions were sound asleep, and in this way too I was able to help myself without arousing further criticism.

We eventually arrived in Granada more or less simultaneously with the spring. If I had found the Carmargue, the Pyrenees and the little Hispanic towns we had passed through lovely in quite different ways, the beauty of Granada far exceeded anything that I could possibly have imagined. But we could not stay there long as the strength of the Moorish army far exceeded our own, and we rapidly realised that our small numbers did not stand a chance against their massive ones. Our leader reluctantly decided that the re-conquest of Granada would have to wait, but he said that we should not be discouraged since the defence of the Holy Land was another important task for us.

******

From Granada we headed to the coast. The name of our port was Alicante, but on the way we made brief stops to battle with Moors in various smaller places. One that took my fancy particularly had the odd name of Calp. It was only a little fishing village, but it was dominated by the most enormous rock jutting out into the sea and visible from many miles round about. I felt an overwhelming desire to climb to the top of this *Penyal d'Ifac*, as the locals seemed to call it, for the view from its summit would clearly be phenomenal, but alas I soon realised that its top part was sheer rock face and there would be no way for any normal human being to scale it. On reaching Alicante, we set sail for the Holy Land, feeling very satisfied with the contribution we had made towards freeing the Iberian Peninsula once more for Christendom.

CHAPTER TWO - AFRICA

The Iberian Peninsula had seemed a far cry from Burgundy, but my travels through it had been so full of interest and excitement that I had not really had much time to be homesick. Now, however, this new continent was a completely different, and alien, world. Besides, the sea journey had been tedious, and our supplies of food were inadequate. How I yearned more than ever for one of those smuggled jars of *vin nouveau*! The North African sun seemed completely relentless and, whereas at home I never tired of it and longed each year for winter to end, here we were in constant search for shelter from the sun. I seemed to have a permanent thirst, and hunger was now a thing of the past. I knew Mother would worry on my return to see how thin I had become, and my energy for fighting was steadily dwindling. I began to wonder whether I would ever reach the Holy Land. "You should eat more, Jules," said François. "These dates are delicious. It is still a long way to our destination and there is much work for a young man like you. You fought the Moors so nobly in Calp and Alicante, but now your skills seem to have diminished."

"Maybe I am not at heart a true Christian soldier like you. All I can think of at the moment is how weak I am under this sun, and how I long for the farm of my own, full of shady trees as well as vines, that I shall purchase on my return."

"That is <u>not</u> what God has called you on this pilgrimage for," replied François sternly. "Certainly we shall all deserve a little recompense for our labours, but our primary purpose is to reclaim the Holy Land for Christendom. If only you could have heard the great Bernard preaching in Vézelay! His words would have inspired you with a better motivation, and you would feel proud to be following Christ in Bernard's footsteps."

"So you really believe, do you François, that your purpose in this massacre is to follow Christ?"

"But of course."

After that I deliberately "lost" François and the companions who shared his view of our mission. Though I despised the dark-skinned people of this land just as much as they did, I felt more and more uncomfortable when they discussed the glory of what they were doing. My own glory was in the wonderful gold jewellery and other precious objects that I managed to acquire as I travelled on. I was still keeping up my practice of burying my treasure at night, and I always took more than I could possibly need in case I was unable to find it all again. One night a man who appeared to be a particularly wealthy chief caught me in the act and, though I could not understand his barbarous tongue, I realised from the tone of his voice that he was asking me what I was doing. I had to run away for fear of what he might do to me, but later that night, when I was confident that he had fallen asleep, I crept into his tent and picked up a huge, really beautiful casket. When I opened it I could hardly believe the sight of all the coins it contained, as well as other objects which looked immensely valuable. That night I got no sleep at all, as it seemed preferable to go a very long way from the village before digging an extra deep hole for the casket.

******

On and on I journeyed, all the time more weary, and longing more and more for the comforts of Burgundy with its cool rivers and inexhaustible supply of fresh drinking water. I was not alone in my weariness with the pilgrimage, yet I no longer had any true friends, for those of us who remained together were constantly vying with one another for the spoils. Suddenly one day I decided to give up the attempt to reach the Holy Land. The enthusiasts like François were much better qualified to defend it, and I had surely by now amassed as much treasure as I would be able to carry home with me.

As soon as I had made the decision it became clear that many of my fellow pilgrims were of like mind, so we realised that we would not be forced to find our way home completely alone. Each of us had the same reason for wishing to return by the exact route by which we had come, so there was always someone to follow whenever I was in any doubt about the way. I had, however, to be very careful that others did not retrieve my spoils before I was able to do so myself.

The most frightening moment of all was when we drew near to the village of the wealthy chief. He was riding around on his camel as we passed and recognised me instantly. With a great shout of rage, he urged his camel on and, though I also spurred on my horse, he soon overtook me. I feigned non-comprehension when he was obviously asking where I had hidden his casket and, but for my companions' intervention, I am sure he would have held me prisoner until I had led him to the spot where the casket was buried. I then promised some of my companions a share of the casket's contents if they would accompany me to the spot and hide with me until nightfall, when I could safely retrieve it. This done, my fellows were so impressed with the contents that I decided to forsake them as soon as they had fallen asleep. I travelled on through the night alone, but by good fortune the next morning I came across another group who were heading back to Alicante. Eventually we located a boat sailing from Tangiers, and I bade "farewell" to the African continent with no regrets.

CHAPTER THREE - RETURN TO FRANCE

Once back in Alicante, the first thing I had to think about was a means of transporting all my spoils. My horse had alas fallen sick and died at sea, but in any case he could not possibly have carried it all. I therefore decided to sell some of the gold I had stolen in North Africa and to purchase another horse and also a cart.

"What on earth do you want that for?" asked François and one or two others from Cluny, who had, to my great surprise, turned up in Tangiers just as we were setting sail. I mumbled some excuses, knowing that whatever I said was pointless. I had already lost their friendship since they all had scruples about the little crime of stealing. Still, what were a few friends compared with the value of the mansion I would be able to buy? I found many oranges and other delicious things to eat in the

Alicante region, my appetite returned, and the thought of my new mission renewed my energy. Fortunately my memory was good and on the whole I managed without too much difficulty to locate each spot where I had buried my treasures. My sword still stood me in good stead because, once they had realised what a dab hand I was with it, the locals rarely dared to challenge me over what I was doing. I succeeded in bribing some of my companions to silence by sharing a few of the spoils, but the few remaining with me who were from Cluny itself were too Christian to accept bribery. They, I feared, would tarnish my good name back at home, and the further north I travelled, the more apprehensive I became about returning there. The remaining party was dwindling daily, and I eventually realised that all the Burgundians would be back long before me. They would, I gradually became more and more sure, be spreading evil tales about me, and so my parents, to whom I had promised a home, would perhaps not want after all to share mine. My heart grew heavier, but there was nothing to be done. I did not feel guilty. I had earned my spoils, and in any case how could I possibly return now to being a simple peasant after all the glories of warfare? I needed to buy my own property and live in comfort for the rest of my days.

Eventually I decided, somewhat reluctantly, not to return to Burgundy after all, but instead to settle in the Carmargue – a part of the country which had greatly taken my fancy on the outward journey. No doubt I would not be accepted there immediately, and I would have to learn to speak the local people's ugly tongue, but I knew that wealth was a passport to almost anything. Once I had crossed the Pyrenees I began to sell my wares, so that by the time I reached the Carmargue my cart was almost empty and my pockets were bursting. Only a few days were needed for me to find exactly what I was wanting: a large farm with a wonderful view of the sea, complete with a troop of beautiful white horses. Here I felt sure that I could settle happily and do well running my own farm.

CHAPTER FOUR - REPENTANCE

I was an old man. Old and sick. Old, sick and alone. I had not seen my family since I set out on the Holy War, my fellow pilgrims had all turned against me, I was still regarded as a foreigner here in the south, in spite of my mastery of the language, and I had no true friends. Of course I had been able to live a life of luxury, with farm workers always at my beck and call, but what had really been the point of it all?

I had laughed at those of my fellow pilgrims who had not taken as literally as I had the promise of material gain in return for our services, yet now I was beginning to wonder whether they had not perhaps been right after all. As I lay in my bed increasingly less able to do everything I wanted, the faces of people from whom I had stolen, which I had repressed for so many years, gradually began to haunt me. Suddenly I yearned to make up for the wrongs I had done them. "I would give anything, anything," I shouted aloud, "to get up from my bed, retrace my steps through every country I went to, and return every single object I had taken." I would search high and low, I reflected, for every one of those people, or their descendants, and give them cash equivalent to what they had lost. But alas it was too late. I was now too ill even to walk the length of my own farm.

So what would become of me? Would I now burn in Hell? For my end was surely nigh. No, I recalled the words of my good mother and of the priests who said masses in Cluny when I was a boy. Cluny – how I yearned to be back there! No, I would never alas see my beloved Burgundy again, but at least I need not burn in Hell. For had I not been taught that the mercy of God was infinite? I had only to call for a priest and make my confession before I died. Even if I could not make peace with the people I had killed and stolen from, at least I could make my peace with God. At least, after a long spell in Purgatory, I supposed I could ultimately gain the promise of Heaven. And perhaps in Heaven I would again meet the people I had wronged – the wealthy chief and so many others equally innocent - and perhaps they would accept my apologies and forgive me. For only if that happened could I ever be at peace. Peace.... Peace.... How I yearned for peace!

PART THREE - UNDERSTANDING

When man emerges from the womb of his mother, one does not find any garland around his neck. There are no jewels made of pearls, nor are there glittering ornaments... But there is one garland around his neck. Brahma[1] strings together the consequences of his past deeds into a garland and puts it around his neck at the time of his birth.

Telugu[2] Poem

It was to be nearly thirty years till I began to learn about karma and came to understand the reasons for my poverty – or rather comparative poverty. (Comparative poverty which continued almost until my mid thirties, because the jobs I moved to from London, firstly in Oxford and then in Geneva, were also poorly paid.) Aron Abrahamsen told me about that crusader's life and, looking at it now, I find several features which have had repercussions in my present life, and it is perhaps worth going through them as points of interest for the student of spiritual matters.

---

1. *Brahma* is the creator God of the Hindu trinity.
2. Telugu is the language spoken in the state of Andra Pradesh.

One: I fell in love with Burgundy when I visited it at the age of twenty, working as an *au pair* with a family there. During the five years in which I lived in Geneva, I was able to make regular trips there, as Cluny was only about a four-hour drive and, first with friends and then with David, my future husband, I did a lot of wine tasting in that area. After my marriage and return to England, David was frequently invited back to the University of Geneva to do research in the summer. When the children were young we used to make the journey by car, and I always felt a compulsion to take a route via Burgundy, stopping for a night or two in Cluny.

Two: working for justice and valuing all religions have been strong features of my present life, and I have always felt a violent revulsion to the Crusades.

Three: I loved the Carmargue when I went there, but did not feel the same desire to return as I always have to Burgundy.

Four: I have never felt the same attraction to the Pyrenees as I have to the Alps. (It must have been pretty tough crossing them with a horse and cart!)

Five: for several years we owned a little flat in Calpe (called Calp in Valenciano), which I let at profit to the third world on account of feeling guilty about owning a second home. Each time we had a holiday there ourselves, I walked up the *Penyal d'Ifac* (or Peñón in Castilian Spanish), which would not have been possible before the tunnel, which enables one to get through to the less steep side, had been made. Getting to the top always gave me a great sense of achievement!

Six: though I have never told her this, I have in fairly recent years been able to identify a woman of my acquaintance as a reincarnation of the Moroccan chief from whom I stole the wonderful casket. She was black with a young family and in particularly difficult financial circumstances. She used to telephone me regularly asking for money, and was always so insistent that I never felt able to refuse, even after I had promised myself that the previous occasion would be the last time since we also had a lot of expense with our own young children. She told mutual friends, who commended my "generosity", yet I could never see it as anything but "duty". When one day she finally took my first "No" as an answer and never asked again, I knew that the debt had been paid.

Seven is a more general point. God never needs to forgive us because He loves us just the same whatever we do, but we always need to forgive ourselves. That crusader on his death bed, even without knowing anything at all about karma or that he would have to return to Earth, had a really strong desire to make it up with all the people he had wronged. This is what we all know we need to do for our own satisfaction, and sometimes it takes many lifetimes to find all the opportunities.

The people I killed during all those travels, for instance, would be most unlikely all to be incarnate in England now.

EXERCISES

1. Have you always had a tendency to be short of money? If so, has it ever occurred to you that you may now be reaping the fruits of past greed? From now on resolve to be thankful for any opportunities you have for paying old debts, and rest assured that, once they are paid, your circumstances will change for the better. (N.B. This does not preclude doing exercises you might find in other books aimed at bringing abundance into your life.)

2. However short you feel, remember that there are always people to be found who are worse off than you are. You may learn through experience that generosity is the best remedy for poverty. The statement "Whatever you give comes back to you four times over" may not be the best motive for giving, but it is nevertheless an eternal truth!

3. Do you worry about money? This is not an easy sort of worry to give up, but if you really make up your mind to replace worry with TRUST, you will be amazed at how effective it is. Remember Jesus' words about the lilies of the field and the birds of the air? You could write them on to a piece of paper and stick it somewhere where you will see it frequently. The more you learn to trust, the more you will find that you CAN trust, and finding that trust works will help you to trust even more. It becomes a "virtuous circle"!

VIII
FOCUSSING ON THE BODY

PART ONE - GETTING INTO MY BODY

Because of the ever increasing density of traffic on the roads, driving into a town these days takes longer and longer. On a trip into Hull, with the car almost motionless behind a bus, my eyes fell upon the advertisement with which its rear end was emblazoned. It gave the telephone number of a help line for children who are abused sexually, physically or emotionally. I reflected on the fact that no such thing had existed when I was a child, but it also occurred to me that, even if it had, not only would I never have had the courage to phone up a stranger about it, I would not even have realised that I was being emotionally abused!

I was fortunate in that I was not abused either sexually or physically, but the emotional abuse that I suffered as a child not only from my father, but also from my paternal grandmother and from certain teachers at school, was such that I really believed myself to be no good at all for anything. A help line would have been of no use to me because as far as I was concerned the grownups were right and I was wrong and God, for some reason known only to Himself, had made me ugly, stupid and useless at everything. Even getting a degree followed by a couple of good jobs did little to disabuse me of this notion, and it was not until I was well into my twenties that I met anyone who had the understanding and compassion to give me the help that I needed.

The very first person to give me some real psychotherapeutic help was the late Michael Hollings, who was then Catholic Chaplain to the University of Oxford. In his day the Chaplaincy was home to students, tramps, and peripheral people such as myself, who had moved to a job in one of the colleges in preference to living in London. I had already got to know Michael through organising a national Ad Lucem conference held in Oxford, and as soon as I moved there he asked me to lead the Oxford Ad Lucem group, which I found most daunting. But Michael always treated me as an equal, and I was a regular guest at his Chaplaincy dinners.

At one point I had a very brief romance with a student several years younger than myself, who was receiving counselling from Michael. When he broke it off, he told me that Michael was waiting for me in the Chaplaincy to pick up the pieces. Had the young man not been so insistent, I would probably not have had the courage to take my broken heart to a celibate priest, but this moment turned out to be the beginning of my long needed therapy. For Michael, bless him, put to me the novel suggestion that my being "no good" might have less to do with the way God had created me than with a distorted view drummed into me by my father. A suggestion that was reiterated within a few months by the psychotherapist who saw both children and staff at a school for disturbed children where I went to work briefly soon afterwards.

Throughout my difficult months of working at that school, I almost invariably went into Oxford on my days off for further counselling from Michael. Still he always treated me as an equal, and we kept in touch, erratically, until very shortly before his death in early 1997. The introductory workshop that I did with Roger Woolger was within days of my seeing Michael's obituary in the newspaper, and - since he had expressed an interest in this book - I set myself the goal of finding a karmic link with him.

At that weekend the preliminary exercise took me into a life as a French thirteenth century Dominican. Roger encouraged my partner to move me on soon into another life, "since monks are all in their heads", but she fortunately did not do so before I had had time to recognise Michael as my great companion in that life and to get a very strong feeling that we had had Cathar sympathies. So that explained both his having always treated me as an equal and his interest in my new found belief in reincarnation!

Roger at that first meeting I had with him said that he would not train me until I had done some body work because I was "too much in my head". Later, as I embarked on the full Woolger training, I learnt more and more about how abuse makes people flee their bodies in order to escape pain, and this does not apply only to physical pain. I had previously been aware at times of being detached from my emotions. For instance, when several years previously my sister Philippa's six-year old daughter had been knocked down by a car, had to have brain surgery in Hull Royal Infirmary, and was expected not to live (but has just completed her GCSE examinations successfully!), I was more or less the only person who remained cool and unhysterical from the first moment. In this case my detachment proved useful because it enabled me calmly to make continual telephone calls to other members of the family all over the country and to take tempting meals to my sister at the hospital when she might otherwise not have been persuaded to eat at all.

However, detachment from one's feelings is not generally a good thing. On the one hand it can cause all sorts of physical ailments, since the emotions have to go somewhere. On the other hand it can generate a lack of compassion for others. Refusing to feel one's own pain makes it difficult to empathise with that of other people. Many women – and no doubt some men too, but I believe that men tend to be better than women are at cutting themselves off from their emotions – suffer intensely at the hands of men who hurt them simply because they do not want to face up to their own pain. Sometimes, too, repressed pain can act as a sort of powerhouse of energy. I used to be envious of people who had infinitely more energy than I had, until I realised that their frenetic activity was sometimes simply a ploy for avoiding facing their pain. And it serves no useful purpose in the long term because there are always limits to the extent to which the body can be driven; eventually it will protest and fall ill. A friend of mine once told me how she had come very near to death before finally being forced to "do her work". Now, after much therapy and "inner child" work done on her own, she is a very contented and useful member of society.

Facing one's pain of course takes courage – and the difficulty is compounded when you are unaware that this is what you have been doing, often for so very many years. Although in my first course in regression therapy I learnt most of the theory, the venue was not at all well suited to body work. Lawrence, my homœopath, had already talked to me about the fact that my painful childhood had made me cut off from my feelings, and had done his best to make me work on it, but firstly our sessions could never be long enough, and secondly I was (and am!) stubborn. "Getting into the body" is not easy when you have been out of it for a very long time. My course in London did confirm Lawrence's view, and also I discovered there that my detachment pre-dated my childhood in this life.

As part of my London College of Past Life Regression Studies training I went on a weekend course aimed at discovering one's Life Plan. For this the first step was to get into our most recent past life, work through that and through the death and then to look at the plan we made in the Bardo for our present life. Well, Edwin Courtenay had already told me that he thought I had been one of the first Jews to be gassed. I had been sceptical about that - partly because of having been born in 1940 - and I had subsequently consulted the well known clairvoyant Lilla Bek on the subject. She confirmed Edwin's view, but said that it was a life that was not yet ready to be looked at. When I voiced my difficulty to Helen Wozniak, one of the tutors at the London College, she said "Never mind. Your partner can simply instruct you to go to the most recent life that you are ready to look at.". So she did that, and what was the first scene I got but a crowd shouting "Heil Hitler". I then observed the life just as though it were a video, in a completely detached way, and when it reached the scenes of the concentration camp, despite getting very clear pictures of people being pulled screaming along the ground by their hair, I felt nothing at all. Even inside the gas chamber I could hear the screams and feel the panic of all the people pressing around me, yet I as a teenage boy remained completely unemotional and simply floated out of my body.

Thinking about the regression afterwards, I realised that I had cut off from my feelings very early on in that Jewish life because it was the only way I had of coping with the horror of what was going on. And I assume that I brought that detachment in with me when I returned to Earth very quickly. It served me well for a while as armour against my father and my grandmother, but it ceased to serve me as soon as I decided that I wanted to work in regression therapy. After gaining my first diploma, not only was I still very bad at feeling things in my own body, I also had difficulty in working in this way with clients. Perhaps the people who came to me then did so because of this shared difficulty. I do not know. What I do know is that gradually my Woolger training changed all that. As I found myself increasingly able to locate and describe sensations in my own body, so I got better little by little at getting my clients into previous lives by use of what is known in the trade as the "somatic bridge". I had previously had a considerable amount of success using guided visualisation, but since people vary so much, it is good to have a variety of tools at one's disposal. Also, one of the most important theses of the Woolger method is that our samskaras (karmic residues) are all stored in the body and we need to get in touch with them in order to release them permanently.

PART TWO - AUSCHWITZ

...the lorry stopped, and we saw a large door, and above it a sign, brightly illuminated (its memory still strikes me in my dreams), ARBEIT MACHT FREI, work gives freedom.
We climb down, they make us enter an enormous empty room that is poorly heated. We have a terrible thirst. The weak gurgle of the water makes us ferocious; we have had nothing to drink for four days. But there is also a tap – and above it a card which says that it is forbidden to drink as the water is dirty... I drink... but I have to spit it out, the water is tepid and sweetish with the smell of a swamp.
This is Hell.

Primo Levi[1]

In August 2003 I accompanied my husband to Poland when he was invited to a conference in Warsaw. I had never felt drawn to any of the Eastern European countries, but David was keen for me to go with him, and I always love visiting new places anyway. The professor who had issued the invitation was actually from Krakow and he encouraged us to visit that city as well, even offering us accommodation in a little guest room that they have inside the Mathematics Institute. So we decided to take a train to Krakow from Warsaw as soon as the conference was over. I had never thought seriously of visiting Auschwitz (Oswieçim in Polish) – never even bothered to find out exactly where it was – but as soon as we noticed in our guide book that it was only sixty kilometres from Krakow and that there was a regular bus service to it, a trip there suddenly seemed imperative. David had had difficulty in persuading me to go and see Schindler's List and I was glad that he had succeeded. Yet, moved though I was by that film, I still remained detached from the horror of the Holocaust.

Krakow was every bit as worth seeing as we had been promised, and after a wonderful day and a half of tourism there, we took the early Sunday morning bus to the Auschwitz Museum. The countryside in between Krakow and the former concentration camp is rather pleasant, which somehow amplifies the starkness of the scene that confronts one on arrival at Auschwitz. I had intended to stay only briefly, but that proved to be almost impossible as the museum has been so well done and there is a lot more to see than I had imagined.

It is hard to say which bit of the place struck me the most deeply, but one sight that I know I shall never forget is the glass case full of human hair salvaged from the corpses. It stretches the entire length of one of the large rooms. Much of the victims' hair was sold for the production of textiles, and samples of those are also exhibited.

---

1. *If This is a Man*, Primo Levi, translated by Stuart Woolf, Abacus, London, 1987.

Each country that was involved has done its own section, and they are all very different from each other. The Italian section, created partly by the author Primo Levi, who survived Auschwitz (largely because of his determination to write about it later), was for me the most powerful in a way because it says nothing at all. Well, there is nothing to say about Auschwitz. No human being, no language could ever come anywhere near to completely describing what really went on there. Now that I have seen the place, I find myself wondering whether it would be possible to get fully into the feelings of the victims and remain sane. I have no regrets about the detachment mechanism that I used for coping in that Jewish life, and I imagine that many of my fellow victims did likewise. (In fact I feel that Levi's book confirms that.)

The Polish Army barracks at Auschwitz was converted into a concentration camp when I was about two months old, so I knew already that it could not have been there that I was killed in my last life. I also believe that I had never been to Poland before (hence the fact that I did not feel drawn to it). When I heard the recorded sound of the "Holocaust train" at the Auschwitz Museum, I knew for sure that I had been in one of those trains, but I am pretty sure that it was in Germany. Anyway, that is of little importance. To my mind the only thing of real importance is that people learn from the horror of what happened in the Holocaust and prevent a repetition of it. The Auschwitz Museum is therefore important as education. Although it was a Sunday in August, I had somehow not expected to see many people, but there were in fact vast numbers of tourists, and I was glad.

But another important part of my brief pilgrimage to Auschwitz was a healing mission. I took a little pot of vibhuti[2] with me and scattered it surreptitiously all over the place, saying prayers and trying to tune in to the souls of the deceased. What came through to me as I wandered was that most of the Jews involved were now fine, that the majority of them had reincarnated already, but that many prayers were still needed for the Nazis who had worked there. Victim, perpetrator; perpetrator, victim – it's the luck of the draw really. We have all had lives as both. I happen to know that at that particular time I was lucky enough to be a victim, but I could equally well have been a Nazi and consequently still be suffering on account of the karma created in the concentration camp. So please, let us not condemn, but just learn.

I had heard that birds would still not nest at Auschwitz, and so as we walked round I had a good look, and certainly I did not see a single bird. I did, however,

2. *Vibhuti* is the healing ash that Sai Baba manifests all the time. It also often forms on pictures of Him all over the world, in the homes of very spiritual people.

hear two. The first was a very distinct sound, which seemed to be saying to me "I've come in response to the healing you're offering to this place.". The second was more a subdued twitter, and I got the feeling that it had been there already. So perhaps the birds are slowly beginning to return to Auschwitz? I should be interested to know whether anyone else sees or hears any. Another interesting point is that the film which included my photographs of Auschwitz failed to come out, although there was clearly nothing wrong with the camera. Does that reflect my desire to blot out the place from my memory?

PART THREE - SOUL FRAGMENTATION

There are many close links between regression therapy and shamanic practice. Sandra Ingerman in her book on Soul Retrieval[3] gives an excellent description of the shaman's way of retrieving lost bits of the soul which split off when the person concerned suffered trauma. On my first therapy course we once did an exercise in that, and I found a bit of myself that had stayed in "Box Tree House" when I was probably about seven. "Box Tree House" was in my grandparents' enormous garden in Somerset, and it was, as its name implies, a box tree that had grown into a sort of house – sheer paradise for young children. It had a door – a hole that was just the right size for young children to go through – and a branch with a "u" in it which made a perfect seat. My siblings and I must have had endless tea parties in there, and – apart from the apples which I guzzled endlessly – it was the only thing that made the long summer holidays spent in the cottage on my grandparents' property bearable. No wonder that, when in 2000 my second aunt had died and selling Welham had become imperative, Box Tree House was the only part of it that I felt sad at saying "goodbye" to! But, since the house was purchased by a family with six children, it now it gives me great joy to think of other children being able to make the most of Box Tree House all year round.

It was not until the workshop in France a whole five years later that I found out that part of my soul had also split off in the womb. In the meantime, on a weekend working with fellow Woolger trainees under the supervision of Grace Dixon, I got regressed to my second birthday, which was traumatic because of my mother having to leave for the hospital in the middle of my party in order to give birth to my sister. Here Grace found another case of a spirit attachment, but this time it was not a whole spirit but a piece of my father's soul that had split off when he was also two years old. Soul fragments can make use of a physical voice box in the same way that whole attached spirits can, and my father's story was also a sad one. It sprang from

---

3. *Soul Retrieval*, Sandra Ingerman, HarperSan Francisco, 1991

a sensation in my stomach (at that stage I had already begun to get better at finding them), and when the sensation spoke, it turned out not to be the two-year old Ann but the two-year old Stephen, who was upset at being left alone with Nanny while his parents went away for he did not know how long. This soul fragment had apparently attached itself to me about thirty years later when it saw me experiencing similar feelings of abandonment and, through Grace's expertise another thirty years later, it was able finally to be released and join up with the main bit of my father's soul now residing in Heaven.

The only other spirit releasement that I had experienced before the one described in Part III was in an individual session with Roger. The previous weekend I had been on a stall at a health festival and got into conversation with someone on the adjoining Aura Soma stall, who was somewhat clairvoyant. She mentioned having been in the Holocaust in her last life and, when I told her that I had been as well, she said that she could see me there as a little girl of seven or eight and that that little girl still needed healing. This puzzled me since I was so sure about having been a male teenager, but Roger immediately guessed the reason for it. Without telling me what he thought it was, he regressed me to that life again, and he then released the spirit of my younger sister, whom I was still carrying. Edwin had told me that I had been gassed for my rebelliousness in trying to defend my mother and sister, and it appeared from the second regression that they had died very shortly after me and the little girl had attached herself to me on account of her need for protection and my feeling of responsibility – a responsibility given me by my dying father when I had been about twelve. This regression with Roger also confirmed the origin of my detachment from my body but, being now more aware of my physical feelings, I felt a burden being lifted from my back as soon as Roger had released my sister's spirit. And, interestingly, when I got home from Oxford, I found that the very same weekend David had been watching a television programme which claimed that the gassing of the Jews had started well before 1940!

PART FOUR - THE FARMER'S WIFE

To love at all is to be vulnerable. Love anything and your heart will certainly be wrung and possibly be broken. If you want to make sure of keeping it intact, you must give your heart to no-one. Wrap it carefully round with hobbies and little luxuries. Avoid all entanglement; lock it safe in the casket or coffin of your selfishness. But in that casket, safe, dark, motionless, airless, it will change. It will not be broken – it will become unbreakable, impenetrable, irredeemable. The only place outside Heaven where you can be perfectly safe from all the dangers and perturbations of love is Hell.

C. S. Lewis

So, by the time I had completed the Woolger training I no longer had so much difficulty in using the body as a starting point for past life work. When a group of those of us who had graduated at more or less the same time went off for the second workshop in France in June 2002, I also realised that I had at last finally overcome my fear of men and was very happy one day to work with Kris, with whom I had never previously done a session. When the subconscious knows that the environment is right for repressed traumata to be dealt with, all sorts of unexpected things can come up, and I became aware of a very strong feeling going right down through the centre of my chest from my throat to my genital organs. When Kris got me to focus on it fully and describe it in more detail, the main thing I was able to say was that it felt as though something – or more likely some<u>one</u> – had been wrenched away from me, and I wanted desperately to grab hold of them again and hang on and on and not let them go again.....

CHAPTER ONE - THE CRUEL FARMER

"Isn't my dinner ready, woman? What use is that to a hardworking man? You knew when I'd be back and how hungry I would be!"

"You're at least ten minutes earlier than yesterday and the vegetables only need a few more minutes. I had all the washing to do before I could put anything into the oven. Otherwise it wouldn't have dried in time for you to have clean things to wear to market tomorrow."

"Always making excuses, you are! If you had the washing to do, you should have got up earlier. Here take that.... and that, for your laziness." This time the blows were one on each cheek. Yesterday he had hit me so hard across the buttocks that I still could not sit down for the pain. What had I done to deserve this? I had not had a moment to relax ever since my wedding day a whole seven years ago. It was work, work, work all the time on this farm, and nothing that I did was ever good enough for Tobias.

I had never imagined it would be like this. When my dear father gave me the news that the farmer from over the way had come to ask for my hand in marriage, I was excited. I was already twenty years old and time seemed to be passing me by. My mother kept reminding me that she had only just turned sixteen on her wedding day and that I had been born before her seventeenth birthday. When I replied that there was nothing I could do about it, she would look pleadingly at my father, who would then say "Well, I just wish there were a few more eligible young men in this part of Yorkshire. If we could move to the city of York, I'm sure there would be more choice, but anyway I don't think we would be suited to city life, do you?" Then my mother would have to admit that she could not bear the thought of moving from this part of the countryside that had always been home to her, and I knew that she would retire to her room and return to her mainstay of prayer.

So, when Tobias suddenly turned up at our front door that day and asked to have a good look at me, it seemed like the answer to my mother's prayers. I knew him well by sight – I had often seen him with his calves on market days – and he had always looked a fine figure of a man to me. But it had never entered my head that he might one day show an interest in me – partly because he was known to be close on thirty and many people considered him to be a confirmed bachelor. What had made him turn overnight to the idea of matrimony? Probably the realisation that there was more work than he could go on doing himself indefinitely or afford to pay for, and so he could do with a son and heir to help him and eventually inherit the farm.

And this of course was where I had so let him down. To start with we both took some pleasure in our marital relations. It was new and exciting for both of us, and after a hard day's work Tobias would sometimes enjoy relaxing of an evening over a pint of beer before carrying me upstairs. But as time went on and each month my bleeding started yet again, he began to get angry. Gradually our lying together ceased to be pleasurable; for me it became first duty, then more like torture. "Perhaps we have never chosen the right time," he would say. "We are both fit and healthy and have no reason not to make fine parents, so we must just try more often." Sometimes he would force himself on me when I was more than ready for sleep after a long, hard day; sometimes he would accuse me viciously of being barren.

Although the sexual violence started quite early on in my marriage, it was another couple of years or so before Tobias first took to beating me. It was a terrible shock initially, and for a moment I thought of fleeing to my parents'. Long walk though it was, I knew I could do it, but before any proper plan had had time to form itself in my head, Tobias threatened me. "Don't you dare run off and moan to that father of yours!" he shouted. "If you do, I'll tell him that I caught you in bed with the farm hand." (In bed with the farm hand? I had scarcely ever even looked at the farm hand! It was true, he was about my age and quite handsome, but with my firm Christian upbringing, committing such a sin as adultery would never enter my head for a second.)

Once, when my family had been visiting, my young sister Katie had asked about the bruise on my neck. Before I had had time to open my mouth to reply, Tobias had spun a convincing yarn about a fall, saying how I had not wanted to worry them by saying anything, how he had insisted that I take to my bed for a couple of days, how he had looked after me so carefully. And all the while that he was telling these dreadful lies, he was throwing me threatening glances which, somehow or other, he managed not to let my parents notice.

Oh, if they knew what my life was really like now, how sad they would be! But I doubt if I could bring myself to tell them even if I could do so without incurring Tobias' rage. They who were already so sad at there being no sign of a grandchild! No, I could not tell them. But that did not stop me wishing that I could turn the clock back. Often my mind drifted nostalgically back to those happy childhood days when I used to sit on my father's knee and twiddle his moustache. He was quite a strict disciplinarian with us four children, but he had such a gentle, loving side to him as well. My mother worked tirelessly keeping the home, and he always showed his appreciation of her efforts, never scolding her if the parsnips were a bit burnt or the Yorkshire pudding a bit too soft in the middle. Why, oh why could God not have found me a husband like my father?

CHAPTER TWO - THE FARM HAND

"What's wrong with you ma'am?" The farm hand's voice gave me such a shock! It was very rarely that he came even to the door – never right into the kitchen – but obviously my sobbing had prevented me from hearing his knock. He held a sickly chicken under his arm and it was evidently his concern about that which had brought him looking for my husband.

"The master was called suddenly to my mother-in-law," I explained, drying my eyes hastily. "They fear that she may not survive until tomorrow. What can I do to help you?"

"Nothing ma'am. This chicken is sick, and if it is a disease, I would not want it to spread to the rest of the flock, but the chicken's problems are of little consequence compared with yours. I see that you are badly bruised. What has happened?"

"Oh, nothing really; just a little accident."

"I don't believe it can be no more than a little accident to make you weep so. You must tell me more." The farm hand's voice was so kind, his concern seemed so genuine, and I had been yearning for so long for someone in whom I could confide. I hesitated for a few moments before replying.

"Oh, it was just the master.... Umm... err... He was displeased with me."

"Displeased with you? Surely you cannot have committed a crime so terrible as to deserve <u>that</u>?"

"No, I don't believe I have committed any real crime."

"So what have you done to provoke him in this way?"

"Nothing really, I don't think. Sometimes he complains if his dinner is not placed on the table the very moment he comes in, or if the vegetables are slightly overcooked or undercooked, or if I have not done his washing early enough for it to have got dry... But..."

"But what?"

"Well, I think the real thing he has against me is the fact that I am barren. He so much wants a son to help him on the farm."

"And he beats you for that? I have never heard anything so dreadful!"

"But what can I do? He is stronger than I am and I cannot run away."

"Something must be done. I will speak to him."

"No, no, you must not do that. If you did, at best he would beat me still harder; at worst you would lose your job. There is nothing to be done, but at least it has been good to have someone to talk to. Thank you for listening. Ah, I think I hear him returning now..."

"Oh master, it is good that you are returned. I just came looking for you this very moment because I am concerned about this sick chicken. If the disease were to spread...."

******

Over the next three months or so the farm hand popped into the kitchen to see me whenever he was sure that Tobias was nowhere near. We talked endlessly, and he tried to encourage me to stand up to Tobias or to ask my father to take me home again. I told him that it was useless, that I would only be made to suffer more if I fought back in any way, and that nothing would satisfy him unless I bore a child. He pointed out to me that it took two people to conceive a child, and that I might in fact not be to blame at all – an idea that had never occurred to me. But of course I could not put that idea to Tobias as it would undoubtedly make him angrier.

Gradually I came to live only for the brief moments that I spent with the farm hand. After a very short time I felt as though we had always known one another. He began to talk to me about his own past, his difficult childhood with an alcoholic father, the death of his mother when he was very young, his relief when he obtained the job with Tobias, even though the wage was so meagre... One day he suddenly took me in his arms. His embrace was sheer heaven after the brutal rapes I was now accustomed to enduring almost nightly from Tobias. But we dared not linger in one another's arms, for we knew that we might both be killed instantly if we were caught.

Over the next three weeks we talked hurriedly whenever we could of various options. My loins ached constantly for him, but we both knew that adultery was wrong and punishable by Hell fire. Also, we could not possibly flee together because we would have nowhere to go. And the two of us could not possibly survive for more than a few days on the farm hand's wage. But gradually we hatched a plan.

CHAPTER THREE - THE END

Today! Yes, it was to be today. I rose from my bed trembling with apprehension and excitement, terrified that Tobias would notice something out of the ordinary in my demeanour. It was market day and he had a particularly fine calf that he was hoping to sell for a handsome sum. I found him in the kitchen already half way through a hasty breakfast, and he scarcely gave me a glance before making his departure.

The farm hand and I had chosen the hay stack in the field nearby in preference to either my bed or his, as they seemed far too risky. My love for him had grown so deep that even my fear of Hell fire did nothing to abate my desire. He loved me sincerely too, and no doubt also felt desire very keenly, but his plan had been prompted mainly by his intense wish to help me. "If I were to have success in impregnating you," he had said, "and you bore a son, then firstly your husband would never guess that he was not the father, and secondly he would be so overjoyed that he would surely give up beating you. Then we could continue with our occasional secret meetings just as we have been doing of late, I would have the pleasure of watching my child grow, and I would be equally happy if it were a girl. Any child that had sprung from the woman I love would bring me intense joy even if I were never able to tell her the truth about her conception."

The plan seemed foolproof, I needed to consummate my love even more than I wanted a child, yet somehow fear seemed to consume me. Endeavouring with all my might to repress it, I made myself a hasty breakfast and then set off in the direction of the haystack leaving most of the food uneaten. There was a slight chill in the September air, but my clothes were ample. They needed to be since I dared not take a blanket from the house to serve as a mattress. If I were espied by the milkmaid or a neighbouring farmer who happened to be passing by on his way to market, they would be sure to ask me where I was going. Dressed as I was, I could simply say that I was going to cut a cabbage for my husband's dinner.

Once at my destination I cannot have needed to wait more than ten minutes for my loved one to arrive, yet it felt like an eternity. He had told me the day before that he had tunnelled out a secret chamber in the haystack, and I crept into it eagerly. My heart pounded like a cow in labour. When finally my beloved arrived, I consumed him with kisses and clung to him as though my life depended on it. Then he slowly took off his clothes and I loosened my bodice and pulled up my skirt.

However, just as he was about to make the longed-for entrance into my hungry body, there was a shout of "Aha, I've caught you red-handed! I've had my suspicions for a good couple of weeks now and, after noticing you walking away from the haystack yesterday, I came along to investigate. Then, with a bloodcurdling yell of "How dare you! This is your reward," he whipped out the scythe and, before my horrified eyes, cut off my beloved's genitals. "Now flee from my sight," he continued, "and leave me to deal with her."

Never had I known Tobias' rage so great. First he seized a handful of straw and stuffed it into my mouth. Some of the ends were so sharp that they drew blood. Then he pulled off all my clothes violently and rolled me around on the prickly straw screaming "Whore! How can I have been such a fool as to marry a whore? How dared you? And with that orphan son of a drunk of all people!" Had I not been gagged by the straw, I would have replied "He is kind, not like you, and he wanted to do you a favour by getting me with child", but by now I was choking with blood as well as straw, and the force of his body was also making the straw dig painfully into my limbs and torso. Finally he grabbed his scythe again and slit my throat.

******

The first thing that I did on leaving my body was to run off looking for my beloved. I found him collapsed, exhausted, by the stream several fields away, with blood streaming down his precious legs. I threw my arms around him saying "Darling, don't worry, I'm here.", but it did not take me very long to realise that I was dead and that, since he was still alive, he could not hear me. So then I simply waited patiently, watching his every movement lovingly. He had picked up his jacket but had not been able to retrieve his breeches before Tobias had made him flee, so I knew that he would not be able to go much further. In my discarnate state there was nothing I could do to help him, so I decided that my best plan would be to proceed into the Bardo and then gather some guides to help him to follow me there. Only a short time ago death's gate had seemed like a daunting mystery to me, but now that I had passed through it, I knew that I was in familiar territory.

Just as anticipated, I did not have to wait very long for my beloved to join me.

But he did not do so before I had had time for a very productive talk with my guides, who assured me that I had now paid a karmic debt to Tobias and would never need to meet him on Earth again. They also reminded me that the person I had fallen in love with had been a colleague in Atlantis and that we had been together several times during the interim.

How great was my joy when my loved one appeared! We embraced long and hard, and then went together for healing, I for my cut throat, he for his severed genitals. When that was done, we discussed what to do about Tobias, decided that he had inflicted his own punishment on himself through his actions and that, since we were now so much happier than he was, we need not bear him any grudge.

PART FIVE - THE SAMSKARA

Twice in the last few years I have suddenly been afflicted by a curious phenomenon which completely defied explanation by the medical profession. My whole body became covered more or less overnight with bloody spots and bruises. It was not in the least painful, but several of the spots were inside my mouth, which was inconvenient and unpleasant as I was spitting blood for a few days. Both times it all cleared up of its own accord within a week or so, but it remained a mystery until I had done the farmer's wife regression. Then it seemed to tie in with the prickly straw being thrust into my mouth and my whole body being brutally pushed around in the straw stack. I cannot prove that this is the explanation, but two years have now passed since that regression and the affliction has not recurred. So Deo gratias!

EXERCISES

1. (a) Put on some lively music and move energetically to it for as long as you can manage.

   (b) When you are really exhausted, switch the music off, lie down and scan your body thoroughly. Now take a large piece of paper and three crayons. Draw a body outline. With your first colour mark any areas of pain/ache/strong discomfort. With your second colour draw the energy flow through your body, putting a cross where you notice any blockages.

   (c) You may be someone who can get in touch with your body quite easily. If, on the other hand, you have difficulty in doing this exercise, repeat it on a regular basis. We have chosen to come into human bodies for a reason, and it is therefore good to be as fully in them as possible. Often your body has an important message for you, so it is good to listen!

2. Would you call yourself a "human being" or a "human doing"? Think about it carefully. Do you fill your life with activity and leave yourself little or no time to relax and just be? If so, did you find 1(b) difficult? Could you be blocking off or running away from facing up to certain trauma(ta)? You will have to deal with it/them some time – in a future life if not in your present one – so why not decide that the time for that is NOW? For a start you could

- work (preferably with a friend or therapist) through John Bradshaw's book HOMECOMING – *Reclaiming and Championing Your Inner Child*[4],

- or book yourself on to a workshop (Woolger/Louise Hay/Brandon Bayes, etc.)

- or find a good therapist and keep going regularly. It's no good making just one or two appointments and then deciding that you can't afford it, or that it hasn't changed anything. Perseverance is essential even if it is a matter of years – and if it's what you really need, believe that the money will not be an obstacle. Prioritise. You <u>must</u> learn to put yourself first. We can be of much more use to others once we have sorted ourselves.

---

4. Piatkus, London, 1990.

IX
RENEWING OLD RELATIONSHIPS

PART ONE
GENEVA AND "THE LOVE OF MY LIFE"

After three years of working in London, I moved to a job in Oxford, which still felt like my home town because ever since leaving it soon after the end of the War, I had made regular visits to an elderly cousin there. I made new friends and was happy in some ways, but the work was less interesting and rewarding than my previous job. So after another three years, having lost hope of finding a husband, I decided to spread my wings and go abroad. I thought of Australia, but then a post turned up in Geneva with an American Catholic organisation. It sounded just up my street, but in fact was a disappointment – not least because it was virtually impossible to live on the salary – and in due course I moved to a slightly better paid job as an editor with the World Council of Churches. In the meantime I fell violently in love firstly with Geneva itself, where I was at last able to escape from the oppression of my family, and secondly with a Spanish priest whom I will call Juan.

Juan and I met in July 1970 in Monaco, where we had both been invited to act as translators at a conference. Midnight bathing was the first thing that we enjoyed together, and initially we both thought of it as no more than a "holiday romance", but before the return train had reached Geneva (he had to go on to Lausanne), we had arranged for him to come and visit me the following week. Besides a love of languages, we shared a passion for music, particularly that of Bach, and he was very accomplished on the guitar. So my joy the following week, when on the evening of Juan's day off he played me some Bach on his guitar, was tinged with sadness at his not being free on account of the Catholic Church's absurd rule on celibacy for priests. Over the ensuing months our friendship deepened, and he tried (rather vainly!) to foster in me hope of the celibacy rule changing. At that point in his life friendship with a woman roughly his own age was sufficient, but I wanted a great deal more. I wanted constant companionship, not just one visit per week or fortnight; I wanted security; I wanted children by a man I loved, but most of all (I realised years later), I wanted the love that my own father had been unable to give me.

PART TWO - FOURTEENTH CENTURY ITALY

CHAPTER ONE - THE CONVENT

"Sister Anna! Sister Anna!" Mother Ambrosia's voice rang loud and clear along the corridor; then she knocked on my cell door and walked straight in without waiting for a reply. "Are you not up yet? It's your turn to fetch the water this morning, and it's only half an hour now till Matins."

"I'm sorry, Mother. I don't feel at all well."

"What's the trouble? Should I fetch the physician?"

"I don't know what it is. I tried to get up just now, but my head started swimming and I was afraid I would fall."

"Right then. I'll ask Sister Chiara to fetch the water, and we'll send for the physician straight after mass. It's a bit early to get him up now. You stay in bed for the moment. We cannot be too careful."

Had the same thought entered Mother Ambrosia's head as it had mine?, I wondered. It could not be the Black Death returning to Florence, could it? When Mother and my brother and sister had died, they had clearly been much sicker than this. Yes, but had they fallen desperately ill straight away, or had it started gradually? I could not quite remember. I had been so young at the time, and it seemed so long ago now. So long ago.... Of course it was. Florence had been declared quite free of the plague, and things had been getting back to normal for quite a few years now. The woollen trade was flourishing once more, the banks had reopened, Orcagna's new tabernacle for the *Madonna del Pilastro* – the painting which was believed to work miracles - had just been completed in the new Orsanmichele building... Father said all about it when he visited. He said it made him proud to be Florentine, so beautiful was the Orsanmichele now, with the grain traders cleared out, a profusion of statues and pinnacles, reliefs and mosaics, precious stones and rich marbles....

Riches? Yes, Florence was certainly full of those, as well as of wonderful art and architecture, cloths and crafts. But who benefited from all these riches? Certainly not Father, even though he had worked so hard all his life! He had never been able to earn enough to keep us all, and after Mother and Pietro had died from the plague and there was only Carlo old enough to earn a little from weaving alongside Father, and poor Giulia had had to cook for us all, he said he really had no choice but to put me in the convent. Mother Ambrosia had welcomed me from the start, but she did find me difficult to deal with. Our energies conflicted so – she so dynamic and stormy, I so quiet and peaceable – and anyway her faith was so much stronger than mine; she could not understand why I found it so hard to pray.

******

Mother Ambrosia and the physician had gone outside into the corridor. "So you're sure it's not the Black Death?" I heard her ask in a low, anxious tone.

"No, no, Mother, don't worry yourself. She'll be fine again in a few days' time. The Black Death really has left Florence for good now, thank the Lord. Just keep her quiet and give her plenty to drink and some herbs which I'll send round to you."

"Thank the Lord! And we can thank the *Madonna del Pilastro* too."

******

"You must get up today, sister Anna. You've finished your herbs, and the physician said a week's rest should be enough to put you right again."

"But what is there to get up for, Mother?"

"Get up <u>for</u>? What on earth do you mean? There's <u>everything</u> to get up for! Praising the Lord that you were not seriously ill and that the Black Death has finished, coming to mass, cleaning the kitchen, fetching the water... Sister Chiara hurt her back fetching the water last week while you were in bed. She's really a bit old now for that job; it was a mistake of mine to ask her."

"Why does it always have to be me cleaning the kitchen? I much prefer to cook."

"It's not for you to decide who does what in this convent,"she snapped.

Oh well, I suppose I had better get up. It was true, I was not faint any longer, and it would not be fair on my fellow sisters to shirk my share of the work. But what was the point of this life here? It was just so boring; every day the same: drudgery interspersed with prayer… And even the prayer seemed like drudgery really.

If there really was a God, surely He meant us to be doing more interesting things than just cleaning the kitchen and praying. When I was a child living at home with my family, life was hard and we were often hungry, but at least I could get out into the streets of Florence and watch what was going on. It was never boring. Even just watching the grain come down the chute from the Orsanmichele pilaster was fun, and there were always hordes of people to-ing and fro-ing, bargaining, buying and selling… I would almost prefer the fights and riots, which used sometimes to frighten me when I was small, to this – this nothingness. Sometimes, when Mother had sent me to buy a little wine or, when we could afford it, some cloth for a dress for my youngest sister, I would linger a while on the Ponte Vecchio, enthralled by the beautiful metalwork and jewels. Then, at other times, my older brothers and sisters and I used to chase each other round and round the Campanile. True, my family was very religious, but religious celebrations at home were always very lively affairs compared with ours now in the convent.

******

Now Matins was over and I was cleaning the kitchen again. It almost always seemed to be my turn to clean the kitchen! "It's good for your soul, Sister Anna," Mother Ambrosia would say. "If you do it joyfully, I'm sure the good Lord will grant you several months off Purgatory." Off Purgatory? Surely Purgatory – whatever it consisted of – would be less boring than this? Anyway, how was she so sure that I had a soul? What evidence did she have? Perhaps it would be worth discussing it with her? If she could convince me that I was ultimately destined for eternal happiness, perhaps it would make this constant drudgery seem more bearable.

******

"You must have FAITH, Sister Anna, FAITH. Of course I can't <u>prove</u> to you that you have a soul given to you by Almighty God, I can't prove it any more than I can prove that I have an immortal soul myself. But think of the wonderful paintings of Fra Angelico, think of the works of my uncle Giotto. Did <u>they</u> need proof that Jesus

Christ was the son of God? Did they ever have any doubt that they would one day see the people they were painting with their own eyes? If they had doubted, would they have been able to execute such wonderful works?"

"I am not an artist, Mother, and it's absurd to compare the work of cleaning the kitchen with the painting of Fra Angelico or your esteemed uncle. Anyway, if there really is a God, why did He make my dear father so poor when he's always worked much harder than any of the rich merchants of Florence?"

"If there is a God! How can you possibly utter such words, my child? Your good father knows as well as I do that he will find true riches in the next life. He cares so much for you, you must believe, if only for his sake. And can you not see that even the most menial of tasks are worth while if they are done to the greater glory of God? Go to your cell now and pray about it. I will pray for you too, for you worry me. I am sure that my beloved Lord Jesus will help you soon to see the Truth and to be grateful to Him for all that He gives you."

Why did I have so much difficulty in sharing Mother Ambrosia's Faith? Yes, it was true, Mother Ambrosia did really care about me. And as for this man/God Jesus, whom she adored as though she had met him personally, why did I have so much difficulty in sharing her faith? In understanding the way she felt? If everything that was said about him was true – that he had healed the sick, communed with the poor – he must truly have been a wonderful person, whether or not he was God. Whether or not there was a God. Yet, despite that, despite admiring everything that I had ever heard about him, I simply could not share the faith of Mother Ambrosia, all the other Sisters, Father, Fr. Marco and all the other priests.... It was Lent now and how I hated saying the Stations of the Cross. Instead of reflecting as we were told to do on the suffering Jesus underwent for us, I sometimes found myself feeling almost resentful about it all.

Resentful? Was that what I really meant? It made no sense! But yes, I could not think of a better word to sum up my feelings when Mother Ambrosia was leading us round the chapel saying the Stations. Her face was so filled with devotion and she seemed really to be living the agony herself. Yet, instead of sharing in this agony, I felt almost as though Jesus had stolen something from me, Stolen from me personally the thing that was most precious to me in all the world[1]. I could not understand it; certainly I could never explain it to Mother Ambrosia. Ah well, I supposed all I could do was to keep on trying to pray. Mother Ambrosia had confided to me that

1. This will be clarified in Section XII.

even Sister Chiara had once lost her faith for a while, when her mother had died so suddenly. She had regained it through prayer, Mother had told me.

CHAPTER TWO - DEATH

Pope Urban V had been forced to return to Avignon, where he had died soon after. Mother Ambrosia was so distressed about it, yet I did not seem able to care.

My life? How much longer was it going to drag on? Not much longer, I felt. That fainting trouble had returned, and I was very weak. Father was so worried. I wished I could go back home with him and just sit on his knee like I used to when I was little. But of course he could not afford the doctor's bills or any extra food, and anyway there was no question of my being able to leave the convent now. It would almost be worth making the effort to stay alive just for Father's sake, but on the other hand, if all Mother Ambrosia and he said about Heaven was true, we would be together for ever eventually anyway, and without all this suffering. Mother Ambrosia was very concerned too, though she did not let on to Father. "Don't worry, Giovanni," she would say each time he visited, "we'll soon have her back to normal, you'll see.". She kept fetching the physician, but he could not find anything wrong. "Perhaps she's just lost the will to live," I heard him confide to Mother Ambrosia in a low whisper at the end of one of his visits.

"Boom. Boom." What was that? I know. Of course it was *La Vacca*, the great bell with its low tone, summoning the people to the Piazza della Signoria. What would it mean this time? Yet another uprising? A call to arms against a neighbouring state, or simply a summons to discuss a matter considered to be important? I hardly cared. What difference did it make to me here, enclosed between these cold walls? Winter time in Florence was so bitter, and there was nothing I hated more than the cold.

I heard a lot of shouting and scuffling. Eventually curiosity got the better of me and I climbed slowly out of bed and peered through my cell window. It was not quite dawn and hard to see, but eventually I made out the figure of a prisoner being escorted through the street. I knew exactly what was happening: he had obviously been condemned to death and was being taken to the Mercato Vecchio to say his last prayers before the *Madonna del Pilastro* painting on his way to the executioner.

Would that I could take his place! Total nothingness would surely be better than this <u>cold</u> nothingness....

PART THREE - HEART BREAK

It was to be over twenty years before I would find out about the life of that poor nun who died so young, and realised that her beloved father had returned to me in this life to give me real love again. So no wonder that when, as a child and teenager, I had gone weekly for instruction in the catechism to Mother Campion at our nearest convent in Bristol, I had shuddered at the mere thought of becoming a nun! No wonder that, when travelling around Europe in more recent years, the site of tall monastery or convent walls always sent shivers down my spine.

Now, though I yearned to become Juan's wife, what I was remembering subconsciously was the strong father-daughter bond that I had with him, and it was that (I realised many years later) which made him so attractive to me. Our relationship continued for more or less exactly two years, and during the latter part of that period the psychotherapist whom I was seeing at the time extracted from him a promise not to keep me waiting for more than another two years. It was obvious to both of us that there was little chance of a change in the celibacy rule in the foreseeable future, and it was also clear that Juan was not really cut out for celibacy. He, however, was very much under the influence of his mother, who was extremely proud of the fact that her son was a priest and so, while on holiday in Spain during the summer of 1972, he wrote me a letter which left me completely shattered. The letter said that, since he was committed to the priesthood and I really wanted a family, it would be better to end our relationship. For me it was more like the end of the world and – no doubt like most people who have their first serious heartbreak – I was firmly convinced that I would never get over it. Reluctantly I obeyed my psychotherapist's orders firstly to return the ring that Juan had bought me for my previous birthday, and secondly to destroy all my photographs of him. We both believed that he had never really loved me after all – a belief which did little for my already fragile ego!

But we were proved wrong on that. Juan and I lost touch for about eleven years, and during those years I married David, who was already becoming a good friend even before the break with Juan, and we had a wonderful family. When we met, David was on a two-year contract with the University of Geneva, and between 1978 and the present day he has been invited back there to do research during the summer vacation about fifteen times. It was on one of these trips that I suddenly took it into my head to look Juan up in the telephone directory. Because of the way in which the Swiss do their directories, I could tell immediately firstly that he was married and secondly that he was a teacher. Delighted, I wrote to him, telling him all about my own family. It took him over a year to reply, and his letter moved me intensely. His regrets about hurting me had been so great that he had made up his mind to make up for it by helping another woman who had been hurt. He had consequently left the priesthood and married a divorcee who had three little boys. In due course the two of them had had another son.

Alas Juan's story does not end entirely happily, as after a few more years, during which we corresponded spasmodically, his beloved wife died of bone cancer. The letter giving me this sad news made it clear that he would have loved to have me back, so we did not finally meet until he had acquired a new girlfriend. By this time seventeen years had passed since our break-up, but when he came to Geneva with his new partner and his son to have dinner with my family, it felt as though time had stood still. It is often thus with bonds that have endured over centuries, and we would possibly still be in touch now if we were both better correspondents. On the other hand, another meeting in his Lausanne flat a few years later made me disinclined to pursue the friendship, because Juan made it clear to me that his wife and I were the only true loves of his life. It seemed sad to me that the flat contained no photographs of his deceased wife, and I attributed this to the apparent insecurity and jealousy of Juan's new partner. The only photo that I saw of her was in his car, when he drove us to the station, and as the train drew in, Juan whispered in my ear that his feelings for me would never change. This was flattering of course, but I had found a better partner in David, and I no longer needed a father in the way that I had done when I was thirty.

EXERCISES

Are you in a relationship which you regard as not wholly satisfactory? If so:

1. Examine your motives for entering it. Were you seeking a father/mother figure, or simply trying to fill a gap in your life? Was the original attraction mainly physical and do you now find that you have little in common? Were you looking for challenge? Someone to dominate? Someone to give you security?

2. Look at whether the relationship is one of equality. Does it prevent you from being able to be fully yourself?

3. When you have done a full analysis, discuss your findings with your partner. If he/she is unwilling to discuss it, this may in itself be a bad sign, for which a drastic remedy may be appropriate. Only you can decide.

4. If he/she is willing and able to have a reasonable discussion and has strong reasons for wanting to maintain the relationship, make a list firstly of the bad points about it and secondly of the good ones. Hopefully the latter will be the longer! If so,

(a) endeavour from now on to focus more on them

(b) ask yourself what you have to learn from the things which you regard as the negative aspects of the relationship – e.g. patience, tolerance, compassion. Could you be making more effort with the learning? (At the end of each life we score more Brownie points for having made the most of difficult relationships than we do for having lived in a relationship such as mine with Giuseppe.)

X
FINDING KARMIC LINKS WITH FAMILY MEMBERS

PART ONE - MARRIAGE & FAMILY

And he said:
Your children are not your children.
They are the sons and daughters of Life's longing for itself.
They come through you but not from you,
And though they are with you yet they belong not to you.
You may give them your love but not your thoughts,
For they have their own thoughts.
You may house their bodies but not their souls.....

"The Prophet" – *Kahlil Gibran*

David and I first met soon after his arrival in Geneva in 1972 – ironically through the Scottish Church, which neither of us attended, but which put on a good social programme for ex-patriots. Initially David made friends with a whole group of us single girls and joined in a number of weekend trips in my little Beetle, of which the most memorable was to Châteauneuf du Pape, where a market grew up round the VW during the night. Needing to set off quite early in order to get back to

Geneva, we were alarmed, but the beefy stall holder whom I approached about the problem was not alarmed in the least. He simply called upon a few of his mates, and between them they lifted the car out of the enclosure as though it was an every-day occurrence!

Our mutual partiality to good wine in due course took just the two of us, after my heartbreak over Juan, on a weekend of "dégustation" in Burgundy, and it was here that we first broached the question of marriage. Aided no doubt by the wine, we even agreed on two names for the children we were both eager to have – Paul and Alice – and neither of us thought better of any of these ideas even after we had sobered up! On the contrary, we clinched it by repeating the trip not long after the wedding, by which time I was already pregnant with Paul. Hence perhaps (although I did take care not to overdo it) his partiality to good quality red wine!

David was engaged in mathematical research at the University of Geneva, on two years' leave of absence from the University of Hull. I had never been as far north as Hull, and that was in fact the university I had shunned in favour of my home town of Bristol, but one compensation for leaving my beloved Geneva was the fact that David had bought a nice little bungalow in the area. So accommodation was one thing we did not have to worry about when I arrived there heavily pregnant. Much though I wanted the baby, I did not enjoy pregnancy, and, with what felt almost like an "alien being" inside me, I was puzzled by the pro-abortionist women who claim that the baby is their body.

Our courtship was comparatively short, yet David and I did not need to be together long before we felt that we had always known one another. Alice came along twenty months after Paul, and he greeted her with as much excitement as we did. They have always been the very closest of friends.

PART TWO - EIGHTEENTH CENTURY LONDON

CHAPTER ONE - DINNER WITH POLITICIANS

"Why on earth does Denis want you to dine with the Earl of Chatham?" asked David. "I'm sure he'll never be Prime Minister again, and anyway he's a Whig."

"It's not only Chatham who's going to be there tonight. He's invited the Earl of Bute as well, who's still one of us even though his period in office was so short. We shouldn't regard Whigs as enemies just because our opinions differ, and I think Denis feels sorry for Chatham. His nervous illness is really quite serious, you know. Anyway, remember you got on quite well with George Grenville when we dined with him at Denis' house?"

"Oh Grenville, he's all right I suppose. After all, if it hadn't been for his Revenue and Stamp Acts, the American Revolution wouldn't have got going. But I thought your main plan of action at the moment was overthrowing Grafton.

"I don't think Denis was planning this evening as a campaigning one so much as a purely social event. It's going to be quite a big gathering, I believe, and Denis is keen for us to sample some of his new cases of French wine."

"Ah well, I suppose it'll make a relaxing change from trying to instil Philosophy into the heads of boys who would rather be out chasing young girls or scrounging cakes at a festival; and it's always good for you to have a chance to enjoy a meal you haven't cooked yourself."

"You know I cook for pleasure, not from necessity. Joanna was asking me only yesterday why we didn't take on extra staff rather than having me always "slaving away", as she called it, in the kitchen."

"And I can guess what you replied. That you'd really prefer not to have any servants at all, since it's impossible to find any that are up to your high standards, but that firstly it simply wouldn't do for a family of our standing to be without domestic help, and that secondly, with your back trouble, you couldn't possibly manage the cleaning on top of everything else."

"You're right. Of course I couldn't. In fact my backache is particularly bad this evening. I found that Kate had made a hopeless job of cleaning the silver and I had to do it all over again myself. I suppose it must be all the rubbing that strained my back muscles. I certainly shall appreciate relaxing over a meal that someone else has prepared, and Denis' new cook does seem to be a great success so far."

"How absurd to fuss so much about the silver! Sometimes I think you really deserve to have back trouble. But of course I know it wouldn't be any good my trying to persuade you to see a physician."

"What good has any physician ever done me? They're just a bunch of ignoramuses. You remember during Alice's birth how that medicine I was given made the pain so much worse? Paul's and Denis' births weren't nearly so difficult and that was because I wouldn't let a doctor come near me. But it's ridiculous to accuse me of fussing about the silver. You know perfectly well how important it is that all the cutlery should be unblemished."

"That's just a matter of opinion. I think your standards are too high. The goals you set are always unachievable. If you relaxed a bit more and strained yourself less, you might well find your back got better without the aid of a doctor."

"Be that as it may. This is not a time for arguing; we both need to be dressed before the cab arrives. Goodness me, look how sordid that gown of yours has got! It's a pity school masters have to use chalk. I must order some more so that you can put on a clean one every day. I'll just go and ask Lucinda to iron your other one so that it's ready for tomorrow."

******

"Good evening, Ann. How nice to see you again. And how are things with you, David? Have you any budding Newtons among your pupils at the moment?"

"Well I wouldn't put it that strongly, but there is certainly no lack of scientific talent in our school. In fact I seem to be having more success in that field at the moment than I am with Philosophy. My class this afternoon completely failed to appreciate Voltaire's great wit, and as for getting them to grasp the main tenets of Descartes..."

"I'm afraid your boys have my sympathy," I chipped in. "Alice was roaring with laughter over some passages in Candide the other day, but when I read it I did not find it the least bit amusing."

"Your trouble is, Ann," said my brother Denis, "your lack of appreciation of French culture. Perhaps you are not sufficiently logical. After all, it wasn't really logical to believe that our campaigns would be successful in ousting the Whigs last time! Have you heard the saying *Ce qui n'est pas logique n'est pas français*? That is one thing I admire about the French."

"I'm afraid your excellent French is lost on me, but, logical or illogical, I must <u>believe</u> in the chances of our campaigns being successful or I should not have the strength to do all the work involved. Certainly I have never been a Francophile, but why be a Francophile when we have the world here at our feet in Westminster?"

"Why indeed? And your work – illogical though it may be – is much appreciated. And what of your History teaching, David?"

"This week I've had one of my classes discussing the attempts to abolish the Poor Laws."

"A pity they failed if you ask me," chipped in Augustus. Augustus often shocked me, and this time I certainly could not let it pass.

"Are we not now in an age of philanthropy? Is it not wrong that, in a great city like ours, where so many of us are able to live in comfort, eating and drinking as well as we are this evening, thanks to Denis' excellent hospitality, some should nevertheless still be confined to living in urban back-to-backs where they have to share external pumps and privies? I believe that over one family in five in this country is in receipt of poor relief. Is that not a scandal? For instance, the Irish who, having no other means of making a living, come over here in the summer for hay-making and, after that season is over, simply swell the hordes of beggars, hawkers and casual workers with which our London streets are already too full?"

"I firmly believe that in general people would be forced to fend for themselves if there were no relief available. If you feel that way, Ann, why do you not invite some of these people to use your handsome bathroom, or even swap your Westminster mansion for a back-to-back such as you were just describing?"

"It is one thing to feel sorry for the poor, quite another to wish to join them! If we allowed just anyone to use our bathroom it would never be available when we needed it ourselves. We are fully entitled to our mansion since my father worked as tirelessly throughout his political career as Denis is now doing in his, and would either of them have been as successful if it had not been for my assistance? Besides, a schoolmaster's profession is an honourable one, and David also works very hard."

"Don't worry, I was only teasing. This claret is quite excellent, Denis, and the meat truly tender. I should appreciate a little more of both."

"But of course. Everyone must have more. I believe there are another couple of joints still in the kitchen, are there not Doris dear? And I certainly have a whole case full of claret as yet unopened. It is far superior to that sweet Rhine wine we were drinking last year."

"Talking of German wine brings me to the subject of our new king. Well, I suppose he is no longer new. But is it not good to have an Englishman on the throne after so many years of being made to feel we were almost a German colony?"

"Yes indeed. I have heard that George III is a very conscientious young man, if simple in his tastes and unpretentious. I believe he has great moral courage and even obstinacy."

"You are right, I'm sure, and I think he will make much change to our parliamentary system, for he wishes to put an end to government by families and choose his own ministers. It is high time that the political life of this country was freed from corruption."

"Who will be the next generation of politicians, I wonder? Are you producing any, Ann, to keep up the family tradition? Your youngest child is Denis' namesake, I believe. Will he be the one to enter Westminster, as the younger of your two brothers did?"

"I'm sorry, Augustus. Did I fail to tell you of little Denis' sad demise last year? Ann and David, I'm so sorry! Such conversation must still be very painful for you."

"Oh, how sorry I am to hear that. The child was very young, was he not?"

"Yes, he was only three. One never gets over such things. Of course many women go through it again and again, but I couldn't face that. I have vowed to David that I will not have another child. Besides, pregnancy is so hard on my troublesome back. We must be content now with Alice and Paul, who are such good friends with each other."

"And how are they? Is Paul destined for a life in politics, or will he follow in his good father's footsteps and become a schoolmaster?"

"Neither, I think. Paul is his own person and, though he is young yet, so it is early to tell exactly how he will develop, I am happy to say that he shows every sign of being an extremely talented musician. He is already showing an interest in playing the 'cello."

"And what do you think, David? Are you encouraging Paul's musical ambition?"

"Me? I'm neither encouraging nor discouraging. I believe very firmly that people should follow their own inclinations. Personally, however, I have little taste for music. I feel it is a waste of time when one could be discovering the secret of creation."

"Is it not strange that, dearly though I love him, I should have married a man for whom science and philosophy have even greater importance than music? I find David's attitude to Purcell immensely irritating."

"Why should you be irritated by my disinterest when I am so tolerant of your passion? Do I not encourage all three of you to go to concerts as often as you wish, and have I not promised to pay a handsome sum for a good 'cello?"

"Of course you have, my dear, but it would be more fitting for a family of our standing if you were to accompany us to the concerts."

"*Vive la différence*! as our friend Christopher would say. Variety is the spice of life. I am much too busy with my own work to make time for artistic trivia."

"Is Miss Alice musical too then?"

"She has not her younger brother's talent, but she appreciates it much more than her father does."

"Alice has an excellent brain," said David. "She reads a great deal and has a profound understanding of literature."

"Oh yes, Ann was saying earlier that she had been reading *Candide.*"

"Our daughter would make an excellent teacher. It is a pity that my profession is not open to her sex."

"A woman teacher? What a strange idea!"

CHAPTER TWO - A FUNERAL

"I met young Christopher on my way from school just now. He is having problems not only with his class again, but also with his love life. I said it would be fine if he came over for a chat tomorrow."

"Oh not again!" said Alice. "The other week when he was here he kept you both up so late talking about Lucy that Mother vowed to me that she wouldn't let you invite him again for at least a couple of months."

"What does it matter to you, Alice? It was us he was mainly talking to. You went off to bed at your usual time."

"Yes, but the discussion kept me awake. Anyway, it annoys me how he sponges off you. Has he given you back that loan you made him last year?"

"Not yet, but he's sure he'll be able to soon. Anyway, I don't begrudge him the money; what worries me more is his difficulty in making decisions."

"And when he does make a decision off his own bat, it's always the wrong one! Remember how he regretted having taken the job at the school for poorer children when he could probably have got one at your school?"

"Yes, Alice," I commented, "that was a big mistake, but he has such very high ideals."

"That's one thing you and he have in common," said David. "It's only your methods of attaining them that differ."

"I suppose another thing we have in common is that we both seem to fail to attain them."

"You would not feel a failure if you did not always place your ambitions too high."

Rather than replying, I heaved a sigh, for I was fond of Christopher. I would have done almost anything to see him happily settled in a job he found less difficult, with a nice faithful wife to care for him. But just at that moment I had been making other plans, because my father's illness had got suddenly worse and I feared that his death was imminent. I felt it was vital for a former politician of his distinction to be buried in Westminster Abbey and, if that were to be achieved, no time should be lost.

"I think Alice is unfair on Christopher," said Paul, suddenly looking up from his 'cello. "I like him a lot, and I wish I knew French like he does."

"Of course he knows French!" replied Alice. "Teaching it is his job. I expect he's envious of your musical talent."

"Well anyway," said David, "I've said he could come. And it's not Lucy he's worrying about now, but a girl called Emma."

"I suppose poor Lucy wasn't good enough for him! I wonder how many other hearts he's broken in the meantime?"

******

"I agree with you, Ann. Father certainly does deserve to be buried in Westminster Abbey, but I simply haven't time to do anything about it at the moment. This war in America is causing North so much bother, and he and John Robinson both depend on me."

"Well, I suppose David and I will have to organise it on our own."

"Maybe I can think of a friend who would be willing to help you."

"Don't worry. I'm used to doing things single-handedly. Just so long as I'm sure you think it's worth while campaigning for."

"Of course I do. Dear Papa, it may only be weeks or even days that he'll still be with us, but his life will always be an inspiration to us all. I know: I'm sure Godfrey would help you. He's indebted to Papa for his entry into Westminster."

******

How moving the funeral was, and how proud I felt despite my intense grief and that of Mama.

"Well Ann, that was an impressive occasion, and it was all thanks to you, I understand."

"Yes, I suppose it was mainly, but of course I couldn't have done it without David's support and the help of our good friend Godfrey. We didn't have much time for the campaigning because dear Papa went downhill so quickly. Now my ambition is for Paul to be buried here too as one of our country's finest musicians, but of course I do not hope to see that!"

"You should be satisfied with what you've done for your good father."

"Didn't you know? Ann is never satisfied! She always sets much too high ambitions for herself, and whenever she does achieve one of these ambitions, she simply sets another one even higher."

CHAPTER THREE - CHRISTOPHER

I really would like to live in the West End," said Christopher, "I find Robert Adam's architecture overwhelmingly beautiful, and Emma likes it too."

"I thought you'd decided not to marry Emma after all because she wasn't passionate enough for you. Anyway, I don't see how you could afford a house in the West End; and how would it tally with your ideals of caring about the poor? You could have worked in a school like David's, but opted for a lower salary in a school for less privileged boys."

"That's true, I know. I think I did the right thing really, because I am very fond of my pupils, but I often have regrets as I find it so hard to make ends meet. As for Emma, I seem to change my mind about her more or less every day. Do <u>you</u> think I should marry her?"

Alice picked up Merlin, our tabby cat, and left the room with a rather pained expression on her face. She was getting more and more fed up with Christopher's endless problems, and we had already been lingering over the meal for a good two and a half hours. Then Paul, who had been patiently silent for quite a while, finally chipped in.

"It doesn't seem a good idea to me to live somewhere you can't comfortably afford. Surely the beauty of your surroundings wouldn't be worth all the worry? As for marriage, Mama and Papa would no doubt say I was too young to judge, but I would have thought an important factor in the decision was whether or not you really loved Emma."

"Paul may yet be a trifle young to be thinking of matrimony himself, but he has a good head on his shoulders. Just as the wig I persist in wearing is beginning to look a little unfashionable, so is my attitude to marriage perhaps somewhat outdated, but I do regard it as a commitment, and I believe that many of today's present ills would be reduced if more people shared my view."

"Your wig, my dear David, is more than a trifle unfashionable. It really is time you discarded it like the rest of us, but your complete devotion to Ann is something I greatly admire. That is no doubt the reason why I cannot seem to be able to decide to take the plunge with Emma. By the way, why does Alice always take that cat off with her when I'm here? I don't think she wants him to sit on me, but I love cats."

"Well, if you're so unsure," I remarked, ignoring the question about Alice and Merlin, "I think you should break off the relationship. The poor girl is infatuated with you. It simply isn't fair to keep her hanging on in this state of uncertainty."

"I just hate breaking hearts. What about you, Paul, have you not yet embarked on any amorous adventures?"

"Paul is much too busy with his music at the moment to think of such things! We are hoping he may be able to perform with a leading ensemble very shortly."

"You are certainly very full of ambition for him, and I hope you will not be disappointed. If you don't mind my saying so, though, one thing I notice about your family is that Alice always seems to be very much in the background."

I felt my shackles rise. How dare Christopher make such a personal remark in a matter that was none of his business! Especially when he was forever coming to us to bale him out of his difficulties.

"Alice is a girl, and you know perfectly well that it is a woman's job to keep a home together, while it is up to you men to be out in the world making money, educating the younger generation, running the country, making music for our relaxation.... If Alice has left the room now, I'm afraid it is simply because she has got bored with listening to your problems."

"I'm sorry to be a bore, but there never seems to be anyone else I can turn to for advice. You two have been such a wonderful support to me ever since I first met you." My heart softened. Christopher may be irritating at times, but it was impossible not to be fond of him. Now it was David's turn to speak up for him.

"I do know what Christopher means, dear. Alice is so clever, yet her academic abilities seem to be wasted when there is no obvious career open to her. If she had been a boy, you would be pushing her to go into teaching or politics instead of concentrating so exclusively on Paul's future. If only little Denis had lived, you wouldn't be putting all your eggs into one basket."

"Yes, I still haven't got over losing Denis, but at least Alice dotes on her younger brother and appreciates his talents as much as I do."

"I do not dispute either of those points, but I think what concerns Christopher is that she also has talents and they are not being given full recognition."

"Well, I don't know about you, Christopher, but David has to get up early for school tomorrow, and my back is killing me after making all that pastry."

"Your apple pie was delicious. But why don't you see a physician about your back trouble? I know one I can recommend."

"You know Ann doesn't believe in doctors, Christopher. Why didn't you ask Alice to make the pastry for you? Or Lucinda? Surely Lucinda wasn't busy the whole afternoon?"

"Yes she was. She had all the linen to iron. Anyway. As for Alice, she doesn't enjoy cooking as much as I do."

"Well, you take too much on yourself in my opinion. But you're right, it is time I got going. It's a pity we haven't had time to talk about the French Revolution. I'm really excited about it, you know."

"Of course, as a French teacher you naturally take more interest in events in that country than I do. But I hope it's all going to work out all right."

"There is every sign of that. Have a good night's sleep, and perhaps I can see you next week?"

"I hope by next week you will have made a final decision about poor Emma. Goodnight."

"You're right; I suppose I'll have to. Well goodnight, and thank you for everything."

******

"No, I'm quite sure of it. This really is the real thing. Jeanne is so much more exciting than any English girl I've ever met, and I'm sure she's just as much in love with me too. The trouble is, now that the Revolution is safely over, she seems quite set on returning to her native country. She says she simply can't adapt to many of our strange English customs."

"Why she should find any of our customs strange I can't imagine, but if you really love her, why don't you go to live in France? You wouldn't have any problem with the language, and you could surely find employment teaching English?"

"Perhaps you're right. The idea of post-Revolutionary France certainly has some appeal to me and it is more than time that I settled down."

"It certainly is, Christopher. Are you going to bring Jeanne to meet us? We would all dearly love to make her acquaintance."

CHAPTER FOUR - VISIT TO FRANCE

"I really think Ann, that we should take a holiday. You have been working so hard recently. How about us going to visit Christopher and Jeanne? I have been hankering somewhat after seeing France, and they have been urging us to come for a long time. Would you not love to meet their daughters?"

"Perhaps that would be a good idea. Alice's wedding was lovely, but the preparations were very tiring. I've often thought I should like to travel, yet there never seemed to be the time. I'm not sure whether France appeals to me that much, but I should certainly like to see Christopher again now that he is so happily settled."

"Right, that's decided. I'll write to them this evening."

******

"And what is Paul doing with himself these days?" asked Christopher as we were relaxing over a particularly fine Burgundy.

"Paul is making a very successful career for himself writing about music. He still plays in a small orchestra regularly for enjoyment, but was forced to give up the idea of becoming a concert artist."

"I'm sure that must be one of the hardest professions to get into, but I am glad he is well settled. I've always had a soft spot for Paul, you know."

"Yes, you two always did seem to understand one another. But, talking of being settled, nothing pleases me more than to see <u>you</u> so happily married and gainfully employed. As for your three lovely daughters, they are a credit to you."

"I'm glad to say that they all seem to have Jeanne's looks and my brains!"

"Your looks have never left much to be desired, and as for Jeanne's brains, they must be pretty good if she can handle you so well."

"I am so happy with *mon cher Christophe*. Now tell me, please, about this executioner of your acquaintance that David wrote about. In France since the Revolution we have been working hard to abandon such barbaric practices."

"Indeed, in England, I am glad to say, the numbers actually executed are diminishing, but that is no thanks to Saul, who to date has failed to heed anything I say to him. Another problem that we have in England is appalling conditions in the prisons. They are simply rife with disease, so some do not even achieve the chance of being sentenced to death at the gallows. How are your prisons in France? Do they have segregation of the sexes? I believe that is something we should aim for...."

Note

For this section I am indebted firstly to Aron Abrahamsen, the American who gave me the bare bones of this lifetime in my first clairvoyant reading, and secondly to *English Society in the Eighteenth Century* by Roy Porter, Penguin, and *London, A Concise History* by Geoffrey Trease, Thames and Hudson.

PART THREE - COMPLETING OUR FAMILY

After Alice was born in September 1976, I tried very hard to share David's contentment with just two children – "a pigeon pair", as people said. I even gave away all the clothes and baby gear as soon as she had outgrown it, but it did not work! Obviously I was very aware subconsciously that I had chosen to have three children this time round (possibly to compensate for the loss of little Denis), and this eighteenth century life gives good reason for our having selected Christopher as our third child. I had liked the idea of adopting for a long time, and David was easily converted to it. Also, since most of my paid working life had been connected with helping Third World countries, I fancied including a black child in our family. Christopher was born in Hull to two university students, of whom the father was from Sierra Leone, but they had already split up before she knew that she was pregnant.

This political lifetime is the one which seems to relate most directly to the structure of my family as it is this time round. Although I learnt about it initially from the first clairvoyant reading I had, in 1992, I found most of the details gradually myself. I do not appear to have been a very pleasant person then, but at least I had some social conscience even though I was a Tory! We no doubt all go through the whole gamut of political orientation, as well as religious belief, during the course of our many lives. This time I was born into a very Conservative family, but inclined more towards Socialism quite early on, while David was born into a working class family and has voted Labour all his life. His devotion to me remains unchanged, and this time, fortunately, he is just as keen on music as I am and our tastes in that are more or less identical.

Alice still has great academic ability, but now, thanks to major changes in our society, she is able to make the most of them. She obtained a First Class degree in

Linguistics followed by an M.Phil. in Publishing, and now has a good job as an editor. Paul gave up his piano lessons at an early age and does not share our taste in music, preferring House and Dance to Bach and Purcell. Though we develop abilities over many lifetimes, which explains the fact that so often people's talents appear innate at an early age, we become more rounded characters by making use of different specialities from time to time. Paul, like his father, has always had a scientific bent in this life, and he is now a Mathematics teacher. Christopher is not a French teacher this time round, but a professional basketball player. However, after doing his degree on a basketball scholarship in the United States, he immediately got himself a job playing in France and is now working hard at mastering the French language! He has recently married a beautiful girl he met during his second year at college. Her name is not Jeanne, but Jeanette. (I first wrote this story some time before they met!) Their daughter Delilah Jade (our first grandchild) was born in August 2004.

Because of a subconscious feeling of having been rejected at birth, it is the norm for adopted children to exhibit behavioural problems. When Christopher was about twelve and we were at the height of our difficulties with him, I did wonder very much whether I had a big karmic debt to him, and that was part of my reason for seeking a clairvoyant reading. The answer that came was "No. You have tried to help him in the past and are now continuing to want to do that." Well, in the eighteenth century he eventually sorted himself out successfully, and this time, fortunately for all of us, he has done it much more quickly. Thanks to that, he and Alice have been able to work out their rather prickly karmic relationship and are now extremely good friends. (Merlin, incidentally, is now our family dog. Animals also evolve and make karmic links with human beings. We feel that he is ready to become human next time!)

Alice's and Christopher's friendship took some time to develop. Paul was almost five and Alice was just three when we first got Christopher, at the age (lucky us!) of only two weeks, and at the time I attributed their very different attitudes to him to the fact that Alice was used to being the baby. But that was before I knew anything about karma. As he grew into a large (he is now six foot eight and a half!), boisterous child, my sympathies were always with our quiet daughter when her books and toys got borrowed and damaged, her sweets were stolen, and her privacy was invaded. What always seemed more difficult to explain was Paul's remarkable tolerance of Christopher's undesirable behaviour, but my clairvoyant friend Edwin Courtenay told me that they also have very strong links as blood brothers.

I have well made up for my anti-French feelings in this lifetime by being sent to

France by my parents at the age of nine, learning to speak the language fluently at that early age, and then doing a degree in it. In any case that attitude was only temporary, as I have found many lifetimes in which I was French. As for my backache caused by stress, this has not changed, but firstly this time I am learning to cope with it better by trying to avoid overdoing things, and secondly there is a lot more to it than just this one past life.

EXERCISE

1. Think about the relationships in your own immediate family – either the one into which you were born or the one you have made for yourself more recently. Which are the more comfortable ones? Which the less comfortable? Does it make sense to you to think that some of those "close" to you are really old friends, while the others are either more like "new acquaintances" or people with whom you have previously had difficulties?

2. If there is someone who falls into the latter category, think of something you might be able to do to improve the relationship. Write a letter or make a phone call? Remember their birthday for the first time for a while? Or simply pray for him/her?

3. If he/she appears to have some sort of grudge against you which seems quite irrational, reflect on the fact that it could well date from a previous life in which it was justified. You may well find that changing your own attitude to him/her as a result of this notion will also produce change in the other person.

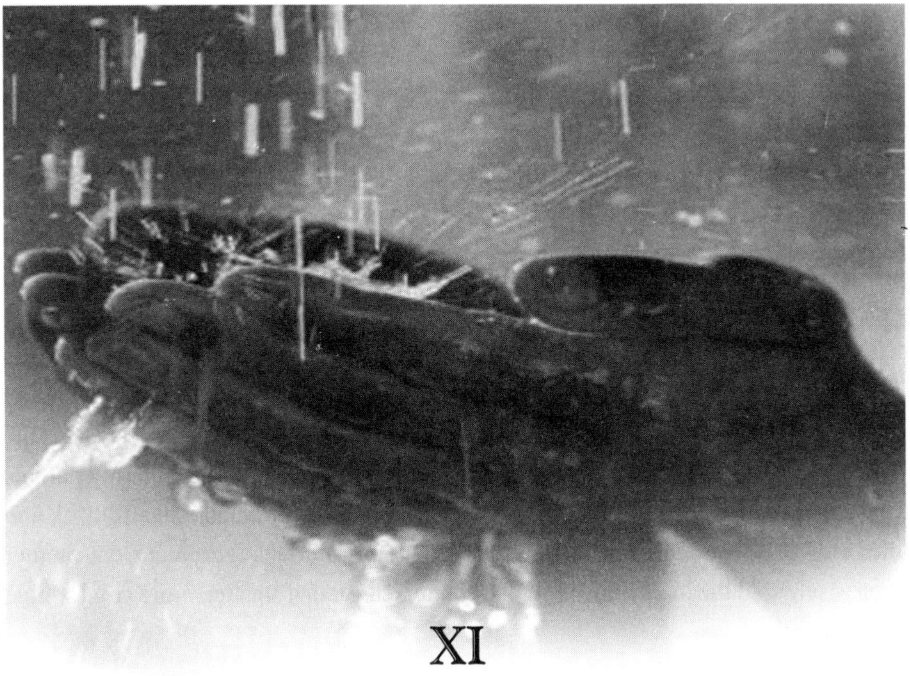

XI
FINDING REPEATED PATTERNS
PART ONE - BACKACHE

Do you think I would confront you with pain if there were not a reason for it? Open your heart to pain as you do now to pleasure, for it is My Will, wrought by Me for your own good. Welcome it as a challenge. Do not turn away from it, do not listen to your mind, for mind is but another word for "need". The mind engenders need; it manifested the world because it needed this. It is all My plan, to drive you by the pangs of unfulfilled need to listen to My Voice, which when heard dissolves the ego and the mind with it.

Sathya Sai Baba, Thought for the Day - 11.06.03

The backache, which is basically what started my "spiritual quest" in this lifetime, began during my first pregnancy, in 1974. This was a time of great excitement, as David and I were both so looking forward to the arrival of our first child, and fortunately I was not troubled by any common problems such as morning sickness. But as soon as the baby had begun to make his presence visible I started to suffer a great deal from back trouble. I was disappointed when, after the birth, this showed no sign of improvement, and a visit to the doctor was not at all helpful. He sent me for an X-ray, which showed there to be nothing wrong, and enrolling for a weekly Yoga class did not help either. So I just went on enduring it until 1987, when my mother's death from cancer first triggered my interest in alternative therapies.

My parents had moved back to Oxford on my father's retirement, having been left the house in Park Town in which we had lived during the War. This house had belonged to Great Aunt Judith Anne (after whom I had been named, but my parents had turned the Christian names round so that my initials would not be JAM – a thing for which I have always been grateful). We rented the upstairs flat during the early 1940s, and when Aunt Judith died shortly before our move to Bristol, the house was passed on to Cousin Phoebe, who was also single all her life. My parents welcomed the chance to move back to Oxford, but my father had a heart attack and died very suddenly when only about eighteen months into his retirement. My mother then wisely sold the huge house and bought herself a much smaller, more comfortable house nearby.

It was in this house that I nursed her during the last week of her life. My sister Philippa also lived in Oxford at the time, and she had been studying homœopathy and was herself receiving treatment from an alternative therapist. Philippa had persuaded my mother also to see her therapist, and he had told Philippa that he could probably have saved her had he been able to treat her earlier on. Hearing that my mother was a "classic case of a cancer victim" (a very private person who suppressed her emotions, dedicated her life to helping others, never putting herself first, and who was also full of fear), naturally aroused my interest, and when Michael made a brief visit while I was looking after her, I took to him instantly. I asked whether he could recommend anyone nearer to the Hull area who could treat both my backache and Christopher's asthma, and that was how I made Lawrence's acquaintance. In retrospect I realise that I owe most of the most important things in my life to my backache!

On my very first appointment, Lawrence corrected my pelvis, which he said had been "out" ever since Paul's birth, and the next morning, for the first time in over thirteen years, I got out of bed without any pain in my lower back. The upper part of my back, however, did not improve, and over the next several years I tried every therapy that I heard about. Besides the osteopathy and homoeopathy in which Lawrence is expert, I experienced massage, aromatherapy, Alexander Technique, shiatsu, acupuncture, psychic surgery, Bowen Technique.... None of them made any difference to my chronic backache, but goodness me, how much did I learn in the process – both about myself and about healing in general! It would of course be nice in some ways to end this part of my tale with the announcement of a sudden and total cure of my back pain – especially since one aim of this book is to show the effectiveness of regression therapy - but life is not always quite that simple. Very many people in this world do suffer from apparently incurable problems (physical or otherwise), and I have gradually come to realise that cure need not always be an important aim. Healing in any case does not always involve cure (sometimes the healing can even be death!), and so, when the problem really does seem to be intractable, we need to think firstly about what we can learn from it, and secondly about how to live with it. Or perhaps the other way around? So now I will look briefly at some of my own learning.

Firstly, the fact that the backache led me to sample so many different therapies gave me some useful knowledge that I have been able to share with others (both friends and clients), some of whom have consequently found cures. Secondly, receiving regular treatment for my back from Lawrence has brought countless benefits besides temporary relief from pain. Some of these will become apparent in later chapters. And thirdly, another thing that I learnt gradually over these years of seeking a cure for my back was how we carry over memories of pain and trauma from lifetime to lifetime. I had not been born with a bad back, but weakness in that area had been imprinted on my physical body by my etheric body, and the seed of my etheric body was in the bodies which are more subtle still and which hang on stubbornly to past traumata until we are ready to release them.

This last was one of many things that I learnt firstly with Dr. Keith Hearne and Helen Wozniak, who at that time jointly ran the London College of Past Life Regression Studies. This course was held in lecture rooms at Regent's College, sitting on uncomfortable chairs, which made any real body work impossible. These two teachers are both also hypnotherapists, and so we were taught to use mostly hypnotic induction for regression, which I personally believe gives less firm direction than Roger Woolger's methods, but it was a very good introduction to the therapy and I did myself gain some useful insights from the course.

PART TWO - THE FISHERMAN'S DAUGHTER

It was getting late and Father was not back yet. He never liked me to worry about him, but it was difficult not to when his work was so hazardous at times. Besides, a storm seemed to be brewing. The meal was all cooked apart from the fish I was waiting for him to bring home, so I might just as well go down to the beach to see if there was any sign of him. There had been so little to do ever since Mother's death, and I often felt very lonely. If only my parents had managed to have one or two more children, they could have kept me company. On the other hand, it was hard enough keeping just the two of us alive. Our village was so small, there was no work other than fishing, and there were almost more people to sell the fish than to buy it. Father sometimes travelled inland a bit, where there were always customers to be found, but in summer time it was impossible to get very far before the fish went bad. Anyway, now Father was getting a bit old for travelling far inland. Mother had entrusted me on her deathbed to take care of him, and take care of him I would until the day that he died too. So now I just <u>must</u> go out and find him, storm or no storm.

It was dark on the beach, and the wind was lapping the sea furiously into waves that looked even taller than Father. Dimly I could see a little speck being tossed hither and thither. Was it Father's boat? Hard to tell, but it certainly could be. I shouted as loud as I could, but my words were lost on the wind. Now there was a big flash of lightning and the thundercloud finally burst. I walked closer to the sea's edge and shouted again....

******

"My dear, foolish child. Haven't I told you not to worry about me? You would have been much safer indoors, even though our little hut is not the sturdiest."

"What happened?" I asked my father feebly.

"You came too close to the waves and an extra big one knocked you completely flat. You fell heavily on the rocks, which knocked you unconscious, and as for your back... Your poor back, I fear it is badly broken. I saw you waving, but could not reach you in time before you fell. Then I had to carry you carefully home with the sack of fish on my back as well. What a trouble you are to me!"

"Oh Father, I'm so sorry! It's because I love you so much that I worry, and besides, I often get lonely in the evenings waiting for you. I'll have to get better quickly, because I promised Mother that I would always look after you, but Oh dear, how my back hurts!"

"Don't worry about me, my child. The Lord always takes care of me."

******

"But I do worry about him," I said to my guide on reaching the Bardo. "And I feel so guilty about breaking my promise to Mother."

And then my Earthly guide, my teacher in Regent's College, directed me to move on a little in time and return to the little fisherman's hut to see how my father was doing on his own. "Yes," I said, "he seems to be getting on OK. He misses me badly of course, but neighbours bring him vegetables in return for fish. Anyway, he really is very old now. I don't think he is destined to live much longer."

"So that's all right. Now you can go and find your mother." I did, and we embraced. How good it was to see her again! I told her how bad I felt about letting her down, but she said that she quite understood, that it wasn't my fault, and that we would all three be together again before too very long.

PART THREE - THE POISONED PRINCESS

During the weekend at Regent's College the following month the hypnotic induction took me to a banquet in a castle.

******

How happy I was to be getting engaged to the man I loved! Handsome, noble, charming and brave... What more could a young girl look for in a man? He loved me too - I knew that for sure - and my father's pleasure in the match gave me great joy as well. I was much more fortunate than many girls of my status, whose parents' choice of a spouse did not coincide with their own! My younger sister Abigail had had her eye on Mark too. Jealous little bitch – she always wanted everything that I had and more. But now that the beautiful diamond ring was on my finger and the banquet had been called to celebrate, I need not bother my head about her any more. She may be even prettier than me, but as the first born girl I was entitled to marry first.

The table was so heavily laden with sumptuous dishes and fruits, it was a feast for the eyes. My prince took me by the hand and we walked in and took our seats in the places of honour. Abigail's greedy, crafty eyes seemed ever to be on my fiancé, but I must not let that spoil my enjoyment of this wonderful banquet. My father always imported the very best wines from France, and the one we were being served today I knew had been maturing in our cellar for quite a long time, in anticipation of this so special occasion. My father raised the toast "to Mark and Anna" and I took a sip. To me it tasted slightly strange, but I was no expert, and my beloved prince smiled sweetly at me in approval, so I knew the wine must be a good one.

After the soup came the fish course, but suddenly I felt a little queasy. I murmured an excuse and went outside to get some air. How I loved our big gardens with all their trees and flowering shrubs, the roses, and the river which flowed so gently past the rose garden until it speeded up to tumble over a waterfall. Feeling not quite myself for the moment, I went and sat down beside it. Suddenly I lost my balance. The next thing I knew I was floating along with the fishes, my long fair hair trailing behind me, my beautiful cream-coloured dress clinging tightly to my legs, and the flowers with which I had adorned myself drifting hither and thither. It was a rather pleasant sensation until I reached the waterfall, when I found myself being hurtled at breakneck speed over jagged rocks, which tore through my clothes and into the flesh of my back. The pain was excruciating.

******

"Ophelia. Talk about archetypal images!" I said to myself as the regression was drawing to a close. Shortage of time was always a big factor when we had our fairly brief practice sessions in Regent's College. So I had to wait until I got home, and could put on the tape my clairvoyant friend Edwin Courtenay had made me for regressing myself, to get the end of the story. And I found that Abigail did marry him – the bitch! Not wanting to show my lack of appreciation of my father's very best wine, I had drained the goblet so well that no-one ever suspected that its contents were the cause of my demise.

But did Ophelia hurt her back too? No reason to think so, I reflected, but anyway did it really matter whether my memory was a true personal one or an example of "cryptoamnesia" (making one's own something one had read in a book or seen in a film)? It did not matter! The purpose of regression therapy is neither historical research nor proving that we have lived before. To me at this moment it was useful to know that my backache had a long history, and that I was not "making a fuss about nothing", as the GP had tried to make me believe.

The therapist to whom Roger Woolger had sent me for body work had a hunch that the regression to my birth might reveal something in my upper back which could have been released. When, however, I returned for the next session saying that the pain was no better, he asked me to focus on the time when it had started, and I told him how it had intensified to almost unbearable proportions during Paul's actual birth.

PART FOUR - CHILDBIRTH IN EGYPT

My husband had left me alone with some of the servants and a physician. He loved me so much that it hurt him beyond words to see me suffering, and in any case his duties at the Pharaoh's court were calling him. He was excited at the prospect of the arrival of our first born child, but he knew that he could be sent for if he were needed. So here I was lying in bed, with the baby's kicking and writhing making me increasingly uncomfortable all over, and the pain in my spine and dorsal rib area causing me to cry out incessantly. Our physician said that a conscious birth was better for both mother and child, so he was reluctant to drug me, but I was conscious of nothing but the agony I was suffering and could not imagine surviving it.

I did survive it of course, but only by leaving my body just as the baby's head started to emerge into the world. What a relief it was to be free – suddenly completely free of pain – and what a beautiful sight was this tiny baby boy with his legs and his fists so tightly curled! Enthralled, I watched my son being pulled out from between my legs, but then suddenly there was panic. Handing the little bundle to an assistant, the physician hurriedly started working on my heart. "Quick. Fetch her husband," he said, and all around there was running and scuffling. Suddenly I panicked too. Was it too late for me to return to my body? Would my new son have to be brought up without a mother? The physician said "Look what an enormous baby! No wonder that she could not take it. Her pelvis is so small, it's amazing that we got him out safely at all." Then, on seeing my husband, he continued "Congratulations, you have a fine son, but I am very sorry to say that there is nothing now that I can do for your wife. Childbirth can be very dangerous, you know, and in her case the weight of this big baby was too much for her back. She was in an enormous amount of pain, and I fear she has suffered a fatal heart attack."

My husband wept. I put my arms around him, whispering in his ear, that I was now free of pain, that I would always love him, but that my time had come. I explained that he needed to learn to cope with loss, and that we could always be together again at night when he left his body in sleep, but his grief prevented him from hearing me. I lingered while my funeral arrangements were being made, overjoyed when I saw the young woman I recognised as my husband's future bride, perceiving her to be an ideal stepmother for my son. But, once the funeral was over, there seemed to be no reason for delaying my journey into the next world.

And into the next world I took with me firstly the memory of the intense back pain which had started well before the birth, and secondly those words of the physician – "Childbirth can be very dangerous, you know."

PART FIVE - THE ACCIDENT IN BATTLE

The battle was raging much too near the cliff edge for my liking, but we had no choice but to attack the enemy where they were. My trusty steed seemed to have no fear at all, and I had precious little time in which to think about the dangers. Suddenly, however, an enemy horse came much too close for comfort. My own horse reared so violently that I was hurled backwards, not at first realising quite how close to the cliff edge we had come. The next thing I knew I was lying flat on the beach with the most almighty pain in my back. The beach was mostly sand, but I had been unlucky enough to land on some rocks. I was fortunate to have survived at all, I supposed, but that was poor consolation for this appalling pain and the degradation of coming off my horse. I gave a huge scream, and then I must have passed out.

The next thing I knew I was on a stretcher. Some of my companions had scrambled down a path at a point where the cliff was less steep, and they carried me slowly and carefully back to the tent. "He's probably broken a few ribs, I guess," said one of our men, "and very likely his spine as well."

"He must be pretty tough not to have been killed outright," said another. I was too shocked and stunned to say anything at all.

Over the next few days – or was it weeks? I know not – I lay in that tent with the battle continuing to rage around me. I drifted in and out of consciousness, thinking only of the pain and of the picture of my dear wife and two small children standing at the gate sadly waving me farewell. How I yearned to get back to them! But that was out of the question at least until this war was over – or until my broken back was sufficiently healed for me to be able to ride again. They brought me food and water whenever they could, though there was scarcely enough now even for those who were fit enough to fight.

As the days and nights wore on without change and I drifted in and out of consciousness, I reflected on the meaning of life and death, on the purpose of war, on relationships, on joy and grief, on loss... Having always regarded myself as being exceptionally fit physically, this loss of mobility, this indescribable pain, were hard to bear, yet I felt sure that there must be some good reason behind it. Perhaps, when my life had ended (which – I feared increasingly now – might be soon), I would be better able to understand. Just now, when the pain was particularly bad and I was only semi-conscious, archetypal images floated into my mind. I saw myself as a pillar being hacked at by men with axes and no feelings. (The church or the temple, so important to all civilisations, could not continue to stand if its pillars crumbled.) Then I saw a sailing boat rocking on a stormy sea. At times I was no more than a passenger in this boat, at times I was the boat itself, at times I was the sea... What did it matter since all is one? But then, suddenly, an extra strong gust of wind shattered the mast so that the boat could no longer carry me, the passenger, to my destination. What was my destination? Did I need a physical vehicle to carry me?"

******

"No you don't," said my guardian angel. "Physical bodies only serve you during your sojourns on Earth. You can leave them, and all the problems that come with them, behind each time you come Home for a respite.... But by suffering so much at the end of that life, you can be happy to have paid off a big karmic debt now...."

PART SIX - PREPARING FOR THE WOOLGER TRAINING

Two lives in a single session – that was more than I had ever been able to get during my training at Regent's College!

"Your first pregnancy could well have triggered that Egyptian memory," said my therapist, "and I wouldn't be surprised if it had made you scared of childbirth."

"Oh yes, I was terrified, and I wouldn't have got pregnant again if I hadn't been so determined to have at least two children. Alice's birth was a lot easier of course...."

"Well yes, you knew by then that it was possible to survive it." (I hadn't thought of that!) "But I still had terrible backache during the second pregnancy too. That's one reason why adoption seemed a much more attractive option the third time."

"And what about that soldier? Was his back pain in the same place as yours now?"

"Oh yes, exactly."

"Well, isn't it now time to let go of it?"

******

"How I would love to let go of it," I said to my good friend John the next time I saw him, "but for some unexplained reason I just don't seem able to."

"Perhaps you haven't yet learnt all you need to learn from it," John replied with a smile.

"Anyway, Sai Baba says that, if our lives on Earth were too comfortable, we might not bother about the fact that our destiny is a final return to the source we originally came from. So that's a good enough reason for my backache, isn't it?"

"It could be," replied John. "If you really believed it! And how about acceptance?"

"Umm... Yes, I know that all our *samskaras*[1] come from saying "No" to what is. That's something I still need to work on in several areas besides the back pain. At least I've got some material for Roger's next workshop, which is going to be focusing on the body!"

PART SEVEN - THE BUILDER

Now that both our parents were dead, I had to look after my younger sister as well as myself. Our house and little plot at the foot of the mountain were tiny, and it was a struggle growing enough even to feed ourselves, let alone have anything left over to sell. When my father was alive he used to earn a little bit cutting wood in the forest, leaving me to work the garden and care for Mother in her sickness, but it was not possible for me to do that as well as growing our food and looking after little Katia.

******

Another couple of years had gone by, and Katia and I were still struggling. One day a rotund, wealthy-looking man appeared at the door of our tiny cottage. "I'm looking for strong young men to help me build my house at the top of the mountain. You look as though you would be a good candidate. I'll pay you handsomely. What do you say?" Katia's face had such a pleading expression, how could I refuse?

"Right. So you can report at seven o'colock tomorrow morning just by that gate at the edge of the forest over there. We'll have to start by carrying the stones for the foundations up the mountain. I won't want any loitering."

"I didn't like the look of him," I said to Katia as soon as the man had gone, "and is it right that anyone should have a big house with the best view when those of us who really belong here have to struggle so to keep body and soul together?"

"But it need not be for very long, and perhaps you'll be paid enough to be able to build us a bigger house – one that would be big enough for you to be able to rear a family of your own. Isn't it time that you were looking for a wife?"

"A wife? How could I ever afford to have a wife? It would be nice, though, I admit."

---

1. The word *samskara* in Sanskrit literally means "cultured traits" or characteristics, but it is also used to indicate "karmic residue", i.e. the problems that we have brought in with us from previous lives.

"Well, let's wait and see what happens tomorrow."

The next evening I arrived home aching and exhausted, but with a small handful of coins in my pocket. Katia had prepared a particularly nice meal, so I did not want to upset her by letting on how hard the work had been. It was the height of summer, and carrying heavy stones on one's back right to the very top of the mountain was thirsty work as well. Fortunately the route we took ran past a beautiful clear stream, but when I stopped to drink from it for more than a couple of minutes, the master's voice would ring out "I said I wasn't going to stand for any loitering." I prayed that a good night's sleep would ease the pain in my legs and back, and that Katia would not start to resent having to attend to the chickens and the vegetable patch single-handedly.

The weeks dragged on and the work did not get any easier. Building could not start, the master said, until we had brought up enough large stones for the whole of the foundations. They must then be completed before the snow started. Since the house was to be massive, this meant an incredibly large number of stones, and there were not very many of us young men in the village ready or able to do it. My little store of coins was growing, but this seemed poor consolation for my bent back, my aching legs and the constant blisters on my feet. "Would any potential wife even look at me twice now?" I wondered. But I could not disappoint Katia, and in any case the master threatened beatings if we failed to turn up on time each morning.

Finally one day the master said that it was time to start digging. This was hard work too of course, and we were not allowed to walk up the mountainside to the site empty-handed. That would be a waste, the master said. Each of us was to carry a sackful of bricks with us every time, so that gradually there would be enough up there to really get going on the house as soon as the snow had melted. The weight of those sacks was unbelievable. It was a wonder that my back had not broken completely by now. In fact one or two of my companions did give up, but then they had to flee the village to avoid the master's ire. I could not possibly leave Katia! We were only just completing the foundations when the snow started to fall. Still the master would not give us any respite. "A bit of snow won't hurt you. You're all young and strong." And none of us dared to argue with him. So now the path was treacherous as well as steep, and I had started to be woken regularly from precious sleep by nightmares of slipping before I had reached the top with my sack of bricks. One day the nightmare came true, and the next thing I knew....

******

As a prelude to locating our weak spots, Roger had had us doing some vigorous exercises to music. Then we had drawn an outline of our bodies, and the "points to notice" were marked on it in different colours. When I scanned my body, I was surprised to find that my legs at that moment were even more painful than my back. I became less surprised when the regression started and I found myself struggling up that steep mountainside day after day with the heavy load. For verisimilitude Roger had me hold a large cushion over my shoulder, and then my partner pulled it downwards while I walked around the room. Then, after I had slipped in the snow and died (so young!) and we had done a session in the Bardo where I expressed my feelings of anger against my employer and met up with my parents, my partner took me back into the life and had me shed the burden.

But now my task was to find analogies with burdens in my present life. Looking back through my sixty odd years there was never any shortage of those: having charge of all my younger brothers and sisters, cooking for a family of eight when I was only a young teenager, examinations, jobs with a great deal of responsibility... Then later on my own children, my clients, getting my books published.... Did all that really have to be a burden, or had one's attitude to it been programmed over centuries? It seemed to me that the latter was undoubtedly true, and that now was the time to break the pattern. (Roger, after regressing me previously to the life of a woman running an orphanage single-handedly, had asked whether drudgery was another of my patterns, and I had realised that it was.) I had already helped several of my own clients to recognise and then break their own patterns. These were so common, and often I found that people did not become aware of repeating undesirable patterns in their present lives until they had observed the same sort of occurrences in previous ones.

For yes, though we do have to accept pain and the payment of our karmic debts as a part of life as much as joy is, we do not have to be victims all the time. That fat woman who was always over the kitchen sink could surely have taught her orphans that helping with the washing up could be fun. Had the princess found a previous life in which she had caused her younger sister's jealousy, perhaps they could have been good friends instead of coveting the same man. If we cannot change the past now, at least we can recognise that we are entirely responsible for our own future. I feel that mental patterns, once detected, can be easier to change than physical ones if the weakness (such as that in my back) is deeply implanted physically, but making change where one can and accepting what is where one cannot, is the way to avoid creating new *samskaras*. Through these regressions triggered by my back pain, I have come to a realisation of a need to work harder at acceptance of it. So often have I struggled to fight it, bashing on at the computer when I could just go and lie down for half an hour. Also, there is one thing for which I can be very grateful: a good night's sleep always cures the pain temporarily.

And those recounted above are not the only lifetimes I have found that are relevant to this particular topic. If you care to read on, you will find the sad story of a slave who got beaten to death by his cruel master, of a future astronomer who was ragged as a child and thrown backwards on to a sharp rock. Oh, that poor old back yet again! I have sometimes wondered how many lifetimes I have had where it has not been hurt or injured. But never mind: Sai Baba says that one of our aims in being born is not to be born again; and He says that while we are on Earth happiness is merely an interval between two pains. He also on occasion reverses that statement, and of course it is entirely up to us which we focus on mainly.

One of the things that people such as the Buddha and Sai Baba come to Earth to teach us is that we are not the body. No matter whether we choose to call it the "soul", the "atma", or anything else, the point is that the real "you" (or me!) is an eternal essence untouched by pain. Sai Baba very occasionally becomes ill or has an accident. Normally when this happens it is because He has generously taken something on for somebody else who would not have been strong enough to cope with it. In 2003, however, He broke his hip extremely badly and had to have an operation, from which He recovered remarkably quickly. On this occasion He explained afterwards that, rather than having taken on an accident that was really someone else's karma, He did it as a demonstration of one of the points that He is here to teach us: that we are not the body.

Sai Baba went into the hospital with a huge smile on His face, and He refused to complain of any pain, leaving His doctors dumbfounded. Would that I had exactly the same attitude towards my backache, but I have at last learnt that this is what I should be aiming for. There is always a good reason for everything, and I would certainly not be writing this book if it were not for my backache!

EXERCISES

PROBLEMS

Have you got some intractable problem that you would really rather be rid of?

(a) Think about what you have learnt from it. Can you make a list? If you can't think of anything, just keep trying!

(b) If you don't feel you have learnt anything yet, but can think of something you could learn, how about working on that?

ACCEPTANCE

How do you react when the weather is not to your liking? Do you say for instance "Oh no. It's raining <u>again</u>!"?, "How I loathe the cold!", or "You can't do anything in this heat!"? Acceptance of what we cannot change is always to be recommended, so you could

- buy a better umbrella
- wear warmer/cooler clothes
- do warming exercises
- relax, drink a lot more water, take a cool bath or shower, or go for a swim.

PATTERNS

Have you found yourself caught in any repeated patterns in your present life? e.g. Have you fallen for a series of men/women who reject you?, dominate you?, are over-dependent on you?

Are you in the habit of making wrong choices?

Do you splurge money on ambitious projects which then fail?

Have a really good look at your life and try to identify the patterns. Are you aware that they are of your own making and that it is consequently up to you to break them? If you really want to break a pattern, you have only to see clearly what it is, make up your mind to break it, and then you can do so.

Let us take the first example. (Anyone with a different problem can try to apply the same principles.) Look back and see where it started. Did your father/mother reject you? If so, it is very natural that you should have formed the notion "men/women reject one", but now you need to realise that it is always inadvisable to make generalisations from a single example. The likelihood is that the people who have continued the pattern for you have simply been fulfilling your own expectations, so is it not now high time to change those?

Have a good look at your pattern of behaviour in the relationships. Did you test your partners by trying to see how much they would take? Did you enter the new relationship thinking "The last one rejected me, but this one's different; he/she seems to really accept me."? This is a common pattern, and then you test the person by pushing more and more until they finally break too. On the <u>conscious</u> level you think and hope it is going to be different this time, but on the <u>sub</u>conscious level you are expecting rejection and this expectation is communicated to your partner.

So the answer is straightforward! Start believing in yourself and believing that you deserve to be loved, and at the same time love your partner simply because he/she deserves it too and not because of what you are expecting from them. Sounds difficult? None of the most worth while things in life are easy, but we are here to achieve the best for ourselves as well as for others.

XII
HEALING
KARMIC RELATIONSHIPS

PART ONE - FRIENDSHIP WITH JOHN

Alice and Christopher were not the only members of our family with a karmic relationship to work out. I had a very difficult one with a man I will call Ambrose, who is over twenty years my senior, and who always seemed to "have it in for me" for no reason that I could understand. My relationship with my good friend John, on the other hand, has for long been a great support, even though his efforts to improve my back troubles were unsuccessful. John, who is a Buddhist, is over twenty years my junior, yet he became almost a father figure for me once I had begun to move away from traditional Catholicism and come to believe in such things as reincarnation. Here, as we shall see, is a case of the karmic tables being turned!

PART TWO - ISRAEL

Follow me, follow me, Leave your home and family,
Leave your fishing nets and boats upon the shore.
Leave the seed that you have sown,
Leave the crops that you've grown,
Leave the people you have known and follow me.

Hymn by Michael Cockett

CHAPTER ONE - THE MESSIAH

"He's coming to our village! The man Jesus... The one some say is the Messiah.."

"It can't be true. Not here?"

"Yes, it is true. It's really he... Jesus! Look at all the crowds. No-one but he could draw such crowds...."

The rumours were circulating throughout the town. The excitement was mounting by the minute. Was it really true? I must go and see for myself. If it really was the man Jesus, I must go and hear him. The stories were so amazing. The miraculous cures he had performed; the vast numbers of people he had fed from just a few small loaves of bread. Life was hard for a poor widow on her own with four little ones, but Mother could mind the children for an hour or two while I went out to see what was going on.

I did not have to go far. Here he was, right in the centre of our little town. The market place was filling up rapidly. No wonder! His words were so powerful, his face so full of love. Everyone felt drawn to him; I had never seen anything like it. This was an experience to treasure for the rest of one's life. If only Jacob were still here to see it too!

******

It cannot be getting dark already? Six hours must have passed since I left home. Most of the crowds had begun to disperse, but here was I still riveted to the spot I had taken when I first saw him, unable to take my gaze off this man Jesus, and quite forgetting about my children. Now I must hurry home to them. But what would they do – Jesus and all his friends? They must need to eat and sleep! Still, I could not wait to find out.

"Excuse me, good woman...." I turned to see who was addressing me and thought

I recognised one of the young men who seemed to have come with Jesus. "Have you any bread and water? We have travelled far today and I am hungry and thirsty." He gazed straight into my eyes and I felt an instant attraction to this young disciple, so inspired and eager did he look.

"Yes, I can certainly give you a little sustenance, but I'm only a poor widow with four young children to feed. Who are you?"

"My name is Ambrose. I've come with Jesus. I'm from a poor family too. I lived alone with my mother for some years after my father died when I was small, but now Jesus is my father. I'm travelling with him and when I have learnt all I need and feel able, I shall carry on his work myself. Perhaps I shall even be able to heal people too."

"How wonderful! You must tell me all about it. There are certainly many people in this town who need healing."

I did not want to delay, so we carried on talking all the way to my home. Joy, my mother, who lived with us and was always such a wonderful support to me, had fed the children and they were all asleep, but there was just enough left for Ambrose and myself to eat. He left when we had had our fill, but asked if he could return the following evening.

The next day I decided not to return to the market place, but to stay with the children, who had missed me the previous day. There was not much food left, but with what there was I prepared the best meal I possibly could in case Ambrose really did return in the evening. Why was I so anxious, I wondered? Someone else could surely offer the young man food. There were plenty of women around who could afford it more easily than I.

Time was getting on. Why had I not eaten? Why did the idea that Ambrose might have eaten elsewhere cause me distress? We had only met once. He would move on when Jesus moved on, and everyone said that the Messiah was going from place to place spreading the Good News. I could not expect him to remain in our village indefinitely, so there was no point in getting too fond of Ambrose. I <u>must</u> see him once more, though; I could not bear not to say "goodbye".

"Thank goodness, it's you! I was afraid I wasn't going to be able to find your home again, and I couldn't request directions because I hadn't thought to ask your name. I hope you were expecting me."

"What sort of a man is this, that he spends the entire evening with a woman whose name he doesn't even know? Ann is my name."

"Ann is a beautiful name!" We laughed together. "What's that delicious smell? Can I eat with you again?"

"Yes, you can eat with me today. I've prepared something specially, which I hope you will like. But you won't be able to eat with me tomorrow, for I have used up all the food I had."

"Don't worry about tomorrow. Jesus will provide for us."

What faith Ambrose had in this man! It was impossible not to share it, so contagious was his enthusiasm. This time he lingered longer over the meal, and we talked far into the night. When morning came again, however, I began to worry. Ambrose would need caring for, I desperately wanted to see him again, yet how could I possibly feed him as well as the children? Anyway, what was the attraction? Why should he be interested in a poor widow with more children than she could cope with easily? It would be better if he did not return to my house, but carried on his travels with Jesus. Later he could find himself a wife, settle down and have children of his own. I could forget.

Forget? Could I easily forget Ambrose? Why did he have so much power over me? Such a young man! Much younger than Jacob would have been. Not much older in fact than Jacob had been when we were first married. Dear Jacob, how I missed him! How hard it was having to carry on living without him. But carry on I must. He trusted me always to care well for his children.

Who is that arriving at the door? "Hullo!" I thought I'd come earlier today so that I could meet your children. Look, I've brought some food. I told you that Jesus would provide for us. We can cook it together. I often used to help my mother to cook.

******

A few weeks had passed and Ambrose was still eating at our house every day. The children had grown used to him. Although he was so young, he was almost like a new father to them, and he loved them very much. John, the eldest, had been immediately fired with enthusiasm by Ambrose's talk about Jesus, and begged him to take him with him the very next day. Ambrose was delighted, and that day the two of them did not return until quite late. After that John begged to go with him again and again. Sometimes I let him, but more often than not I felt I could not spare him. With Jacob dead, he was really the only "man" in the house, and anyway he was extraordinarily grownup for his tender years and we all five depended on him a great deal.

Occasionally Ambrose persuaded me to go with him as well. I did love to listen to Jesus, but did not feel that I could leave the children and the chores very often. Besides, Mother's health was beginning to fail a little. She had been concerned at first about the relationship. She felt I should not take on anyone extra, but now she was saying "There's no law against your marrying someone a bit younger than you." She had always felt that, having lost my husband so young, there was no reason why I should remain a widow for the rest of my life.

On the days when John had been off to follow Jesus with Ambrose, he would join in with him in telling us all about it. He seemed to be growing in maturity and wisdom daily, and he would talk to Joseph about plans to change the world until the poor lad was literally falling asleep. Joseph was really interested too, but I felt that a child of his age could not possibly last there for a whole day, so occasionally I took him along with me for an hour or so.

One evening when Ambrose returned on his own, his look was different. The earnestness was as intense as ever, but his usual sparkle was replaced by anxiety. "Jesus says we must prepare to leave. He has done all he needs to do in this town and wishes to move on to the next one. What shall I do? I love you. I don't think I could live without you. Will you come with us?"

"Go with you? How could I with the children?"

"You do love me too, don't you? John is already a disciple, Joseph is a good little walker, and between us we could carry Simone and Selma."

I looked at him. He threw his arms around me and suddenly I knew that I could not possibly bear to see him leave without us. "All right," I said, "we'll come. So long as Jesus doesn't mind."

"That's wonderful! I'll see Jesus about it just before we leave tomorrow morning. So make sure you're ready."

Mother, who had been in the back room while Ambrose was eating with us, came through after he had gone, and she said "Jesus won't want you lot tagging along with him. Anyway, how could you possibly care for them all properly?"

"I don't know, Mother, but Ambrose is always confident that one can manage <u>anything</u> with Jesus, and I love him <u>so</u> much...."

Just then there was a knock at the door. It was my good friend Paula with a present of some of her freshly baked bread. I had hardly seen her since meeting Ambrose, so I decided to confide in her about the whole thing. Together with Alan, Jacob's best friend, and of course Mother, it was she who had been the greatest support to me when I had been widowed. When I had finished, Paula looked very concerned. "It sounds crazy to me," she said. "Anyway, if he really loves you so much, he should be prepared to stay here and devote his energies to caring for you all. Why don't you seek a more mature man if you're really wanting to remarry?"

"But Paula, you just can't imagine how much I love him. He's so full of life, such fun to be with, so caring...."

The Next Morning

Ambrose's dear face looked like a thunder cloud. "Jesus says it's impossible for you all to come – that it would be too difficult. He says that I'll have to choose between you and him. I just don't know what to do." I threw myself into his arms and tears streamed down both our faces. Eventually I looked up at him.

"You must decide for yourself, my dearest. I wouldn't want to influence you. You are a free man."

"Free? How can I be free when I'm imprisoned on the one hand by my love for you and on the other by my desire to follow Jesus?"

"Perhaps there are more ways than one of following Jesus, Ambrose. But you will have to make up your own mind."

CHAPTER TWO - LOSS OF AMBROSE

Ambrose and I had been married for seven months, and together we were just raking a living for the seven of us including Mother. Ambrose had green fingers; all the vegetable seeds he obtained in exchange for odd jobs grew wonderfully under his care in our little patch, and we were never really wanting for food. However, Paula said that her instincts about Ambrose's hot-headnesses had been confirmed. Ambrose and I argued often too – the strong attraction between us was one of total opposites – yet the bond of love which drew us together made up for all these difficulties.

Ambrose was a tremendous talker, and often, after our day's work was over and the children had gone to sleep, he would hold me enthralled with stories of his childhood and of his brief travels with Jesus and the other disciples. Although he had not been with them for very long, he had made firm friends among Jesus' followers. There was always nostalgia in his voice when he talked of these adventures, but sometimes the nostalgia would turn momentarily to enthusiastic plans. "When the children are all older," he would say, "and you and I are freer, we and your John will be able to go out and change the whole world. We'll tell everyone about Jesus:

how he came to bring peace, how he desired justice for the poor, how he came to show us the way back to God.... There will be no more wars, the rich will be made to share all their wealth, no more will there be any need for people to struggle to keep alive as we do...."

Although we were so different in temperament, we shared many interests, such as a tremendous love of nature. We were never happier than when we were able to go out walking, either on our own or with one or more of the children. Ambrose would teach us the names of all the different trees and birds, and we would revel together in the beauty of the sunsets. John knew so much already, but Joseph was really keen to learn, and his stepfather found him a good student. Besides being a good teacher for the children, Ambrose was a wonderful playmate for them, having such a tremendous sense of fun.

At times, however, when he was not busy with the children or his vegetable patch, Ambrose would suddenly be filled with melancholy. I knew that he was missing Jesus and his friends, and all that I could do was sit with him, hold his hand, give him food.... Mostly he appreciated that, but just occasionally I noticed his eyes upon me with a look almost of resentment. After a while I found that these melancholy moods became more and more frequent; I found myself drawn into them and felt less and less able to shake him out of them. Sometimes he almost made me feel guilty.

Then suddenly one day the dreadful news reached our town. The news that the Messiah had been crucified. Everyone was distressed, but Ambrose and John were both quite beside themselves with grief. All night long Ambrose tossed and turned. "It's my fault!" he said. "If I'd been there I wouldn't have let them do it."

"Ambrose dearest, you mustn't concern yourself so. Jesus had lots of other friends; one more or less couldn't have made any difference. If they were so determined to kill him, there's no way anyone could have prevented it."

"You're wrong, Ann. It's my fault. I should have gone with them. Why didn't I? Because of you of course! It's your fault. How could I have been so weak willed as to fall in love with a mere woman? I'll never forgive myself. I'll never forgive either of us!"

He was inconsolable. I felt he was really beginning to hate me, and I started wishing that I had tried to persuade him to go with Jesus when he left our town. He might have come back to me after a while – certainly after this dreadful murder he would have come back.... But now it was too late.

"There's no point in blaming yourself and me, Ambrose. It's happened now. There's nothing we can do about it. But what you can do is preach to our people about Jesus. Perhaps you and John could learn to write. Then you could both put some of the stories about Jesus on to parchment to hand down to our grandchildren and their children. So that his name will never be forgotten."

"Learn to write? What a waste of time, woman! We must act! In fact I must act now. I must go out and find these wicked killers and seek vengeance. I won't return to you until my hands are red with their blood." He was talking so loudly that John heard him from the other room and shouted "Wait, Ambrose. Let me come with you." Ambrose hesitated just for a moment then said firmly "No. You must stay and take care of your family." Then, before John could get in another word, he was gone.

Then day after day dragged by with no news. John was filled with melancholy, and the vegetables were wilting. I kept watering them, but somehow I just didn't seem to have Ambrose's touch. We were all getting hungrier and hungrier. Life did not seem worth living any more. Yet I must carry on for the children's sake.

******

Several weeks had passed now. Surely Ambrose must come back soon? He would realise that there was nothing he could do now that Jesus was dead. Even though he had blamed me for keeping him here, I felt sure his love was still as strong as ever. He would be missing me by now. He must come back. Mother, who understood the trials of widowhood only too well, did her very best to comfort me, Paula and Alan were both wonderful (neither of them said "I told you so"), and Joseph was becoming more and more supportive, but no-one was able to allay my anxieties or give me or John any real consolation. One day little Selma just looked up at me with her huge brown eyes and said mournfully "Ambrose is gone."

*****

"Ann!" It was Alan's voice. "Bad news, I'm afraid. They've just brought Ambrose's body back to the village. It seems he went on the rampage seeking vengeance on Jesus' killers, but simply got killed himself. However, they say that Jesus is alive! That he's come back from the dead! He was seen by the women who went to the tomb, and has since met with some of the apostles. This means he must truly be the Messiah as people said!"

"Maybe you're right, Alan. Maybe Jesus is the Messiah. But how can any Messiah make up for the loss of my Ambrose?"

I wept. The children all clung to me, weeping. "Ambrose! Daddy! Come back! Come back!" We wept.

CHAPTER THREE - LOSS OF JOHN

John had got over his melancholy and had begun to take Ambrose's place as the breadwinner and gardener. He still missed Ambrose and Jesus of course, but he coped with the loss much better than I did, and I was becoming more than ever dependent on him. In fact I often reflected that I would simply not have managed to carry on at all if it had not been for John. One day, however, he suddenly said to me out of the blue "Mother, I've been thinking. I've decided that I must go off now to spread the word of Jesus. I've heard that, after he rose from the dead and appeared to the apostles, he entrusted them with carrying on his work. If I could have seen him too, I know he would have said the same to me. Anyway, someone should make up for Ambrose not being able to carry out the plans we'd made."

I was too stunned to reply. The thought of a second loss - no, a third including Jacob – was too much to bear. "You must understand, Mother. It's what Ambrose would have wanted. Joseph will learn to take care of you and the girls." Something deep inside me told me that I must let go. And that I would never see John again.

"All right, son. I understand."

PART THREE - ENLIGHTENMENT

This life explained so much, it was amazing. Ambrose, who was of course also Mother Ambrosia in my lifetime as an Italian nun, seemed when we first met to remember the love there had been between us in Israel, but this was quickly replaced by what I can only describe as apparent hatred. I found this extremely hurtful and, not understanding the reason for it, I reacted very badly and expressed a great deal of anger – anger which was really the anger against my father that I had repressed for many years and needed to acknowledge before letting go of it. But it was also very obvious that Ambrose was angry with <u>himself</u>. He is an extremely strong Christian, and this story makes complete sense of much of his behaviour. Once I had found out about this past life, even though I could not possibly tell him about it, our relationship changed completely. We no longer meet very often but, when we do, he is completely charming to me! I have met other people who have also found that gaining information about a previous life with someone has improved their relationship despite their not being able to share the information with them.

Occasionally during a regression I recognise people that I know now (such as Patricia/Patrick in my life as the village idiot), but this is not always the case. I did not immediately recognise John as having been my son in Israel, but he is an expert dowser and I decided to consult his pendulum about all the close relationships of that lifetime. (I also use a pendulum myself, but it is not usually advisable to use it for very personal issues, as it too is easy to influence it.) Through John's pendulum I was able to trace both Paul and Alice (as Paula and Alan) and all the members of my family. The four children that I had then are all friends of mine now, though none is as close to me as John; and my mother was my friend Joy, who is now a lot younger than me. In our present life I have been something of a mother figure to Joy, just as John has been a sort of father figure to me.

This story also explains that Italian nun's difficulties about Jesus. In this life, too, although I was brought up a devout Catholic, feeling love for Jesus has not always been easy for me. Finding the reason for that has also made it much easier for me to regard him as a true friend!

EXERCISE

Can you think of someone with whom you have a difficult relationship?

Do you react with anger when you feel that he/she has attacked you with insufficient justification?

If so, try to think who this person might be symbolising for you. Could you be expressing the anger that you also feel against, for instance, one of your parents?

Once you have identified the other person in an earlier relationship, write him/her a letter expressing all your feelings of anger and resentment. Really try to get it all out. Now destroy the letter.

Next time that the first person says or does something to upset you, make a real effort (and this is a case of "Don't do as I did, do as I say"!) to just smile and contain your emotions until you get home.

When you get home, if you are still feeling angry, get a big cushion and give it a really good punching. Then, if you like, write a letter expressing what you wanted to say at the time but held in. Now destroy the letter.

Keep doing this and you will probably find a remarkable change for the better in the relationship. This will not only help your life now, but will also prevent you from accruing karma which may have to be worked out with the person concerned in a future life.

XIII
GETTING BACK ON TO THE SPIRITUAL PATH

PART ONE - JUSTICE AND PEACE

Long before discovering my true spiritual path for this lifetime, I reached the point where my religion became much more meaningful to me than it had when I was young. For many years I went to church, and I prayed (occasionally!) at home more out of duty than anything else – because I had been brought up in fear of the consequences of not being a good Catholic – but none of it helped me a great deal either emotionally or spiritually. As a child one of my biggest nightmares was confession. We were made to feel obliged to go at least monthly, and, being such a shy child, I was always terrified. The most difficult thing was trying to think up new sins to confess, and I invariably ended up repeating for the umpteenth time "I quarrelled with my sister and brother". The only reason I ever felt better afterwards was because of the fact that it was over until the following month. Occasionally my apprehension made me leave six weeks between my confessions, but that made things worse because of the shame of having to begin by saying "It's six weeks since I made my last confession". The act of confession was for me much more frightening than the idea of Hell, because even at the tender age of about seven I could not really accept that notion. It simply did not make any sense to me that a supposedly loving God could condemn anyone He had created to eternal damnation.

Fortunately many things have improved radically in the Church in recent years, and so my own children did not have to go through such torture when they reached the age for going to confession. As for me, Church life took on much more meaning when I joined the Justice and Peace movement. Most of the work that I did before getting married was connected with helping the Third World (or, as some prefer to call it, the Exploited World), and so I was glad when the children began to get old enough for me to have a bit of time to get involved with that sort of thing again. Our diocese had a Justice and Peace Commission which held meetings regularly in York, and I also took to attending the annual national Justice and Peace conference, which I found truly inspiring. I met many wonderful people at those meetings and conferences, and on one occasion I heard a superb talk by someone I will call Bertrand. Although at the time I had not even begun to think about reincarnation, I instantly felt an extremely strong spiritual connection with Bertrand, and he has continued to inspire me by his spirituality, his knowledge of Third World issues, and his commitment to justice.

PART TWO - GREECE[1]

Never try to suppress the Spirit, or treat the gift of prophecy with contempt; think before you do anything - hold on to what is good, and avoid every form of evil.

I Thessalonians 5:1

CHAPTER ONE - FINDING MY VOCATION

My father had returned earlier than usual from the Agora, where he conducted most of his merchant's business and occasionally became involved in philosophical discussion, and I noticed him conferring quietly with my mother, who had just been very busily organising the servants and slaves in the preparation of a large feast. I had risen from the stool on which I had been seated with my spinning in the women's quarters and was walking slowly around the outside of the second storey of our

1. For this section I am indebted to: The Encyclopaedia Britannica
The Ancient Greeks - How they Lived and Worked by Maurice Pope, published by David and Charles.; *Religion in the Ancient Greek City* by Louise Bruit Zaidmann and Pauline Schmitte Pantel, in the beautiful translation from the French by Paul Cartledge, published by Cambridge University Press. (Surprisingly, this otherwise excellent book makes no reference to the Greek belief in reincarnation.); *Hellenic Traveller* by Guy Petreath, published by Routledge and Kegan Paul., and *Blue Guide to Athens and Environs* by Stuart Rossiter, published by Eres Benn Ltd., Rand McNally and Co., and the British Museum..

mansion, looking down upon the courtyard and its altar of Zeus Herkeios[2]. My parents were standing together in the far corner and were unaware of my presence. As soon as Father had gone indoors, Mother returned to the servants' quarters and I descended, feeling suddenly drawn to offer a little prayer to Zeus at the altar.

Father regularly invited friends and fellow merchants to dine with him in the second dining room, but today I had noticed that they were planning to use the first dining room, kept mainly for more special occasions. Neither of my parents had mentioned to me that anything unusual was happening, so I assumed that Father was planning some particularly important deal, or something else that was none of my business. Perhaps I would hear about it at the end of the meal, when I would be called in as usual to entertain the guests with my harp. On the other hand, perhaps I would not. Speculation on the subject did not seem worth while at the moment, and in any case, whatever it was, the matter was unlikely to be of any interest to me.

Having made my prayer at the family altar, I wandered to the second gate at the back of the house and through into the orchard. The peaches were in season, and as I sat peacefully enjoying one, its wonderful nectar pouring down my fingers, my thoughts turned from Zeus to Demeter, the goddess of corn and other vegetation. How blessed we were here in Attica, I mused, with so many delicious fruits to nourish us, and Apollo always ensuring enough sun just at the right time to ripen them. There were the fig trees on the other side of our orchard, with their green burdens gently swelling and turning slowly and assuredly to a superb, deep purple[3] - symbolic, surely, of the divinity which had conceived them initially and was now busy preparing them for human consumption.

Eventually, a trifle reluctantly, I left the orchard and returned towards the courtyard, only to be greeted by my mother, who exclaimed in an anxious tone "Ann! There you are. I thought you were spinning. Your meal has been ready for a full twenty minutes."

"I was bored with spinning." (Mother looked slightly shocked, but said nothing. She had long since more or less given up attempts at arguing with me, often saying to my father - sometimes exasperatedly, sometimes, I felt, slightly enviously - "It's no use arguing. You know she has a mind of her own.")

"What's the hurry?" I asked.

"Father is holding a particularly important dinner party this evening, and you know

2. Zeus Herkeios = Guardian of the Fence or Enclosure. All well-to-do families had an altar to him in their courtyard as the centre of their worship.
3. Purple is the colour of the crown chakra, and is always associated with the spiritual.

you must finish your own meal in plenty of time before you are called in to play for the guests."

"Yes, Mother, I know that, but I can hear the guests arriving only now. It will be quite some time before they are ready for my entertainment. I shall have finished eating long before they have even started on their libations."

"Yes dear, but you could be practising your harp, or learning one of Pindar's Odes to recite."

"Father seemed quite satisfied with my performance last week, and he has made no intimation to me that he wished me to recite poetry to his guests as well as make music for them."

"Well, the women's part of the roast lamb is well cooked now and we are all waiting for you."

******

The lamb had indeed been perfectly roasted and tender, and the vegetables - an even wider variety than usual - particularly elaborately prepared this evening. We women were still sitting at the table in our own quarters, but it was not too far for me to be able to hear something of what was going on in the first dining room. Drinking my watered wine slowly, in due course I heard the meal tables being removed by the slaves, and the bowls of water for hand washing being taken in for the use of my father and his guests. I then envisioned the men perfuming themselves and garlanding their heads. The libations would not have started yet, so I knew there was still some time to go before I would be summoned with my harp. "Pindar's Odes?" I thought to myself. "I remember noticing a volume of that title only the other day when I was returning *The Republic* to the shelf." I had glanced at it, but the handwriting looked a trifle difficult to read and I was seeking something a little less hard going than Plato. Perhaps I should nevertheless go and have a look at it.

"Miss Ann." It was the chief servant's voice. "Your father says can you please come now to the first dining room with your harp."

"But surely the libations cannot have finished yet?"

"I know not. I know only that your father has sent for you."

I rose from the table dutifully, went to pick up my harp, and entered the men's dining room. The men were reclining on their couches as usual, their beautifully painted, two-handled kylixes in their hands and the habitual garlands on their heads, but I seemed to sense an exceptional air of excitement, anticipation and festivity.

"Perhaps Father has just concluded a more than ever successful business deal," I reflected. "Or perhaps one of his colleagues is about to set off to a new country to negotiate new exports or imports. Whatever it is, I am sure their libations are not yet finished. I wonder why I have been sent for prematurely?"

But Father obviously had no intention of enlightening me at this point.

"Sit down please," he said slightly brusquely, "and play us that piece I heard you practising yesterday. It struck me as unusually pleasing."

"Well," he continued when I had finished, turning to the merchant reclining on a couch to the right of him, "does her music please you?"

"Indeed it does," the man replied. "Not only does the music please me, so does the harpist. What think you Xercathon[4], my son and heir?" addressing in his turn a younger, but obese and red-faced merchant, who did not look to me as though he could possibly have any ear for music.

"Of music I am ignorant," the younger man replied, "but the harpist herself is undoubtedly of good appearance. I feel perfectly content with the match."

"Match," I exclaimed inwardly. "Is that what my father has in mind? Is that why I have been called in at this early point?"

Of course, though I had never given it a great deal of thought, I had always been aware that my parents would one day arrange a marriage for me. What had never occurred to me was that firstly I should have been informed of it in circumstances such as these, and secondly that they would choose a man who was so patently undesirable. Xercathon's father was familiar to me. He was well known as one of the wealthiest merchants of Attica, and my father entertained him frequently, but he had always struck me as a tremendous bore, and my first impression of the son was that he seemed to be, if anything, an even greater one.

"So, Ann," said my father, "I have brought you in at this point in our celebrations in order to give you some very good news. We have already made our libation to Dionysius and the Graces, but I wished to have you present at the second one. Why? Because Aphrodite, the goddess of Love, always presides over our second libation, so what more appropriate moment could we choose to celebrate a betrothal? My good servant here, refill all the men's kylixes. My friends, raise your cups, pour the wine in honour of Xercathon and my daughter Ann. Next week I shall arrange for a civic celebration, with several cows sacrificed to Athene, but for the moment let us be content with congratulating the happy couple."

4. I have made up this name! It sounds to me firstly Greek and secondly unpleasant.

"Ann and Xercathon.... Ann and Xercathon...." The names rang round and round the dining room, the wine flowed more and more speedily, the merriment intensified.

After a few minutes my father raised his voice. "Just for this evening let us dispense with the third libation, which is presided over by Quarrels and Disaster. Ann, before you play to us some more and we continue the evening with song and perhaps a game of Kottabos[5], is there a word you would like to address to my good friend here? Or to his son Xercathon, whom he is so kindly offering to us as your husband? A more suitable match for you I could never have hoped to make. You must be deeply grateful both to my fellow merchant and to me for arranging it. The exceptionally good meal we have just been enjoying was in your honour, but I preferred to keep the good news as a surprise for you."

Surprise it certainly was, but as for news, I could think of none worse at that moment. I was speechless. But speak I must.

"I have only this to say, Father. I am grateful for the meal and appreciative of the parental care you have always extended to me, but at this moment I have no wish to marry."

Looks of amazement were passed right round the room. My father opened his mouth, then closed it again. Eventually Xercathon's father said "Perhaps you would prefer to delay the ceremony a month or two? Does Pyanopousion[6] seem a more appropriate time to you for a wedding?"

"Why Pyanopousion?" asked my horrified father. "Why should there be any delay? Both parties are of a good age for matrimony."

"It is nothing to do with age, Father. I simply do not feel any desire to be wed."

"Why not?" My father's tone was angry now. "All young women in our society must expect to marry at about your age. You know that. You should be grateful for the choice I have made for you!"

"I am sorry, Father. I have already expressed my gratitude, but I feel unable to accede to your wishes."

Xercathon's face was now redder than ever. During those last five minutes he had consumed so much he would surely soon be totally inebriated. I could not cause offence by speaking the whole truth, but later, when my father spoke to me

---

5. *Kottabos* = a game consisting of flicking wine from the bottom of a cup to try and sink a saucer in water.

6. *Pynapousion* = mid-October - mid-November.

privately, I would explain my feelings of antipathy towards the youth he had chosen for me. For the moment I could see nothing for it but to pick up my harp and leave the room. Wishing to avoid my mother for the time being, I went straight upstairs, and very soon I heard the party dispersing amidst much confusion and commotion. Xercathon and his father were the last to leave, and I heard the latter's parting words: "Be consoled, good friend. I am sure when you have talked to her that she will come to see reason. Next week I will give a feast at my mansion, and after it Ann can play to us some more and meet my wife and daughters. They will be good to her."

I waited, knowing what was to come, but not flinching in my resolution. Before another half hour had passed, my mother, as I had anticipated, came into the room, where my spinning lay idle.

"Your father wishes to speak with you. He is waiting for you in his sitting room."

My father's face was a thundercloud. "Never in my entire life have I suffered such humiliation! How <u>could</u> you treat me so contemptuously?"

"I am sorry, Father, but I was not intending to be at all contemptuous. And had you consulted me in advance about the match you were proposing, you could have saved yourself the humiliation."

"Never for one moment did it enter my head that you would be anything but grateful. But now I am awaiting your explanation. I was too thunderstruck earlier on to ask for that."

"Had you asked for it, I would not have given it. I have no wish to offend either Xercathon or your friend, his father. The idea of matrimony itself is not abhorrent to me, but I am afraid that that particular young man <u>did</u> fill me with abhorrence."

"Abhorrence! How can you feel abhorrence? Are you not aware that Xercathon is heir to one of the most successful businesses in the whole of Attica?"

"Money is no interest to me, Father. Xercathon did not appreciate my harp playing. My music is the expression of my soul. How could I live with a man who did not appreciate my psyche?"

"It is true," said my father softening slightly, "that for an Athenian his lack of ear is a serious one, but this is surely more than compensated for by his other qualities? When you have a family of your own, you will have other occupations besides your harp playing to interest you."

"Yes Father, I am aware of that. As a virgin I am still somewhat ignorant of such things, but is it not true that if they are to have children, a man and a woman must lie together? Nothing seems more abhorrent to me than the idea of lying with a corpulent, boring, red-faced drunkard such as Xercathon."

"How dare you speak so offensively of my friend's son!" My father's anger had returned. "You have never even spoken with him. What justification have you for describing him as boring?"

"I think dear," my mother interrupted, "that you should let Ann retire to bed now. You will perhaps be able to discuss more fruitfully tomorrow morning."

******

As I lay in bed my father was pacing the courtyard angrily. Even if I had been ready for sleep, the volume of his voice would have made it impossible.

"The <u>humiliation</u>!" he exclaimed to my mother. "You cannot imagine the feeling of humiliation."

"I <u>do</u> understand your feelings, my dear, but perhaps you should make more effort to understand things from her point of view. I did not know you either of course when our match was arranged by our parents, but I have never found you unattractive. You have always pursued the Athenian ideal of physical fitness allied with agility of mind, and even now, in middle age, thanks to your regular practice in the gymnasium, your appearance has in no way deteriorated. I doubt whether young Xercathon has <u>ever</u> been to the Kynosarges, or either the Lykeion or the Akademia for that matter. If he is unattractive to Ann now, he will perhaps be still more so by the time she is my age. For Xercathon certainly does have the appearance of a man more interested in food and drink than in music or philosophy."

"Nevertheless, his father is my friend and he has nothing but a prosperous future assured him. You must help me to persuade her."

"When has Ann ever been persuaded to do <u>anything</u> against her will? Even when she was only a little girl we often commented to one another on her strength of character, the individuality of her mind.... Surely there must be somewhere in Athens another young man equally suitable?"

"Another young man? How could I possibly be pardoned the affront to Xercathon? No, if she will not marry him, there can be nothing for it but to send her to a temple as a priestess. That is the only respectable alternative for a woman from a family of our standing. Yes, a priestess she shall be in the Hephaisteon, even if it means that we ourselves shall have to change our allegiance to another temple. For after the degradation I have been made to suffer this evening, something tells me that I shall have no desire to see our daughter Ann ever again."

The voices became gradually lowered and, before drifting into sleep, I let my thoughts wander around and around the idea that my father had just sown in them. "A priestess? Why not?" The idea was a new one to me, but by no means unpalatable. Certainly much less unpalatable than that of bearing children to Xercathon! Was not the Hephaisteon almost like home to me, so often had we been there for communal worship or family celebrations. There my harp could be of service where it could not be in the home of Xercathon, and I could look after the visitors who stayed in the sanctuary hotel and learn to give counsel. It would surely be a worth while life compared with many, and I did not feel that I would particularly miss either my family or this mansion.

******

"Your father has gone to the Kynosarges early this morning. He slept badly and felt in need of a swim to relax him, but when he returns he has an alternative proposition to put to you. Unless, that is, you have reconsidered your decision about Xercathon?"

"That, Mother, I shall never do. I prefer to hear Father's alternative proposal. Ah, is that his horse I hear returning now?"

"Well Ann, a sorry state you put me in last night! Are you now repentant?"

"I fear not, Father, though I am sorry for the inconvenience my feelings seem to have caused you."

"Sorrow is of no use without action. If you will not change your mind about marrying Xercathon, I have no alternative but to send you away for good to become a celibate priestess."

My father was obviously surprised at the equanimity with which I received his announcement. He had no idea either that I had overheard his conversation the night before, nor that the thought of becoming a priestess had considerable appeal to me.

"Well," he said, a trifle put out, "let us proceed forthwith to the Hephaisteon to enquire whether they can accommodate you. You will require, I think, nothing other than a couple of spare tunics, your chlamys[7] and your harp. The simplicity of lifestyle in the Temple may come as a bit of a shock to you."

7. *Chlamys* = a heavy cloak.

"I do not think so, Father. I have never revelled in our wealth, and I regard the beauty of the Aegean, the blue Athenian sky and the mountains with Athene's olive groves and the beautiful almond blossom as riches far greater than any mansion."

CHAPTER TWO - SETTLING IN AT THE HEPHAISTEON

Normally we would walk to the Hephaisteon but, despite what my father had said about my taking very little with me, my mother had insisted on packing up several things - for instance a few books and the spinning wheel - as she did not like the thought of my ever being idle. This meant travelling in the donkey cart. When my mother kissed me "Farewell" at the front gate, I noticed that there were tears in her eyes. This moved me, but not sufficiently to shed tears myself. I looked at our massive front door, resplendent with its heavy bronze nailheads, plates and knocker, with no regret, for now it seemed clear to me that my destiny lay elsewhere than in the milieu into which I had been born, and I was already actively embracing it. My father, in contrast to my mother, showed not one iota of emotion, and remained silent throughout the journey.

In order to reach the flat-topped hill of Kolonos on which stood the Hephaisteon, we needed to pass through the Agora, from which it lay to the west. The Agora: for us Athenians the focus point, giving us pride and confidence in citizenship. Thence we could lift our eyes to the Akropolis, where the rising smoke from Athene's altar reassured us that our city's protecting goddess, Athene Polias, was playing her part just as we were ours.

On arrival at the sanctuary, my father bade me wait in the cart while he talked with the High Priest. It was not yet fully clear whether I would be accepted in the temple, but the chances seemed high in view of my father's status in the community. The Temple of Hephaistos and Athene, like so many in the nine hundred square miles of the State of Attica, had a very large staff, but of them only a handful were either resident or permanent. Nor was celibacy essential for the priesthood, but I fully understood that, since this was the alternative being given to me following my rejection of the marriage partner I had been offered, I should dedicate life-long virginity to the service of Hephaistos and my fellow citizens.

It was not long before my father returned to the donkey cart in the company of the High Priest.

"Welcome, Ann," said the latter. "One of our resident priestesses has recently died and we are happy to take you on as her replacement. Come, let me show you to what will be your quarters and introduce you to a fellow priest who will make you feel at home and explain your duties to you."

My father helped the High Priest unload the cart, bade me "Farewell" without a kiss, and departed without a backward glance. I felt no sorrow, only elation and curiosity about the completely new life lying ahead of me.

On entering the sanctuary with my belongings, we took water from the lustral basins to purify ourselves, and then the High Priest introduced me first to a beautiful young woman by name of Selma. Among her duties was the care of the snakes, which were an important adjunct to the temple. I spoke briefly with Selma, whom the High Priest then sent to find Patrick, the priest with whom I would be working most closely. He appeared between about five and ten years older than myself, and the twinkle in his eye was a permanent reassurance of his innate kindness, even though one sensed that one would be unwise ever to do anything that would displease him. "As soon as you have installed your belongings in your chamber," Patrick said, "I shall show you around and explain some of your duties to you. I myself do not live here, since I am married, but I work here every day and will always be available up until nightfall to help or advise you."

"So at nightfall you return to your family, do you?"

"I return to my wife Daphne, who is a priestess in the Temple of Demeter. I understand that you have decided to commit yourself to a life of celibacy in the service of Hephaistos?"

"That's right. It was the only choice left to me after I refused the offer of a husband that my father made to me.

"And a good choice you made too. I would never have permitted my parents to force me into a marriage that was not of my own choosing. But failing a love match such as mine and Daphne's, I am of the opinion that a life of celibacy and service is a very worth while one and has many advantages and attractions."

******

"Being by no means a complete newcomer to this sanctuary," said Patrick, "you must of course already appreciate that it is a secure place of worship. Once one has come within the boundary marked by the *horoi*[8], it is forbidden to give birth, make love or die. A sanctuary is also an *asulon*[9], and anyone, be it a runaway slave or a refugee from justice, can seek protection here. In fact assassination in a sanctuary is a crime so heinous that the gods may well inflict a scourge on a whole city in punishment for it."

---

8. *Horoi* = pillars marking the boundary of a sacred place.
9. *Asulon* = Asylum (a safe place of refuge).

"I am sure I should always be happy to care for anyone who sought refuge here. But I am amazed at the beauty and the number of the vases and other objects on display. When I have come here for worship with my family, I have never had the opportunity to look around properly."

"Indeed the dedications are exceedingly numerous. You see that wonderful crown over there? That was the offering of a victorious athlete. And this simulacrum of a hand was brought by a woman just cured of a serious injury to her right hand. Now let me show you the temple. As a *Hereus*[10] of Hephaistos, the god of fire, I take particular pride in his statue, entrusted to my care. You are perhaps aware that, since Hephaistos is the brother of Athene, daughter of the great Zeus, our temple is shared with her priests and priestesses. But come now, let me find Thenis[11] , the guardian of the Temple of Athene. He is better qualified than I to tell you all about the temple."

"No doubt," began Thenis, "you have previously admired our temple, but I wonder whether you have yet had the opportunity of appreciating all of its finest points? Let me show you, for instance, the stuccoed, brightly painted friezes above the exterior of the cella walls. I believe them to be among the finest in the whole of Attica, if not in the entire world[12]. On these frontal metopes you see depicted the Labours of Herakles; on the latter the exploits of the great Theseus. The eastern frieze depicts a battle scene with seated deities on either hand; and the western a *kentauromachia*[13]. Did you know that our temple was older than the Parthenon?"

"Thank you, Thenis," intervened Patrick. "Now let's show Ann the sacred laws inscribed on pillars at the entrance. One of our most important functions as priests is to act as guardians of the sacred law, is it not?"

"Indeed," replied Thenis, "this guarantees the perpetuation of our ancestral tradition. Well, Ann, I am glad to have made your acquaintance, and I'm sure that you will be very happy here."

"Now," said Patrick, "let us return to the sanctuary, where I can explain to you your main duties. We have here a hotel for visitors to the sanctuary who come from a

---

10. *Hereus* = a priest.
11. Kandia (who appears later) is now my adopted son Christopher, and the clairvoyant Edwin Courtenay named Thenis as one of his spirit guides.
12. The Hephaisteon, erroneously called the Theseum in the Middle Ages, is the best preserved Greek temple in the world.
13. *Kentauromachia* = Battle of Centaurs.

distance. You will be expected to help care for them. Apart from that, one of your most important tasks will be participating in the slaughter of the victims for the *thusia*. The actual killing is done by a professional on this *trapeza* here, beside the altar, the victim's head being turned upwards so that the blood spurts skywards and then falls in a stream on to the altar and the ground. You will at times be asked to hold the *sphageion*, a basin for catching the blood, which must then be poured over the altar. Before the sacrifice is performed at the altar, the *thusia* begins with a *pompe*. This procession is led by the priest and the sacrificers, and the priest sprinkles the victim's head with lustral water as he pronounces the prayers. In the act of purification the victim's assent is elicited by a nod of its head, and after the killing, in which you will normally lead the *ololugue* - the women's scream - you will have to sprinkle the thigh bones with a liquid libation and incense. This gives olfactory pleasure to the gods as the *meria* (the thighs) are burnt on the altar. Here you see the *obeloi*, the spits for roasting, and the *lebes*, the cauldron for boiling the meat prior to its distribution. Not only of course is the *thusia* the only opportunity for the poorer section of our community to eat meat, but the parts of the victims which are allotted to us priests and priestesses is both for our own sustenance and for us to resell as a source of income. Though the objects and implements I have just been showing you are not intrinsically sacred, they are, like the sanctuary and the temple themselves, endowed with power through the ritual use we make of them, and are thus brought into relation with the divine. Well, I have surely given you enough to take in for the moment."

CHAPTER THREE - THE ORACLE

A few years had passed since my installation in the sanctuary, and it was almost as though my life prior to that day had never existed. If, on journeys to the countryside or the Akropolis, I ever happened to pass by my family mansion, I scarcely gave it a glance, so alien did it now seem to me. My mother's fears of idleness had been totally unfounded, for my duties rarely left me time for either spinning or reading. In fact I was now a well established priestess, and many came to seek my counsel. The work was pleasant to me, but occasionally I had times of severe doubt about my abilities. "Supposing I gave some misguided counsel?" I would sometimes reflect to myself, "this might have truly disastrous effects". For, though I trusted in the gods, and particularly Hephaistos, to guide me, I was aware of my youth and lack of experience. One day I began to wonder whether a visit to the Delphic Oracle might be of use to me. I knew that my good friend and fellow priestess, Kristina, had consulted it in the past, and I sought her advice.

"It is true," Kristina replied, "that I did find my consultation with the Oracle extremely beneficial, but I was accompanied by my father. Delphi is a long way for a young woman on her own to travel. I have a better idea for you. There resides in the Athenian Temple of Demeter[14], where, as you know, Patrick's wife Daphne dedicates her services, a clairvoyant healer priestess who possesses the rare ability to see people's auras. She is highly respected by the Senate, who make use of her powers for character analysis. She cannot only see how people's past may affect their future, but also detect when they are lying."

"I have no fear of deliberately lying, simply of failing always to give people the best advice."

"Of course, I understand that. I merely mentioned that as an example of how Lilla is so useful to the Senate. From what I know of her, you would find her very sympathetic and easy to talk to, and I'm sure that a consultation with her could be very helpful to you. Besides, the sanctuary of Demeter lies not too far from here. I will gladly show you the way in an *astrabe*, and I would welcome the chance of talking again to Lilla myself."

*****

The journey in the donkey cart had not been too long, and Kristina kindly waited until I had finished. I found the priestess Lilla extremely sympathetic to talk to, just as Kristina had predicted, and she had instilled me with much confidence with regard to my work. I was also amazed at the depth of her understanding of my character, revealed within a few minutes of our meeting. When the consultation was coming to an end, Lilla enquired after my health. I felt this to be normally good, but admitted to some minor problems, such as attacks of headaches "at that time of the month".

"If you care to return another time," Lilla said, "I could give you healing for that. But, better still, I should like you to meet my good friend Bertrand, who is a priest here and a highly respected healer and musician. Wait while I go and see whether he is still here or whether he has gone home. He is among our non-resident staff, being a widower with a house of his own... No, Bertrand has just finished his duties for today and has left. But never mind, none of your health problems is desperately urgent. Could you come back next week?"

"Certainly. I'm sure I shall remember the way now."

"Good. I should like you to meet Bertrand, not only because I feel he could heal you, but also because I am certain that you would find him very compatible. He was

14. This temple is alas no longer extant.

educated at the Academy and is something of a philosopher, as well as having been a professional musician. He would never tell you this himself, but he won musical competitions in the Great Panathenaia."

******

Before retiring for the night, I took my harp to my favourite spot, from which I had the best possible view of the sea, and accompanied myself in a little song of thanksgiving. Kristina's idea had been an excellent one, and I no longer felt a great urge to travel all the way to Delphi. Lilla had not only talked almost like a mother to me, she had reassured me about the value of my work here. How fortunate I was in this life that had been mapped out for me by the gods, and how I was now looking forward to meeting Bertrand and perhaps being healed of these troublesome headaches.

CHAPTER FOUR - BERTRAND

Had my position as a celibate priestess not prevented me from allowing myself to look at him in that way, I would doubtless have found Bertrand attractive. Not more than, I would guess, two or three years older than me, he was tall and fairly handsome, with kindly eyes and an air of great composure.

"So you play the harp, I understand?" he began. "Have you brought your instrument with you so that I might hear it?"

"Oh no! My standards fall far short of those of a professional who has competed successfully in the Great Panathenaia."

"My modest success has, I trust, never caused me to look down upon anyone for whom performing is a pastime rather than a means of livelihood, and since my entry into the service of Demeter, music has for me too become relegated to a secondary position." He smiled, and I felt as though I had always known him. "But you have come here today partly for healing. Tell me what are your chief symptoms, that I may invoke Apollo for a cure."

*****

Bertrand's healing - performed mainly with minerals and crystals - had lasted no less than a full hour, and I was already feeling wonderfully relaxed before he took up his kithara to play and sing for me.

"I always like to end my healing sessions with music," he explained. "It was our great ancestor Pythagoras who was probably the first to discover the healing power of music. He alone, in the whole history of humanity, was able to hear the music of the cosmos, and he imitated it on his lyre for the benefit of his initiates. He also, apparently, had an unbelievably beautiful singing voice. I'm sure I should never be able to play or sing as he did, but how do you like this little piece?"....

"That was quite beautiful!" I exclaimed when Bertrand had finished. "Tell me, how do you know where to put your fingers in order to change the tone? On the harp we have a different string for each note."

"Now that can be explained mathematically and was again beautifully expounded by Pythagoras. You see that, if I hold this string exactly in the middle, its note will sound one octave higher. If I hold it at the two-thirds point, it is a fifth higher; at the three-quarter point, a fourth higher. The tone is represented by 9:8 (5th-4th), that is to say 3/2 divided by 4/3. A semitone is represented by 256:253, that is a fourth minus two tones, or in other words 4/3 divided by 9/8 multiplied by 9/8 in brackets.

Moving on from Pythagoras, Archytas worked out the relationships of the notes in the chromatic or twelve-tone scale, as well as in the enharmonic scale, and this involved minute differences such as that between A flat and G sharp. Can you hear? Now in Geometry Archytas solved the problem of doubling the cube by constructing a three-dimensional model, and the conclusions that he then drew concerning the continued proportions, expressed as a:b equals b:c equals c:d, he applied to musical harmony, which enabled him to discern intervals of pitch in the enharmonic scale. Do you follow?"

"Ye-e-es..." I said hesitantly, not wanting either to display my mathematical ignorance nor to disappoint Bertrand, whose friendship, I already sensed, was to become one of the most important things in my life.

"Pythagoras taught purification of the soul by its means, and of course a pure soul is the inevitable pre-requisite of a healthy body - a fact well understood by my mentor Asklepios, who, incidentally, is identified with Imhotep, the architect and physician whom the Egyptians deified. Did you know that all our knowledge of medicine really comes from the Egyptians?"

"That does not surprise me. Is not Egypt the cradle of most of our civilisation?"

"All of it probably! Though remembering too, of course, that the Egyptians themselves owe much to the great civilisation of Atlantis, not to mention the Sumerians. But returning to Greece: in Hippocratic medicine, too, health is equivalent to harmony of the bodily constituents. For did not Plato describe the soul as the form of the body and the body as the matter of the soul? For Plato the soul was the vital principle essentially united with the body to form the individual person."

"That is all very interesting. I fear that I am no philosopher, though I enjoy literature. Lilla told me that you were a widower. I'm sorry about that. How long were you married? I myself refused the marriage that my parents desired for me, and greatly prefer my life as a virgin priestess to that I would have had as the wife of a well-to-do, unartistic merchant."

"I do not blame you! The Greek freedom of thought and our ability to see the world clearly comes not from wealth but from our philosophy (a word coined, as you probably know, by the great Pythagoras) and our art, which is distinguished by an absence of struggle, marked by calm and serenity. My marriage was arranged by my parents too of course, but I was more fortunate in that Katharina was neither unartistic nor unattractive. I had no great love for her, but during the ten years we were together I grew fond of her, and her death was painful for me. It was partly that which made me resolve to master some of the healing arts of Apollo."

"I'm sure I couldn't even have <u>survived</u> ten years with Xercathon, and I could certainly never have grown fond of him!" We laughed together. "So for you healing and music have more importance than the beauty of a woman?"

"For me truth is beauty."

"And beauty is truth, is it not? I was just admiring the perfection of those pillars there."

"The pillars raise another fascinating mathematical question. Did you know that they were not actually perfectly vertical as they appear?"

"No. How can that be?"

"I could explain it precisely with more mathematics, but would not wish to bore you. The point quite simply is that, were the columns exactly vertical, they would appear to the human eye to be sloping slightly outwards. In order to achieve the appearance to us of verticality, they need to lean inwards in such a way that they would all ultimately meet at a single point. Similarly, if the columns were perfectly straight, they would appear to the human eye as waisted. Consequently they are constructed with an outward curve, which again involves much mathematical calculation."

"Really? I would never have guessed that. How fascinating! And had you and Katharina no children?"

"Alas she was barren, which was a cause of great distress to her. This distress may even have contributed to her early death. I know not. As for me, I should no doubt have been quite content to have been a father, but since I am not, and since my needs are few, I decided to give up my profession in favour of duties in the Athenian sanctuary of Demeter. I have been here nigh two years now and have never regretted my decision.

Returning for a moment to the subject of Truth, for Socrates there was nothing more important than finding it. *To find the Father and Maker of all is hard,* he said, *and having found him it is impossible to utter him.* Truth, I am sure you will agree, is linked to excellence, and Aristotle said that *Excellence must be laboured for by the grace of men.* I'm sure by that he meant to include women too! But perhaps it is now time for you to depart? It would be better for you to make the return journey before nightfall. Could you come for further treatment in a week's time? We cannot expect a single healing session to sort out all your little problems."

******

"Last week, you remember, we were discussing the nature and importance of Truth?"

"I remember," I replied, as Bertrand carefully put his crystals back on to the shelf where he kept them.

"Have you ever read Pindar?"

"I'm afraid not."

"Well, there is a beautiful line in one of his Odes which goes thus:-

> *Forge thy tongue on an anvil of truth*
> *And what flies up, though it be but a spark,*
> *Shall have weight.*

"How lovely! I must remember those words when people come to me for counsel."

"I'm sure you are not in the habit of giving false counsel."

"I certainly try not to, but we mortals are fallible."

"As indeed are the gods."

"As indeed. I should perhaps depart now, but I was thinking of making my return journey via the Parthenon, as it is some little time since I was there and it always fills me with such wonder. Would you care to accompany me."

"*Wisdom is the child of wonder*! So said Aristotle. That is a very good idea. I too have not paid my respects to Athene Polias for some time and, if we were to part there, the *astrabe* would take you back to the Hephaisteon quite quickly."

******

"Aristotle," continued Bertrrand as the *astrabe* was approaching the Akropolis, "identified categories structuring man's language and thought. His chief accomplishment was probably the establishment of the basis for logical thought. He understood even better than Plato, to whose beliefs Lilla, like you and me, subscribes, the need to define language and its use as a creative instrument of thought capable of an ordered structure, and able consequently to confer its own inner law upon nature."

"Look! Is there anywhere a better view than this of the Parthenon?"

"No, I'm sure there isn't. Now you remember what I was telling you about the slope of the columns? Here you have an even better example than in my temple. Can you imagine a greater impression of a *building in repose, content to be at one for ever with the rock which it crowns* ?"[15]

"I'm sure the same comment will be made many centuries hence!"

"Yes, Greek art and architecture were conceived for immortality, were they not?"

"Look at the helmeted Athene! How tall is she? Forty feet?"

"Almost, I believe. The ivory of her face, arms and feet is prevented from cracking in the dry air by that pool of water in front of her, and of course the gold plates from which her helmet and *chiton*[16] are made are detachable in case the State ever runs into financial crisis."

"You see how she holds the Winged Victory in her right hand and the spear in her left? It's no wonder that she was able to defeat Poseidon in the battle for the City! And the round shield by her side has a serpent coiled in its hollow.

CHAPTER FIVE - A NEW FRIEND

"Come, Ann," said Patrick, his bright eyes looking at me with that irresistible twinkle I now knew so well. "Thenis has asked me to introduce you to the new High Priestess of Athene. She is young to have been given such an important position straight away, but she is very dedicated and already respected and honoured. She appears to be a direct channel to the Goddess of Wisdom, and Thenis believes that she will be consulted by statesmen and members of the Senate. Her name is Kandia and she is keen to meet you."

When we left our sanctuary in the direction of that of Athene, Selma was just giving the snakes their final feed for the day and preparing to go home.

---

15. From *Hellenistic Traveller* (see above).
16. *Chiton* = a long tunic.

"Have you met Kandia yet?" Patrick asked her.

"Yes, I was very impressed with her channelling, but she struck me nevertheless as a trifle vulnerable compared with, for instance, Ann here."

"If you are right, that will no doubt become apparent in due course. But in any case we would all be hard put to find a tougher character than Ann the iron maiden, would we not?" Patrick winked at me as he spoke, but I feigned taking his words as an insult.

"I may well be a maiden, but I would prefer the analogy of a diamond to that of an ugly metal!"

"Diamond you shall ever be," replied Patrick, "for diamonds never lose their sparkle."

******

I felt instantly drawn to Kandia who was rather younger than myself. Perhaps it was her vulnerability, which Selma with her insight into character had noted, that made me feel protective towards her. Whatever it was, the attraction appeared to be mutual, for over the next weeks Kandia came frequently to talk with me. Her fame was already spreading and, just as Thenis had predicted, her advice was beginning to be sought by important people. "I try," she explained to me, "only to impart the wisdom channelled through me by Athene with discernment. It would be easy to use it to help gratify people or win political acclaim, but I would not like to reveal secrets to any who might be tempted to make use of the knowledge for darker causes."

"You do well," I said, "but how can you be sure of the people who seek your counsel."

"I trust of course in Athene's own guidance, and I believe that I have a gift for recognising those who are truly in need of her wisdom. My aim is to teach the value of knowledge and wisdom and how to use them to advance spirituality, virtue and the moral discernment of humanity."

"My friends Lilla, Daphne and Bertrand of the Temple of Demeter would approve of your intentions. Would you like me to invite Bertrand to meet you here next time I see him?"

******

"Your visit was well timed, Bertrand. I fear that Kandia is sick. I hope you can do something for her."

"I will certainly do what I can, but all my minerals, crystals, oils and herbs are of course in the sanctuary of Demeter."

"We have some here."

******

I was becoming increasingly anxious about Kandia. A whole year had passed since Bertrand had first given her healing when he had come here to meet her, I had taken her over to his sanctuary several times since, yet now she appeared to be ailing even more seriously. I could not make another visit to their sanctuary today, as it was the day that they were all walking the twenty kilometres to Eleusis for the Mysteries. This was of course the most important festival of the entire year for them. It commemorated the rape of Demeter's daughter Persephone by Hades. Had Demeter not threatened to stop the crops growing, Persephone Kore would never have been returned to her. As it was, she had to return to Hades once a year. This symbolised the grain coming forth from the seed and being reaped to yield bread, for as the young girl was taken from her parents and her virginity destroyed, so new offspring was able to come forth. The vital message for the initiates at Eleusis was that out of every grave grows immortal life. More than that about the ceremonies I knew not. Bertrand, Daphne and Lilla were sworn to secrecy about their Mysteries just as I was about our own. None of us would ever think of asking questions about them of the other.

Bertrand, I knew, would return refreshed and elated from the ceremonies in a few days' time, when both he and Lilla would be very ready to console me, but I wanted Bertrand's consolation NOW. Still, I suddenly remembered what Bertrand had told me about music as a method of healing. So, taking my harp, I walked over to Kandia's chamber. She looked pleased to see me, but when I had finished playing, her fever seemed to be as high as ever. I kissed her "Good night" gently and returned to my own quarters, stopping on my way to make a petition to Hephaistos: "You are the god of fire, divine smith and patron of craftsmen, can you not abate the fire in my friend Kandia? Your good sister Athene needs her as a channel for the wisdom she wishes to impart to mortal Athenians. Help her to recover quickly. Please hear my prayer!".

******

I went to look for Lilla while Bertrand was ministering to Kandia. It would be better to talk to him on another day when I had come on my own again, but in the meantime Lilla would understand my fears.

"Of course I understand very well how you feel. You have grown so fond of Kandia, and she fulfils a need in you. A need to mother someone. But sometimes the cosmos takes things out of our hands. Are you aware that none of us has only one life on this Earth?"

"I have heard that Pythagoras taught reincarnation, but it is not a thing to which I have really ever given any thought."

"Well, I feel that it would be useful for you at this time to learn about karma. Would you care to come and see me again in a few days' time without Kandia?"

"Certainly. Now I had better go and see whether it is time to take her back."

"*A hundred blossoms grew from the roots of it and very sweet was the fragrance, and all the wide sky above and all the land laughed and the salt wave of the sea*[17]." Bertrand was chanting softly as I entered the healing chamber, having just put down his kithara. Kandia looked peaceful, but her breathing still sounded raucous.

"Next time I shall come to her sanctuary," he said. "I don't think she should be travelling much more."

I didn't want to discuss Kandia's condition in her hearing, so I simply helped Bertrand to install her comfortably into the *astrabe*, saying as I bade him "Good night", "Lilla has suggested that I come and learn from her about karma. Would you like to join me for that, or are you already knowledgeable on the subject?"

"No, that is not something I have considered at all, though Daphne sometimes mentions it as something on which Patrick is well informed and which we too should do well to study. If Lilla thinks it would be good for you to learn, I'm sure it would be good for me too. Get the healer priest of Athene to give Kandia a sleeping potion, say your prayers and try not to worry too much. Good night."

Bertrand was still elated by his attendance at the Eleusinian Mysteries, and his faith was very sustaining for me. "Cicero said of these mysteries," he had explained to me, "that *nothing was higher. They have not only shown us how to live joyfully, but they have taught us how to die with a better hope.* You must have no fear for Kandia."

CHAPTER SIX - PYTHAGORAS AND THE BEAN

"Ah, Ann, you bring our good philosopher friend with you. Welcome, both of you! So today the roles are to be reversed, are they? So often it is I who am learning from Bertrand."

"Well, I feel sure that if you have something to teach Ann, it will be of benefit to me too."

17. From Homer's *Hymn to Demeter.*

"Very good. Now, you see the reason that I felt it would be helpful to Ann at this moment to understand about reincarnation and karma is because of her current distress over the High Priestess Kandia, who I fear may die from her disease before very long."

"But how can it be that she should die so young, when firstly she has so much to offer to humanity, being a channel of wisdom for Athene, and secondly she is receiving so much healing from Bertrand, whose powers you yourself have long since recognised? I do not think I have suffered a single headache since he started treating me."

"Now here, my dear Ann, you perhaps misunderstand the full meaning of the word *healing*. To be sure, it can, and fortunately often does, lead to cure, but that is only when the mind of the patient herself is disposed to curing her own body. For healing can never come from without, only from within. The job of us healers is to act as catalysts for self-healing. Our herbs, for instance, can strengthen the body if the soul inhabiting that body has chosen that it should be cured. If the psyche has not so chosen, then death itself may be the healing. And in this case it is the manner of death that is all important. Bertrand's most crucial task for Kandia at the moment is perhaps to aid her transition back to the life of spirit."

"But I don't understand. Surely no-one's soul could choose to leave its body so prematurely? Kandia is younger than I am, and I believe myself to be barely at the prime of my life."

"That is precisely why I felt you needed to appreciate the fact that we all have many, many lives. That another time it could be you dying young while Kandia lives to a ripe old age. You see, for the soul to attain its full evolution and completion, it is necessary for it to experience every possible aspect of the Earthly condition."

"I see. So why are we not all taught this from an early age? Why are we brought up to regard early death as an unfortunate disaster?"

"That is quite simply because not everyone has yet come to recognise the fact of reincarnation. That is, not everyone in our society. The Egyptians of course do recognise it universally, as did the great Atlantean civilisation before them. The esteemed Pythagoras, whom Bertrand so admires as a mathematician and musician...."

"Indeed, Pythagoras, besides demonstrating beautiful melodies to his disciples, showed them the beauty of mathematics, the perfection and symmetry of certain geometrical forms. In fact, I believe that he saw numbers as gods and thought that it was they and the stars that created the music of the spheres, which he was able to reproduce on his lyre...."

"You are right. In fact for Pythagoras everything was number. He formalised a form of Astrology, that I personally find fascinating, which is related entirely to Number. But, despite the interest you both have in Astrology, I will not go into that at this moment, for we have come together this time to talk about karma. So now let me go on. Pythagoras, as you may know, was a great mystic. So much so that his followers regarded him as superhuman. Well, because of his powerful mysticism, he actually remembered all of his own previous lives, and it was because of that that he knew all about reincarnation, despite the fact that it was not generally taught in the society in which he was born. Now we call this capacity for remembering *anamnesis*. I myself have it to a certain extent - it is normal for this ability to go hand in hand with the gift of being able to see auras - but I only tend to recall my own past lives when a particular memory seems useful to me. For instance, the three of us have obviously all known one another before. Otherwise we would not be sitting here together discussing these things at this moment. The memory that comes to my mind just now, looking at you, Ann, is that we were well acquainted during a lifetime we both had at the time of the final destruction of Atlantis. You were then working as a healer and you had certain clairvoyant powers, which enabled you to prophesy. Indeed you prophesied the fall of Atlantis before fleeing yourself to Egypt. I was considerably older than you at that time and had acted as midwife at your birth. You were a man then, by the way. We change sex regularly through our different incarnations. As you grew up we kept in touch, and you often came to me for advice. So now in this lifetime, you see how we are continuing in those roles we had in Atlantis?"

"How fascinating!"

"Yes, it is fascinating. You also knew Patrick in that lifetime. I feel that you and he have been colleagues several times already, but in that Atlantean incarnation you formed a particularly strong bond because, when you prophesied the fall of Atlantis you were much maligned by a powerful man named Saul, and Patrick defended you against him. Patrick and Saul both worked at that time in the Temple of Clairvoyance, whereas you were in the Temple of Healing, although also clairvoyant yourself, and Patrick had great artistic ability. You were good friends then, which is why you so rapidly became good friends again, and you will find that your friendship will continue over many lifetimes to come, as will your friendships with, for instance, Bertrand, Kristina and Selma. So you see, if Kandia does die - and of course I greatly hope she does not, for I would never like definitely to predict such things, and while there is still life there is always hope - but if she does die, you must not think for a moment that that will be the end of your relationship. In this lifetime you have chosen to help her - you see yourself as a sort of mother figure to her. Well, it is extremely likely that in a future life you will be a real mother to her. She might well become your adopted son."

"So is that the meaning of this word *karma* then?" asked Bertrand. "Is it the continuation of relationships."

"It is more than that. Perhaps the best way to define it is the *law of cause and effect.* This is a universal law from which no-one can ever escape, and it is one of the reasons why it is advisable to lead as upright a life as we can. For everything that we do or say comes back to us. Let me explain. Supposing - the gods forbid! - that one of you should suddenly take it into your head to poison me, you might happen to profit from it, or think you profited from it, in this lifetime. For instance, if I were no longer here to heal people, Bertrand might become even more sought after for that purpose than he is at present, thereby achieving for himself greater Earthly glory (assuming that no-one found out that he had murdered me!). But in the future he would at some time have to have a life in which he himself got poisoned."

"I'm sure Bertrand would never desire to poison anyone - least of all you!" I laughed.

"Of course he wouldn't. I simply took that as an example. A very extreme example. But karma works equally for our good deeds as for our bad ones. In this life Bertrand has given you healing. So in a future life it may well be that he will receive healing from you."

"I see. You said that you had a memory of having known me before. Can you also remember a past life when you knew Bertrand?"

"Just at this moment nothing comes to my mind. But that is probably not because there has not been anything of great significance, but simply because it is not relevant to our relationship at present."

"Ah, so no wonder that, as soon as I met Ann, I felt as though I already knew her really well."

"It is no wonder. Your relationships have nearly always been close ones, but they have also varied considerably in their nature. For instance, in the past you have had children together, and I'm sure that you will do so again. This will make up for any little sadness either of you might feel at not being parents this time round."

"You were talking," said Bertrand, "about Pythagoras' understanding of reincarnation. I've heard it said that, as well as being strictly vegetarian, Pythagoras would not eat beans in case one of them was, for instance, his grandmother. Is that true?"

"It is true that Pythagoras and his followers abstained from beans as well as from meat, but the reason you have heard is not the correct one. Pythagoras of course believed in the interconnectedness of all nature, and he had a tremendous love of animals, whose language he claimed to be able to understand. That is why he did not like to eat meat, and I approve of his sentiments there, though I do not actually share them, for of course our beloved Demeter likes us to sacrifice pigs to her. Pythagoras said that all life was imbued with psyche, and he believed that we have all ourselves experienced every form of it. In fact it is said that he once recognised a deceased friend of his in the form of a dog he encountered in the street, and consequently stopped a man from beating it.

But the bean is a special case and is among the many notions that Pythagoras learnt from the Egyptians. For, as you no doubt know, he travelled very widely before establishing his community in Croton. Well, the Egyptian idea that creatures came forth from primeval slime, thanks to water combined with the heat of the sun, was taught to Pythagoras by Thales. Within this primeval slime, it was said, humankind and the bean were intimately related. Pythagoras himself claimed to have proved this when he buried some beans in mud and, digging them up after a few weeks, found that they had developed the shape of human embryos. It is for this reason that to him eating beans was nefarious."

"I see, though it seems a rather strange idea," said Bertrand. "But how could he prove his own past lives? Surely his so-called anamnesis could simply have been his imagination?"

"That is an interesting point for which, I am glad to say to you, as a typical scientific sceptic, that there is an answer. Pythagoras once happened to see a shield hanging high somewhere, and he said to the companion who was with him: "That shield was mine when I was Euphorbus. If you take it down, you will see that on the inside it has an inscription saying that it belongs to Euphorbus." And so it was."

"Fancy that! That sounds like pretty good proof to me."

"Now to continue. Pythagoras had one belief that I do not personally share with regard to reincarnation. He said that we return to Earth exactly every 216 years. Now I am sure that you, Bertrand, will appreciate the significance of the number 216."

"Yes of course, it is two cubed times three cubed, and also...."

"Do not bother to explain now. I know that you have for long tried to interest Ann in Mathematics, but I do not think you will be successful this time round. For this lifetime she has chosen to work on other things, and that is fine. For instance, she is using her musical ability and her understanding of and compassion for people."

"So we work on different things in each lifetime, do we?"

"Yes, we do, and that is why I cannot go along with Pythagoras' concept of a regular 216 years. You see, if we come to Earth each time in order to learn new lessons, we need to choose the best possible circumstances for learning those lessons, and those may not occur with complete regularity. That is why Astrology is important when we are planning an incarnation, for we need to choose the characteristics of the planets governing our birth in accordance with those we are needing for our lessons."

"Yes, Plato believed, did he not, that the soul falls to Earth from a star and that, in passing through the planets, it acquires their properties: sloth from Saturn, combativeness from Mars...."

"Voluptuousness from Mercury..." I added.

"And so on," said Lilla. "And besides choosing the characteristics needed from the planets, the soul needs to choose to incarnate among the people with whom it still has karma to work out. So now do you feel you understand what I am trying to say?"

"I think so," I replied. "My understanding is that, just as I have come to you for advice in the past, so I am doing again, and while I am caring for Kandia in her illness now, so I might be her parent in the future. But on the other hand, since Bertrand has given <u>me</u> healing this time round, I could give it to <u>him</u> in the future, since, although I am not a healer now, I have been one in the past and so could be again."

"That is quite correct. For subconsciously we remember everything we have ever done. No-one can use all their abilities in every lifetime - they would not have time - but those which they are not using each time are still there in a latent form, and it may only need a little trigger to revive them when they are needed."

"Well, this is all fascinating, but perhaps I should return to Kandia now."

"Perhaps you should. In any case we have probably done enough learning for today. I look forward to seeing you again soon."

Kandia did not linger much longer after that day. Anticipating her demise, she was taken from the sanctuary of Athene back to her parents' home. Like Thenis and the other members of their temple, I did my very best to console them, though this was not easy for me as I shared their grief so intensely. "At least she died a beautiful death," they said. "So peaceful!"

"That was thanks to Bertrand's healing," I replied, remembering what Lilla had told me. "You see she must have <u>chosen</u> a short life this time, before she came in, and so Bertrand's job was to help her to carry out her destiny with as little suffering as possible. It is hard for us who are left behind, but where she is now all is light, and, until we see her again, she will be enjoying the music of the spheres instead of my harp or Bertrand's kithara."

Soon afterwards Bertrand made one of his fairly rare visits to my sanctuary. "It's you who could do with some healing now," he said. "Lie down while I place this crystal at your head and sing to you." What a beautiful voice he had! How blessed I was with his friendship.

"You remember our conversation with Lilla about Pythagoras?" he asked when he had finished. "Well, whereas Pythagoras had only seven notes - that was one for each planet including the sun and moon - Plato based <u>his</u> cosmic music on an eight-stringed lyre."

"Oh yes? And Plato admitted women as members of his Academy, did he not?"

"Indeed he did. And you know, there's another thing I've found out since the lesson Lilla gave us the other week on karma. As well as having himself the gift of anamnesis, Pythagoras encouraged it in others and he helped many people to recollect some of their previous incarnations. Furthermore, Plato popularised this practice. In the dialogue entitled *Meno*, the Platonic Socrates reminds a slave of the geometrical knowledge he had previously acquired. You see, both Pythagoras and Plato believed that <u>all</u> knowledge came from recollection of previous experiences."

"How interesting! That is work that I would love to do - exploring my past lives and helping others to explore theirs. If I never find time to do it here, it is nice to think that I might do it in a future incarnation!"

"I'm sure you would be very good at it," replied Bertrand.

"Do you prefer reading Plato or Socrates?" I asked. "I know you admire both of them greatly."

"As a matter of fact Socrates didn't actually write anything! He spent nearly all his time in the street, marketplace or gymnasia, speaking with young men of promise as well as with politicians, poets and artisans about their notions of right and wrong. Did you know that, before he had become fully aware of his mission, the Delphic Oracle pronounced him to be the "wisest of men"?"

"Really? Well, if he was so wise, why did he neglect the city's gods? I do not of course believe that it was right to have gone so far as condemning him to death, but surely there was some case against him?"

"I do not think so. You see, isn't everyone right to follow their own conscience? Socrates is remembered for his admonition "to know thyself. Socrates understood better than anyone else to my mind the secret of true happiness, because he could see that knowledge of the absolute good was the one most vital thing. He pointed out that people failed to achieve felicity simply because they did not appreciate what it was. That is to say, they mistook wealth or power for good. For that reason he believed that all wrong-doing was involuntary. This ties in of course with Lilla's notion of karma, doesn't it? Socrates said that if people knew true good and did not confuse it with anything else, then they would never use strength, wealth or anything else wrongly. And understanding of karma would of course prevent them from committing a crime. This was the purport of Socrates' message, which, as I said, he never wrote down himself, but which has been handed down to us mainly in the great writings of Plato. His assassination for so-called "corruption of the young" (as well as so-called "impiety" or neglect of the gods) is one of the greatest tragedies in the history of Athens."

"Never mind: remembering what Lilla has taught us, Socrates will be getting his own back on his assassins in due course!"

"In view of the sort of person he was, I would rather trust that he has forgiven them. In which case it would be from someone else that they would get their return."

"How right you are. Forgiveness is always preferable."

We strolled out of the sanctuary towards the temple. Looking from the Hephaisteon up to the Parthenon standing out so clearly against the pink sky, tears sprang once more to my eyes. Reading my thoughts, Bertrand said "Of course Kandia is with Athene herself now. Has not the smoke rising in her honour taken on a more joyous appearance?"

"Maybe," I replied, choking back the tears.

Then Patrick appeared. "I'm sorry to interrupt you, Ann, but the High Priest is asking for you."

"Work must go on," said Bertrand, "and in any case it is time I was getting home."

"Yes, work must go on. Good night, Bertrand, and thank you."

"It's time for me to go home too," said Patrick, "though I hate to leave you in distress. When you've finished with the High Priest, go and find Kristina. She is always so comforting to talk to. Kandia's death has grieved me very greatly also, but I do appreciate that you were the closest to her of all of us, and so must be feeling the loss the most keenly. Although I'm leaving you now to go to the High Priest and then Kristina, while I myself return to Daphne, you do know, don't you, that I shall always be there for you? And that applies not only to this life but also to future ones. Daphne tells me that Lilla has been teaching you and Bertrand all about reincarnation and karma. She has decided to join in the lessons too."

"Has she? Oh good! It's certainly true that this new understanding has helped me a great deal, for Lilla assures me that Kandia and I will come together again in the future. Do you really think that the same applies to you and me, Patrick? I should love to think that you will always be a good friend to me!"

"Of course I do, and of course I shall. Indeed, in future lifetimes I might be more than just a friend to you. We might find ourselves as brother and sister, husband and wife.... Who knows?"

"Who knows? You'd make both a lovely brother and a lovely husband, Patrick. Infinitely preferable to Xercathon!"

"I don't take that as much of a compliment!" Patrick laughed.

"Well then, you can give me a kiss to cheer me up. Then you had better hurry home to Daphne, the good wife to whom you have wisely committed yourself for this lifetime, while I see what it is that the High Priest wants of me. Then it will be agreeable too, as you suggest, to have a chat with Kristina. Good night."

"Good night, Ann dear. I'll see you in the morning." As Patrick bent to kiss me, the tears flowed again, but they were not only tears over Kandia's death but also tears of joy in the wonderful friends with whom I felt so blessed.

PART THREE - SIGNIFICANCE IN MY PRESENT LIFE

This Greek life is probably the most significant of all the previous lives I have found out about so far. I fell for Greece very strongly on my first trip there in 1971, and returned the following year with the same two friends and my little Beetle so that we could see rather more. The Acropolis completely bowled us over, as did the temple of Cape Sounion, where I felt so at home that I wonder whether it has something in common with the Athenian temple that I was in.

The priestess Lilla is now the well known clairvoyant and author Lilla Bek, and in my present life she gave me a great deal of help and encouragement when I was first embarking on writing and regression. She taught me, among other things, about Numerology, about karma and about twin souls, and she also gave me good advice when we were in the midst of great difficulties with our son Christopher. In fact she and Edwin Courtenay both told me independently about his and my previous relationship as priestesses in adjoining Greek temples. Since there is no feminine version of the name Christopher, I have adapted his second (Sierra Leonean) name – Kandeh – to make it sound like a girl's name. It has always been obvious to me that Christopher is a very evolved soul, and this brief life confirms that.

Kristina is my very good friend Christine, who has done the cover illustration for this book, and has also given me a great deal of encouragement in my work. For many years she has felt that she should have been named Christina rather than Christine! Also, for fifteen years she made a prilgrimage to the Acropolis on her way to Skyros, where she taught yoga, meditation, art as therapy, and some psychic development. She was one of the first people to bring spiritual healing, psychic development and crystals into the Centre in Skyros, and she has always felt deeply connected to Greece's history. In this life she was born both with great psychic gifts and with past life memories.

Selma is the same Selma who was my daughter in Israel. (It was she who first felt that she had once been my daughter.)

It took me a long time to find Patrick. This was because I had not yet met him when I first worked on this life! When, however, I did meet him, I identified him almost immediately, and he was of course, I found out later, also Patricia in my life as the village idiot. (In addition he was a much loved brother of mine in one of the lifetimes I have had to discard for lack of space.)

As for my own personality, there is much correlation between the two lifetimes. I am still very stubborn and strong-willed, and of course I am aiming towards a highly spiritual life again, even though I have never this time had any aspirations to the priesthood. Apart from the fact that I can sing, my musical talent has not alas been so much in evidence in this lifetime, (my violin lessons at school were misery for all concerned!), but music has nevertheless been my biggest source of consolation and relaxation since I was very young.

So in Greece I seem to have had natural spiritual inclinations, whereas in this life it was much more difficult initially. As a child and young person I always felt guilty about what I saw as a lack of spirituality in myself, but later on I came to appreciate that it is not easy to feel God's love when one has not experienced its expression through human love. I was always blessed with good friends, but that never quite makes up for the lack of love that every child needs. Later still I was given the gift of human love by my own family, which did a great deal to change my life for the better, yet there still seemed to be something lacking. People like Bertrand, who did such wonderful work for Justice and Peace as well as being intensely spiritual, could and did inspire me, but at that time – before any of these subconscious memories had begun to surface – I felt inferior to them.

About seven years must have elapsed in between my first meeting with Bertrand and the realisation that all such people who struck deep chords in me were souls that I had known before in previous lives. The trigger for my rediscovery of reincarnation was a talk at a health festival by John Walsh of the Edgar Cayce Centre. Hearing that Edgar Cayce had been such a strong Christian aroused my interest, and the two books on him which I bought at that fair were the start of a long period of research which culminated firstly in embarking myself on writing books and secondly in my training as a regression therapist.

However, throughout those years of the early nineties, even though I had already taken up daily meditation seriously, I still did not see myself as a spiritual person, still felt God to be a rather remote figure despite holding a strong belief in His/Her existence. What gradually changed all that was my discovery of Sathya Sai Baba, which began in about 1995, but more on that in a later chapter!

EXERCISES

> *Whenever your mind wanders in the maze of myriad worldly thoughts, patiently lead it back to remembrance of the indwelling Lord. In time you will find Him ever with you – a God who talks with you in your own language, a God whose face peeps at you from every flower and shrub and blade of grass. Then you shall say: "I am free! I am clothed in the gossamer of Spirit; I fly from earth to heaven on wings of light." And what joy will consume your being!*
>
> ***Paramahansa Yogananda***

Are you as spiritually minded as you would like to be, or do material things have a greater hold on you? It is fine to enjoy the things of this world but, since they can never bring total satisfaction, it is not a good idea to let ourselves be dominated by them. Finding God and serving Him/Her brings more lasting contentment.

Is it difficult for you to believe in and experience the love of God? Have you ever tried practising meditation? If your answer is (as mine was for many years!) "Yes, on and off", I strongly advise a resolution to make it more on than off from now on. In fact if you make it a daily practice, you should find firstly that your life will begin to work better generally, and secondly that you will worry less and be more contented.

1. How about attending a meditation class? (If you live anywhere near a Buddhist Centre, for instance, it will surely offer them, and it would not necessitate becoming a Buddhist. I believe that <u>everyone</u> can learn a great deal from Buddhism whether or not they feel any strong affinity with it.) Or alternatively you could get hold of a good book on meditation? I particularly recommend *Sai Baba's Teachings on the Direct Flight to Divinty.*[18]

Failing either of those, here are a few hints:-

Start by getting up that little bit earlier each morning. Most people find that before breakfast is the best time to meditate – before our minds start to get too crowded out by duties and events. Begin with just ten minutes if you like, and then gradually increase it to half an hour or even an hour. (After a while you will find that your half hour feels no longer than the ten minutes did initially!) Always use the same spot for meditating.

Find a comfortable position in which to sit. Meditation stools, which have a

18. *Sai Baba's Teachings on the Direct Flight to Divinity*, by Sai Anoos, Sri Sathya Sai Publications Trust, India, 2001.

slight slope and on which you have to fold your legs so that your feet are facing backwards, are excellent, though I personally need a cushion on top (perhaps my buttocks are extra delicate!). But some people are more comfortable cross-legged - with or without a cushion, though we Westerners are generally better off with one.

Keep your spine as erect as you can. It is important to stay alert and not fall asleep.

Begin by lighting a candle or an incense stick, or any other starting ritual that you fancy, such as ringing a bell or saying the Lord's Prayer.

You might then – though this is by no means essential – like to have a second starting ritual, such as breathing in white light through one nostril and expelling grey mist through the other three times. I myself always begin with the 'Jyothi Meditation', which comes from India. *Jyothi* means light, and you begin by visualising a shaft of white light descending through the top of your head, through all your *chakras* (energy centres), and then out to form a circle right around your body. Then imagine it spreading to encircle every object in the room, the house, every person in your village/town, then country, the world, the universe... Then, when my half hour has come to an end, I imagine the light returning, coming back into my body, shrinking into a tiny ball and then residing in my spiritual heart (located on the right hand side of the body) for the rest of the day as a reminder of my innate divinity.

There are numerous ways to meditate and you would do better to consult an expert, but here are a couple of suggestions:-

- Simply watch your breath as it goes in and out. Your mind will wander, but each time it does, don't get cross with it or with yourself, but just gently bring it back. Say to your thoughts "I will deal with you later.".

- Have a picture, or make one in your mind, of whichever holy person fits your own spiritual path (Jesus, Buddha, Sai Baba... It really doesn't matter. Just so long as it isn't Saddam Hussein or Osama Bin Laden!) and focus your full attention on it. (Sai Baba advises "one name, one form, one pose". So if you choose, say, an image of the Buddha seated with his hand held in the blessing position, stick to it.) See yourself as one with this marvellous being and let His love embrace you and permeate every cell of your body. Don't let the constant undercurrent of thoughts in your mind bother you. Observe them but don't get involved with them. If you like, put a bubble round each thought when it comes and just blow it away, or stick a label on it marked THOUGHT and let it drift away of its own accord.

When your allotted time is up (yes, you are allowed to open your eyes to look at your watch! As a matter of fact some schools of meditation advise against closing the eyes completely.), don't get up in a hurry. Use a closing ritual of your own choosing, then blow out your candle or snuff out your incense stick. Do a bit of stretching if you like, and then go and have your breakfast and turn your thoughts to the matters of the new day.

> *I am neither a man of letters nor of science, but I humbly claim to be a man of prayer. It is prayer that has saved my life. Without it I would have lost my reason long ago. If I did not lose my peace of soul, in the midst of many trials, it is because of the peace that came to me through prayer. One can live several days without food, but not without prayer. Prayer is the key to each morning, and the lock to each evening. It is a sacred alliance between God and us. Let everyone try this experience, and they will find that daily prayer will add something new to their lives, something which cannot be found elsewhere.*
>
> ***Mahatma Gandhi***

2. Meditation (listening to God) is generally agreed by all spiritual Masters to be the most important, but Prayer (talking to God) is also a good idea. You can of course pray at any time of day or night, and in any position, and at the same time as doing other things, such as the washing up or driving. Which form of prayer you prefer is likely to depend on your religious upbringing, if any, but God is not the slightest bit interested in the words you say, only in the intention in your heart. It's fine to ask for things for yourself.* but I also strongly recommend getting into the habit of praying for others, and for peace in the world. If you haven't been in the habit of praying, once you start you'll probably be surprised at how often the things you request are granted. The more you think of God as a friend who is always there ready to listen, the more He/She will make His/Her presence felt to you. And why not try too asking questions and just seeing what answer comes into your head. Again, you may be surprised at how often the "Yes" or "No" is accurate.

---

*My requests for a parking space are invariably answered, but I always begin with a "thank you" for it.

XIV
OWNING ONE'S SHADOW

PART ONE - DEALING WITH RACISM

When Christopher was very young, we were fortunate in having friends who had also adopted black children, as well as a few who were in mixed race marriages. Together we formed a local branch of the national anti-racist organisation called Harmony, went to their annual conferences and held regular meetings in each other's houses. Some of these were in the evening, when we discussed issues of race, while others were social gatherings where all the children were included. This helped Christopher to realise that he was not alone in being a lovely shade of brown. Harmony stressed the importance in our racist society of giving our children a strong black identity - feeling good about oneself inside is excellent armour against any form of abuse - and thanks to that organisation we bought books about black children and also such things as appropriate birthday cards for them. Giving a black identity to a child who is being brought up in a white family is obviously more difficult, and it was partly for that reason that, when Christopher was ten, we had a family holiday in Sierra Leone. He still has fond memories of that trip and comments on the odd fact that no-one there noticed that he was black.

Christopher was happy at nursery school, but problems began as soon as he moved up into the primary school. At play times the abuse was such that he would sometimes flee to the part of the playground reserved for Alice's class, and then got into trouble for doing so. My constant visits to the Head simply brought the reply "They get it from their parents. There's nothing we can do about it."! Is it any wonder that black children in this country so often become aggressive in school?

When I first became involved in the Justice and Peace movement, I felt overwhelmed by all the world's problems and wanted to try and tackle them all. Jointly with my friend Josephine (whom I identified as my son Joseph in the life in Israel), I formed the Cottingham One World group, which had members from all the churches in our village, and we held monthly meetings, studying mainly the excellent educational materials put out by CAFOD (the Catholic Fund for Overseas Development, (London)). This tied in with the work I had done in Geneva, but gradually, as Christopher was being subjected increasingly to racism at school, I decided to concentrate my efforts mainly on that issue. One of my co-founders of the Harmony group and I organised a teachers' conference on Education and Racism (thanks to which we moved Christopher at the age of seven to a little Catholic school in Hull which had a strict rule against name-calling, and where he was much happier); and my friend and I were both also invited to be on a panel which was giving anti-racist input into the new national Religious Education programme.

PART TWO - THE SLAVE

How appalling were the conditions in this ship! Shackled to each other with scarcely enough room to lie down on the hard wooden floor, it's a wonder that so many of us survived the journey. In fact I often wished that I were among the many slung overboard because they were either dead or too sick to be cared for. At night, when everyone was trying hard to sleep, I thought nostalgically about my family and life at home in Africa. I had been seized without warning and not even given a chance to say "goodbye" to my parents. How I worried about them! I resolved to return somehow, but obviously there would be no chance of that while I remained imprisoned in this wretched ship. The journey seemed to be endless, and the stench was indescribable. There were but a few buckets between dozens of us, and only when the mixture of urine, shit and vomit made walking around dangerous for our captors was any effort made to clean the floor. Then of course it was one of us who was made to do it, his shackles being removed for no more than a few minutes. I had a pretty tough stomach, but sometimes when the ship was ploughing through an extremely rough patch, I could not stop myself from vomiting too.

The worst thing about it all was not having any idea where we were going or why. These strange colourless men, who treated us worse than animals, spoke a language we did not understand and made no attempt at all to understand ours. In fact they spoke to us more with kicks and beatings than with words. Sometimes it was hard to believe that they were actually human beings at all.

******

Now we had reached our destination – that is those of us who were still alive - but it was instantly clear that life in a country where everyone is this strange pastey colour showed no sign of improving for us. Our chains were not removed, and we were driven like cattle from pillar to post and then inspected by men who were obviously wealthy before being taken off one by one to goodness knows where. The man who picked me had a particularly brutish expression and lost no time in beating me and trying to make me walk more quickly to his carriage. Where on earth was he taking me and why?

******

Well, it did not take me long to find out why! At home I had always worked hard looking after our crops, but I was always allowed rest when I needed it, and my mother always cooked good meals for me even when she was overworked and tired. How I yearned for one of those meals now that I had not been fed properly for more weeks than I could count! I was still as determined as ever to get home again, but how to do so was a major problem. Twice I had slipped away from the fields while my master was not looking, but had hardly run more than a couple of miles before getting caught by a neighbouring farmer and brought back again. And the second time the wholopping I got was even worse than the first. My master had this terrible whip which cut into the flesh on my back. The pain was unbelievable. Nevertheless I <u>would</u> find a way to get back to Africa, because that was where I belonged.

******

Oh, what a relief – I'm back home at last! I had begun to give up hope. "Yes," said my dear mother, embracing me, "but it's not your physical body that's come Home. That young body failed to survive your brutal master's last beating. You can't imagine what your father and I suffered during those years before we died, wondering what on earth had happened to you. In fact the worry and despair precipitated our deaths, but it was wonderful to get here and be able to find out. We kept visiting you over there in North America, trying to tell you that what you were enduring was only temporary, but you couldn't hear."

"I thought the spirits had abandoned me, Mother, when I left home. I couldn't hear anything except the brutal shouting, or feel anything other than the whip. Thank goodness it's all over!"

"Yes, thank goodness. Now you can forget the suffering and think about what you've learnt from it. When you feel ready, you can meet your master, express your anger about the whole business of slavery, and point out to him the errors of his ways. But remember that forgiveness is always very important too... What would you like just now, though? Some healing on your sore back?".

*****

Oh, that poor old back yet again!

Sometimes it is quite extraordinary how strong are one's experiences in regression, and this can extend to the therapist as well. At one point while I was being taken through the scenes on board ship, I could actually smell sick. I was only just becoming strongly aware of it when Jen, my partner at that point during the workshop, asked "Have you been sick?"!

Anyway, no wonder that I had always felt so strongly about racism, had wanted to adopt a black child, and had educated myself so thoroughly in ways of combating this particular evil. HOWEVER, was this all there was to it, or was there another side to the story?

PART THREE - THE SLAVEMASTER

Individuality, not individualism, is the cornerstone of community. Individuality is synonymous with uniqueness. This means that a person and his or her unique gifts is irreplaceable. The community loves to see all of its members flourish and function at optimum potential. In fact, a community can flourish and survive only when each member flourishes, living in the full potential of her or his purpose. To honour and support its members is in the self-interest of any community.

***Malidoma Patrice Somé*[1]**

I prided myself on having some of the fittest, most hard-working slaves in the whole of Bristol. They had not looked so fit when I had first bought them (and at such a bargain price too – irresistible!). Far from it. Skinny they were, and just cowering there as though we were lions about to pounce and gobble them up, rather than dignified English gentlemen. So I brought them home and fattened them up quickly. Well, it was worth spending money on some good food to strengthen them after getting them for a song. Some of my business friends and acquaintances

1. From *The Healing Wisdom of Africa*, Malidoma Patrice Somé, Thorsons, London, 1999.

thought I was daft, "wasting money on creatures who have no more appreciation of good food than animals", but I was rewarded for my generosity. Now I had a good strong team at my beck and call and a woman with whom to satisfy my urges when the wife was with child, asleep, or simply not in the mood. Well, could one really use the word "woman" for such an ignorant creature? Perhaps not, but at least she served the purpose for my strong libido, and she was quite useful in the kitchen as well. Veronica, my wife, had high standards for our entertaining, and she worked hard for many months at training the bitch to keep to them. Whenever she had fallen short in any aspect of her duties, I only had to lick her into shape with a beating after I had had my pleasure.

Another difficult task my wife and I had both had was to instil into these pathetic creatures the most vital phrases of the English language. A few slave owners of my acquaintance had even gone so far as to teach them to read and write, but what purpose could it serve? I was perfectly capable of writing all my own bills and accounts, and the Bible and our wonderful works of English literature would be completely wasted on these jungle-reared monkeys. Besides, getting them to be truly articulate could even be dangerous! Even if – Heaven forbid – that wretched Wilberforce succeeded in getting his Bill against the Slave Trade through parliament, at least he didn't advocate emancipation of the slaves. But rumour had it that a former slave who had somehow managed to get free – I believe he had some strange name like Equiano or something – was travelling up and down the country preaching in allegedly good English (though that seemed hard to believe!) all sorts of lies about slavery. I had heard that he had even succeeded in organising gatherings of niggers and was egging them on into fighting for their freedom. Please God he wouldn't come anywhere near our fair city of Bristol! This port where so many important businesses had been enabled to flourish thanks to the importation of these African labourers. My good friend Mr. Perkins said "Never mind old Wilberforce. I fear it may ultimately be the niggers themselves who put an end to slavery." As I say, Heaven forbid!

PART FOUR - FACING THE TRUTH

Horrors! But yes, it must undoubtedly have been me. The picture of that well built, so-called gentleman had been so clear, and Roger's aim in getting us all to do that particular regression was to find our "shadow". So it was not just having been a victim of racism that made me feel so strongly on the subject; I obviously also had at least one karmic debt to pay in that domain. Well, hopefully those long years of writing letters to the papers, buying up racist books in second-hand shops, campaigning against golliwogs and for formal anti-racist policies in schools, would have brought me quite a long way towards paying it. I could have had many lives as a brutal slave owner, but right now just one was enough to uncover, thank you very much! Realising that we ourselves also have a shadow side inevitably makes us much less condemnatory of others.

It was after doing that regression that I suddenly realised the reason for something which had previously been puzzling me. The question in my mind – I have no idea to what extent it is the same for others – had been "Why is it that in some regressions I feel emotion very strongly, while in others I simply get images without feelings?" Now the answer was clear: where there were only pictures from which I felt detached was on the whole (the Holocaust life being an exception) in the lifetimes that I felt ashamed to own. Precisely those "shadow characters" who, Roger was teaching us, needed to be identified and recognised as just as much a part of ourselves as the more palatable ones. I had had a similar experience at a workshop in France the previous year, when Grace had begun a session by getting us to draw a picture of a person towards whom we felt antipathy. I had endeavoured (I am no artist) to do a portrait of Margaret Thatcher, and in the subsequent regression I had found myself as a dictatorial queen or something equivalent.

Personally I do not believe that it matters how much we relive the <u>feelings</u> of those unpleasant people, just so long as we are willing to recognise them and identify them as parts of ourselves. Nor need we be ashamed to own our shadow, once we realise that even the most saintly people have them too. My dear friend Lawrence tells me that he actually has a memory of chopping off people's heads in China. Owning our shadow does not mean either that we have to live any more such lives. All the Masters say that we are free to step off the world at any time, and God's grace is always at hand to flush away our karma, however undeserving we feel. After my regression to the life of the Bristol slave owner, my partner took me into the Bardo, where I met the black woman I had treated so badly and received her forgiveness.

EXERCISES

(a) Think of someone who irritates you. Try to pinpoint in your mind the nature of the things about the person that irritate you. Now go deep inside yourself and look for those very same qualities. Realise that the cause of your irritation may be that the other person is mirroring things about yourself that you do not like.

(b) Forgive both the other person and yourself for these imperfect qualities, remembering that no-one is perfect.

(c) Think of some good quality(ies) that the other person has and endeavour to focus on it/them.

(d) Think of someone for whom you have an intense dislike. Draw a picture of him/her. (Don't worry if you can't draw at all.)

(e) Act that person, endeavouring to really get inside their skin. You may find yourself moving away from the person into another, similar, character. Let whatever wants to come just come.

(f) Realise that the person you have drawn may be mirroring one of your past-life personalities - an aspect of yourself that you have been suppressing. Appreciate that there is nothing shameful about our shadow side; it is through living both good and evil lives that we learn the difference between them.

(g) Realise that you have now learnt the lesson that being unpleasant does not serve you, and resolve in future to lead lives of service (both to others and to yourself).

PART FIVE - DREAMS

> *I have come not to disturb or destroy, but to confirm and vindicate everyone in his own faith. Let the different faiths exist, let them flourish, let the glory of God be sung in all languages, in a variety of tunes. That should be the ideal. Respect the differences between faiths and recognise them as valid so far as they do not extinguish the flame of unity.*
>
> ***Sathya Sai Baba***

It is not only in regressions to previous lives that our shadow side can manifest itself. It can also appear in dreams. Lawrence's expertise in dreams includes not just interpretation but also getting his clients to do some of the work themselves. I used to find dream interpretation extremely difficult, but gradually, under Lawrence's guidance and encouragement, I have begun to improve. We worked together on a dream of mine on the very day that I was travelling to the 2003 annual national Justice and Peace conference, and the discussion which took place while Lawrence was working on my back forced me to give some thought to my shadow side, while the latter helped me with the subsequent longish drive down to Derbyshire. The previous weekend I had been to a reunion lunch of my school year, which explains the appearance of two of the characters in this dream. Here is a brief account of the dream.

I walked into Lawrence's Natural Health Centre as though I owned it, and Lawrence's therapist wife walked through to her own room, saying "Hullo" and then leaving me to carry on with what I was doing. This involved mixing a cream for my great friend Crystal to put on to her spots, and I was doing it according to a prescription written by another former member of my class at school whom I will call Felicity. Then Lawrence walked in and I realised that I had better clear out quickly as he needed to be using the room with his own clients. So I moved into another room and carried on with the task, thinking that when the stuff was made up I would leave it out with a note on it for Crystal. I had in mind that Lawrence would see what I had done, and there was also a distinct feeling of wanting his approval of it.

When I told David about the dream, he commented "You don't need to defer to Lawrence all the time", to which I replied that that was indeed something of which I was very aware and was working on. Lawrence himself was pleased that I was aware of that, but he also reminded me that characters in dreams tend to represent different aspects of oneself. Lawrence himself was easy. He was the "authority figure" and the brain. Crystal I described to him as the most unique person I know, and I also told him how she used to mother me when we were young at school and I was very small for my age, so she was the "unique bit" and the back (which supports). Felicity, when I met her again after forty-five years, was exactly as I remembered her from school: very pleasant and friendly and talked a great deal but without saying anything of great substance. So she was the one "who is happy at cocktail parties" and the face. As for Ann, she was the bit of myself that was "doing the down-to-earth nitty gritty bit", and the uterus.

Well, the unique bit of Ann had something wrong with her (spots) that needed attention; we all need remedies for things at times. The down-to-earth, motherly aspect of Ann was doing the nitty gritty bit of mixing the prescription, but she felt a need firstly to defer to her more intellectual side, which she regards as "superior" (cooking a meal is much easier than writing a book!), and secondly needed her approval of even so menial a task as mixing a cream according to a prescription. As for Felicity, here is where the shadow came in. Lawrence challenged me with the question "When in your life do you follow prescriptions given you by the person who is most happy at cocktail parties?". I was unable immediately to think of any instance of that.

HOWEVER....! As I said, I was on my way to a Justice and Peace conference – weekends which are always enjoyable social occasions as well as inspiring. In preparation for the "partying" on the Saturday evening I planned to change into the Indian dancer's costume that I had had made in India for the party when Roger had ordered us to dress as one of our most outrageous or neglected past-life selves. In the event I did not do so after all, because it was a lovely evening and I got into conversation with people who preferred sitting outside to joining in the dancing. Not until I was driving home the next day did it occur to me that the idea of wearing such a costume at a Christian gathering had been prompted by the "cocktail party" aspect of myself. I then realised, following Lawrence's challenging question, that I had once more faced my shadow and owned it. Owning our shadow is one of the most important things that the human race in general needs to do. Men who fight wars (and I say "men" of course advisedly!) are really simply fighting their own shadow, and until they have come to recognise that, there can be no hope of peace in the world.

But sometimes, I think, the shadow can sort of get twisted. The night immediately after the conference I had another dream. This one I interpreted myself. I was at a largish conference and queuing for a meal, which my sister was serving. I went and sat down, but got up after a bit, presumably to go for another helping, leaving my knife and fork behind. Then I was holding the plate of food and looking for the knife and fork with which to eat it. I found them on the ground, picked them up and was concerned that they had got a bit dirty, but started to eat anyway. Intent on the task in hand (eating), I noticed that Bertrand (my priest friend in the Greek life) was standing nearby talking to another woman but nevertheless observing me in a way that I felt to be critical. Then for some reason I suddenly let my hair down, had to walk past him, and felt distinctly embarrassed about my hair. Then I was walking side by side with my sister, who was talking to me about the drudgery of the job she had been doing. She said to me "Even Kathy (my cleaner) recognised that dealing with all that pizza was an awful job". We were both surprised that "even Kathy" should think that way about it. Then the scene changed completely. I was walking with a group of people and we were all reciting the Gayatri mantra. It seemed to be a sort of pilgrimage and we had a definite destination. We were taking a direct route, which involved walking straight through a monastery. A monk opened the door to us and let us through, obviously realising that we were serious pilgrims even though he did not share our feelings about what we were doing. When we came out the other side of the monastery there were some really huge steps to go down. They were not even, but some were so big that it more or less entailed jumping down, which did not appear to be an obstacle to me.

Firstly, here is how I analyse the characters in this dream using the same principles as Lawrence had used with me for the first dream. Bertrand, whom I respect and admire, is the authority figure and the brain (just like Lawrence, he has an extremely good one), but in addition to that he represents the Catholic Church – a part of myself which I have fairly recently left behind, though it still has quite a big effect on me. My sister, who is a very earthy, motherly sort of person, represents the breasts, but she also symbolises the hands and takes me back to the drudgery theme of Section X. Because a great deal of her life is, alas, in her eyes, just that. (What an onomatopœic word that is – "drudgery"!) Kathy, who loves cleaning but hates cooking (just the reverse of myself), is a wonderful, ever cheerful, person, who talks non-stop about inconsequential things, and she is therefore the "Felicity" of this dream. The monk who kindly opened the door to let us through represents my spiritual side and the heart. As for Ann, she is also the hands but a different aspect of them. Hands have of course many functions, some of which can easily be drudgery if we let them be, but we use them a great deal too in the most important tasks of life. The feeling associated with eating that meal in the dream was not one of enjoyment but more simply of "just getting on with the job". We have to eat to live and I needed tools (the knife and fork) to do this. Similarly, in order to convey information and ideas to others, I have chosen to write this book. The knife and fork may be a bit dirty, but they are the ones I was using already for the first helping of food that I had and they worked all right. So I used them again, even though cleaner ones might have been preferable. I would love to be able to write poetry like T. S. Eliot or Philip Larkin, or prose like Martin Prechtel or my other sister, Philippa, but I can't, so I just get on with the job in hand in my own personal way, using the tools already at my disposal.

So where is the twisted shadow, do you ask? Well, the fact of having moved away from conventional Christianity to belief in things such as reincarnation and Sai Baba gives me two different personas. Nowadays, when I am for instance with a client, engaged in my writing, at a meeting of the Integral Regression Network or a Sai Baba group, I feel able to be completely myself – my new self, which feels more genuine than the old Catholic self. However, when I meet with the sort of people who used to form "my world", I am not only unable to talk about my "real self", I even feel almost ashamed of her. What does the phrase "letting one's hair down" mean? It means running wild, and I am now (in the eyes of the Church anyway!) "running wild with Sai Baba". So I felt embarrassed and almost ashamed as I walked past Bertrand with my hair loose. I was feeling his disapproval of my "shadow". In the dream he represented the still Catholic bit of me which almost despises the "real" bit, regarding it as a shadow which should not be owned.

This dream was for me a very unusual one because, as well as giving voice to the "problem", it later provided the solution! Suddenly the scene changed and there I was with a group of people who were all singing the Gayatri mantra and walking firmly towards a known destination. The Gayatri mantra, which is the oldest prayer in the world, is a prayer for enlightenment on all three levels and it is the one used when saying the 108 beads of the *japamala* (which is the Hindu equivalent of the rosary). Baba says that it is the most important prayer and, though I am not by any means a Hindu, I recite my *japamala* each morning for whatever intention is topical (the troubles in Iraq, finishing this book satisfactorily.....) The monk who opened the door to my little praying group had a completely different attitude towards us than Bertrand had had just beforehand. He recognised us as different, but found us acceptable. So it should be between all the different aspects of our personalities. So it should be – and hopefully will eventually be – in the world. When we came out the other side of the monastery the steps were big, but they were going downwards and were not too difficult to manage. We were intent on our goal. There are always obstacles in life, but if we know where we are headed (back to the Source whence we came) and have the word of God on our lips, we can make it reasonably easily! My shadowy, whacky, side can co-exist quite happily with the more conventional persona I so often have to present to the world, and I need not be ashamed of it.

EXERCISE

1. Think of a dream you can remember clearly – preferably one in which at least four characters figured.

2. Try to relate each of the characters to a different aspect of yourself.

3. Having done that, see whether you can identify the character who represents your shadow.

4. Embrace him/her, recognising him/her as a part of yourself that you can now own every bit as much as the more likeable parts.

5. You might like to think of attending a dream workshop or getting hold of a good book on dream work.

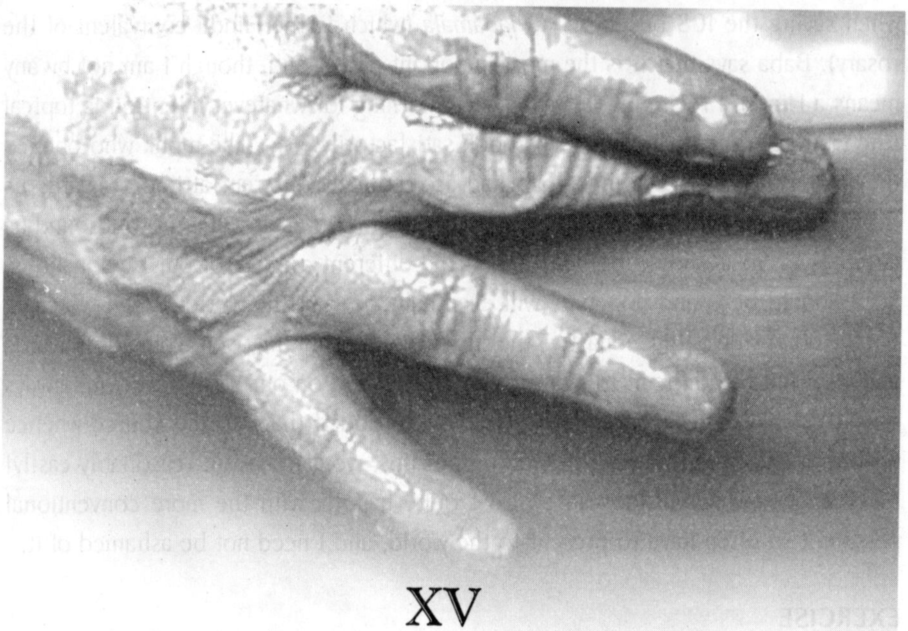

XV
REVIVING OLD TALENTS

PART ONE - HEALING

> *He called the Twelve together and gave them power and authority over all devils and to cure diseases, and he sent them out to proclaim the kingdom of God and to heal..... So they set out and went from village to village proclaiming the Good News and healing everywhere.*
>
> ***Luke 9 1-3,6***

Although I had been into alternative therapies for over five years and had already started writing the original version of this book, I knew little about healing. My sister Philippa had been using her healing gifts for a while, but I imagined it to be something that some people had and others (the majority) did not have. So when my friend Selma, who was my daughter in Israel and my fellow priestess in Greece, suggested that I attend the *Reiki*[1] weekend which she was about to hold at her house, I was sceptical. I agreed, however, to go along to the introductory talk, and was surprised at how strongly I felt the vibrations when the *Reiki* energy was demonstrated. Still sceptical as to my own ability, I nevertheless paid my fee and went along for the weekend.

---

1. *Reiki* is a Japanese word meaning *universal energy*. It was discovered by someone named Usui, and has spread throughout the world in recent years.

My doubts were blown away instantly. The moment that the *Reiki* Master carried out the first "attunement" on me, I felt the healing vibrations coursing right through my body just like electricity. Then, when I laid my hands on somebody else, it started up just as strongly. Now at last I understood how it was that Jesus had told his disciples "Go thou and do likewise": the healing energy of the Creator (or of the universe – whatever one liked to call it) was out there ready to be tapped into, and all we needed to do was to channel it where it could be used, just as we use oxygen for our own purposes. Gradually I realised that I must have made use of healing power in many of my previous lives. So often do we revive old talents at the same time as developing new ones and working out our karma. How else can one explain child prodigies such as Mozart or Yehudi Menuhin?

PART TWO - NINEVEH[2]

CHAPTER ONE - RETURNING HOME

May your silver be lost for ever, and you with it,
for thinking that money could buy what God has given for nothing!

Acts 8:20

I arose from my bunk and looked out eastwards over the great river Tigris. The sun was beginning to rise, and I could tell from the contours of the trees and other familiar landmarks that I could now just pick out in the dim light that there remained but a few miles to go before Nineveh would appear, gleaming invitingly to the north-east of the boat. It was time to go and attend to Faithful and to sort out all the oils and perfumes that the inhabitants of Sennacherib's palace would be eagerly waiting to purchase from me.

I still thought of the "Palace without a Rival" as Sennacherib's, though he himself had long since perished. So what good had it all done him? Spending the whole of the first two years of his reign enlarging the city and building his magnificent palace, embellishing the latter so richly in gold that it made the entire city shine like the sun.... Sennacherib, the *mighty hero clothed in terror*, who destroyed Babylon only to be later assassinated himself in the very house of Nisroch, his god. For such were the ways of men! Had we not seen it throughout the entire course of history? People who had come to Earth to learn would get trapped in the lust for possessions and the delights of the flesh, completely forgetting in the end what it was they had come to learn – indeed the very fact that they <u>had</u> come to learn – and

---

2. For this section I am indebted to *The Luck of Nineveh*, Arnold, Brackman, Eyre Methuen, London, and *Road to Nineveh*, Norah Kubie, Cassell, London.

would simply hang on to their earthly "delights", believing them to be the only source of happiness, until these were finally wrested from them by death.

For Nineveh, besides being the seat of great libraries filled with noble works on Mathematics, Astronomy, Astrology…., was a very hotbed of misuse of Earthly power and riches. The Emperor was unimpeachable, his word being law. The rulers were all lustful and sadistic, and they practised human sacrifice. The palace was guarded by eunuchs, and royal guests feasted their eyes on the sight of young women – even the wives of noblemen – dancing naked before them.

So had Sennacherib's entire life been wasted on account of his preoccupation with wealth and power and his bloody end? Indeed no! His palace, with its seventy-one halls, walls panelled with alabaster recording all his wars, triumphs and great deeds, its almost two miles of *bas-reliefs*, and twenty-seven portals formed by colossal winged bulls and lion-sphinxes, was no doubt an extravagance of unprecedented degree, yet it was Sennacherib who had introduced cotton into Assyria. The *wool-bearing trees* which our people could shear and whose produce they wove into hard-wearing garments. Sennacherib it was who had drawn water from another river to add to that of the Khosr, which joined the Tigris at Nineveh. In order to give these waters a course through the steep mountains, Sennacherib had cut through certain places with pickaxes and directed the river's outflow to the city's great plain. This had enabled all the orchards to be watered in the hot season, and within these orchards, more than in their native habitat, vines, other fruit-bearing trees, and herbs throve luxuriously. Sennacherib himself might be gone for ever, but his name and the fruits of his labours would undoubtedly live on for generations.

******

Faithful was now fed, watered, groomed and all set for the brief ride home, heavily laden with the precious oils and perfumes which together we had travelled so far to obtain. And lo and behold there already lay Nineveh, gleaming white before our eyes with the morning sun shining so brilliantly behind it. Nineveh, encircled by its five walls and fifteen hundred watch towers. Walls so thick that three chariots could ride abreast atop them! And the *Palace without a Rival* was only one of a great number of majestic palaces, temples and gardens that the city boasted. Thirty temples, each shining with silver and gold; fifteen gates guarded by castellated ramparts, three moats…. No wonder that my heart leapt within my breast each time that I found myself once more approaching home at the end of another long period of travel.

Yes, there was no doubt about it: I <u>was</u> attached to the city of my birth. About as attached as I was to my beloved horse Faithful, who had been the equivalent of family for me for the last eighteen years. How appropriately had I named him! Yet my attachment was in no way akin to that of Assyria's kings and noblemen who had built Nineveh. Each time that I was invited into one of the palaces to sell my wares, dine sumptuously, explain the healing properties of my merchandise and impart to my hosts some of the pearls of my accumulated wisdom, I was struck almost dumb at first by the wonderfully carved winged man-headed lion and bull on the doorway of the palace of Ashurnasirpal II, the winged deities kneeling beside a sacred tree, or the fish god on the entrace of the temple of Ninurta. Yet I remained always detached; an admiring spectator rather than someone caught within the thrall of the ephemeral material world. For the ability that I had developed over the years to read the Akashic Records had reinforced the knowledge that I had always held deep within: that everything in this world – even so well built and strong a city as Nineveh – was ephemeral. I had never wanted to make a career from this gift that I had acquired, as did the diviners employed by the royal household, nor even to devote a great deal of time to using it for my own purposes, but sometimes, when I was relaxing after a long and tiring day, I would let my mind open itself to visions. Visions of the past and even occasionally of the future. I knew from these visions that I had had many previous lives: in Atlantis and possibly even earlier... in Egypt.... And from these visions I knew too that great civilisations which had imagined themselves to be indestructible had in fact sunk without trace beneath the waves. So would Nineveh, alas I felt sure, one day perish too – if not under water, at least under ground.

In a sense of course, I was not completely detached from the wealth. Were I to be, I would have to surrender my comfortable house – the house I had had built to my own design as my very own home. I would have to dismiss the servants who had served me so faithfully for so long, and whom I had always treated well in return. Many spiritual seekers would no doubt do this; would be content to live from hand to mouth with never the assurance of a roof and a meal to which to return. I, however, had worked hard for my wealth and, after the rigours of travel, of weeks on end spent alone with my horse and with only a rolled up blanket to spread out under a tree or the stars at night, I felt I deserved a comfortable home to which to return now and again. A home, too, in which I would finally be able to end my days once I had become too old and weary to travel any more. I sensed that that day was still quite a long way off, despite my already advanced years and my white hair and beard, for I was still energetic and sprightly and had as yet no desire to retire from my merchant's career, but the years were now passing ever more quickly and, when the inevitable day did finally come, I would want to be well cared for.

I could of course have married many years ago rather than choosing this life of celibacy, but I did not feel that raising a family would really have been compatible with my chosen career. Binding oneself to a woman entailed responsibility for an upright man, and I had no wish to curtail my freedom by any such responsibility. I knew that I had been married (both happily and unhappily), had raised families, many times in the past, and that I would no doubt wish to do so again in the future; but for this lifetime I had been content to live on my own, to travel the road just with my horse, keeping company occasionally with people in many high places within the Empire and beyond, learning from some of them, teaching others, nurturing and expanding the wisdom that grew from within, and increasing continually in self-sufficiency.

As we descended from the boat, Faithful let out a delighted neigh in recognition of his home ground. I mounted carefully so as not to disturb the precious bottles with which I had already bedecked his sides, and off we set, Nineveh's gleaming white stone walls beckoning us ever more invitingly. Today would be a day for relaxing, for feasting on the wholesome meal which my good cook would prepare with care as soon as he saw that I had arrived, and for decanting my wares into smaller containers so that they would be ready for the noble purchasers. Then a good night's sleep in the bed that would seem so comfortable after all these weeks of hard ground or the boat's bunk, and tomorrow I would be ready to start on my round of the local palaces.

CHAPTER TWO - DEATH OF A NOBLEWOMAN

> ***Yes, remember your Creator now while you are young, before the silver cord of life snaps, and the gold bowl is broken, and the pitcher is broken at the fountain, and the wheel is broken at the cistern; and the dust returns to earth as it was, and the spirit returns to God who gave it.***
>
> ***Ecclesiastes 12: 6-7 (The Daily Walk Bible)***

I had spent the entire morning in Sennacherib's palace. So many people there had been interested in the exotic oils and perfumes imported from the Far East which I had been able to purchase from the merchants who landed in the Persian Gulf at the mouth of the Tigris. In fact I had had to wait a whole week for that boat to arrive, but it had been well worth it. After so many years of dealing in these goods I could detect the finest quality ones from a single sniff, and these were indeed among the very best that had ever been brought to our land. No wonder that the noblewomen and all their friends had been so enthralled. Following a morning in which I had probably made enough profit to live well for a number of weeks if not months, I had declined the king's invitation to dine, preferring instead to return for some rather more simple fare in my own home. No sooner, however, had I put my feet up at the end of my meal when there arrived a messenger at my door.

"Julius, please come with me quickly. My master Gadaziok has sent me to urge you to attend to his young wife who is very ill. He has already tried all the leading physicians in vain, and he says that you have certain knowledge and healing powers that are beyond the ken of anyone else around here."

"Right, I will come. Just wait a moment while I gather a selection of my most potent healing oils.

******

"Well, Gadaziok, I fear that there is little more that I can do now for your good wife. This oil has obviously alleviated her pain somewhat but, you see, her aura is very depleted. In fact I can scarcely see it at all any more, and I have, I am afraid, to tell you that this is a signal that the soul has already realised that the time has come to leave this particular body and return to its true home."

"What do you mean, its true home? Jacinta's true home is right here, with me. I love her the most of all my wives. She is so fair and but twenty-five years of age. Our son has only just learnt to walk."

"Man's plans, I fear good Gadaziok, do not always coincide with those of Jehovah. Only He is Lord, and if our life plan was a short one this time, He will call us when our time is up. The only thing that I can do for her now is to aid her transition. In fact you could help me to massage her feet and her neck with this delightful oil I have here. She would appreciate the attentions of her beloved husband more than my own. It is very painful for you, I know, but it is through pain that we learn and grow. You must not hang on to Jacinta now, or her soul will not be free to go where it has to. One of your other wives can surely become a mother to your son?"

"Yes, that is so, but she loves the child so..."

"It is hard indeed, but know that the child too had made his choice even before entering Jacinta's womb. He will have known who was to be his foster mother and will go to her with joy after he has been given time to grieve. I suggest you call him now to her side, so that he too can bid her "Farewell". This will be an important part of the healing process for both of them. Then, when she has gone, you should not touch the body for three days. The etheric body requires three days fully to detach itself from the physical one, and that will be a good time for you too to continue to detach yourself and give Jacinta the freedom she needs to move on.

Letting go is always one of the greatest manifestations of love, though probably the hardest. In this universe there are no true farewells, only temporary partings, and our loved ones who move on to higher planes do not forget us but are always there to guide us when we need them. You and Jacinta will still be able to communicate even when she is no longer visible to your eyes, and at night, when you leave your body in sleep, she will again become visible to you. Then you will be able to communicate even better than you have ever done down here, and you might even find, with practice, that you can remember some of these conversations upon waking."

"You mean dreams? I nearly always remember my dreams, and of course I do not doubt that I shall dream of Jacinta, but dreams are not reality, only fiction."

"You are wrong, Gadaziok. Dreams are never fiction, but always important messages from the Higher Self to the Lower Self, that is from one's spirit being to one's soul and mind. But I am not speaking now of dreams; I am speaking of real contact. I can see that I need to explain further.... But wait: it is now happening before our very eyes. A truly wondrous sight! I am fortunate in having been trained to see with the eyes of the spirit, but perhaps it is not completely invisible to you either. Go fetch the child quickly... Good, you have brought him just in time. Look, child. You know that your mother was very ill. This meant that the time of her physical presence with you was coming to an end. She is being called back to the other side. Do you see that wonderful white light just above her, and the silver cord extending from it to her body? Now embrace her."

The child did not speak, but his eyes were fixed on the light which I knew to be Jacinta's soul. I knew that young children often had clairvoyant ability which they lost later on. His eyes were brimming with tears, but at the same time gleaming with joy at the beauty of what he was beholding. Then he threw himself upon his mother's breast and wept.

"Let him weep," I said to Gadaziok. "Tears are important at such times. He has witnessed his mother's soul leaving her body, and this will not only help him to accept the loss, but also make him realise that it is not a real loss since the physical body is only clothing. Our essence is soul and spirit. The child has seen his mother's soul set off on its journey back to her spirit. He may even still have memories of his own journey from spirit into this world. He is still young enough for that.".

"I am feeling somewhat bewildered."

"There is no need to be bewildered. It is really very easy to understand. You see, when the spirit sends a soul into a physical body in order to gain further experience of the physical world, this soul attaches itself to the chosen body with a silver cord. The soul is, however, still free to come and go at will, and it generally takes at least the first year or two before it is firmly anchored. Then, even after that, it still almost invariably leaves the body during periods of sleep. At these times the soul returns to its true home, where it can meet with friends and relatives who have passed over, as well as with other souls who also still have bodies on Earth, and where it can do important work."

"What sort of work might it be?"

"That will depend very much upon the level of evolution of the soul in question, but it will often be, for instance, helping people who are in the process of passing from Earth back into spirit."

"So do you think that Jacinta is receiving such help just now?"

"I am certain of it. As well as seeing her soul as a white light above her body, I have been aware of other lights coming to meet her. But now they have all left my field of clairvoyant vision, and you can feel that her body is beginning to grow cold. The massage that we just performed undoubtedly eased her transition, as did your love for her. It is hard for you to accept, I know, but you must understand that we all have and need the experience of brief lives. So please remember what I have said – that you will be able to meet with Jacinta again each night – and if upon awakening you have memories of conversations or actions you have performed together, trust them as true memories and be thankful for the joy that they will bring you. Now I must go, but I will return tomorrow with some oil with which it will be useful for you to embalm the body before the funeral."

CHAPTER THREE - THE MESSIAH

> *"You are a priest of the order of Melchizedek, and for ever.".... having been made perfect, he became for all who obey him the source of eternal salvation and was acclaimed by God with the title of high priest "of the order of Melchizedek".*
>
> ***Hebrews 5: 6-10***

A couple of months had passed since Jacinta's death, and poor Gadaziok was coping very well despite his intense grief. I had been a guest of honour at the funeral and had visited the household several times since, doing my best always to bring consolation. The child was doing well in the care of one of the other wives, who I felt sure would grow to love him as her own.

One evening I was invited to dine not at Gadaziok's palace nor at the *Palace without a Rival*, but at one of Nineveh's other handsome palaces, whose noble owner had also invited a number of astrologers and other learned gentlemen. It promised to be a more interesting experience than the usual orgies at the King's palace. There was dancing laid on for our entertainment, and the young women artists were not naked, but dressed very beautifully in the richest colours. Even some of the older and most scholarly guests were enthralled.

"Julius," commented one of them, "I am surprised that you, such a handsome figure of a man, quite seductive looking this evening with your curly white beard and fine white turban, should remain so aloof to the charms of these young ladies. Have you really never felt tempted to abandon your life of celibacy?"

"No," I replied. "I am not, as you suggest, impervious to their beauty and charm, and have greatly been enjoying the entertainment, but I do feel strongly that affection is not something to be trifled with, and the sexual act without affection is empty and meaningless. In my opinion a sexual relationship – especially if it produces offspring – entails responsibility, and in this lifetime I have never felt inclined to take on such responsibility on account of my travels."

"I admire your attitude," commented another guest, "but does it not bother you, now that you are beginning to grow old, that you will have no family to care for you at the end of your days?"

"No, it does not. I have good and faithful servants whom I have always paid and treated well, and I trust them to carry on taking care of me. Besides, I have always taken good care of my health, never indulging greatly in unwholesome food or excessive drink."

"Julius is wise in many ways," remarked another. "Can you advise me how best to treat my troublesome insides? And can you perhaps sell me some castor oil? If you think that could help."

"Castor oil is good for very many things, and I can certainly sell you some of the very best quality, but I would advise you also to cut down on rich food as well as on wine." (The man who had just spoken was corpulent in the extreme.) "You realise of course that I do not need to travel far afield in order to purchase my castor oil? Remember the story of Jonah and the castor oil tree which sheltered him at Nineveh?"

"Yes, but the tree did not shelter him for long! I trust that you would not sell anything from a withered tree."

"Fear not. All my products are of the very finest quality."

"Talking of Scripture," carried on another scholar, "have you read or heard of the recent prophecies concerning the coming of a Messiah? A Prince of Peace?"

"No. Tell us. We could do with some peace in this kingdom, I feel. When is he to come and who is he to be?"

"When" I cannot answer, but as for "who", I am told that he is to be a reincarnation of the great Joseph – he of the coat of many colours – who in turn was a reincarnation of the great Melchizedek[3]."

"That's right," interjected one of the astrologers. "A priest of the order of Melchizedek. I trust that I shall be around to see him!"

"This prophecy may not yet be fulfilled for several centuries," replied another astrologer, "but I do believe that when he comes it will be with an important mission to change the world, and he will be greater still than he was as Joseph."

"How exciting!" I commented. "I fear that I shall not still be here when he comes. But on the other hand, perhaps I shall. Perhaps I shall return to Earth at that very time. Who knows?"

"Who knows?" echoed my fellow guests in unison.

PART THREE - PERSECUTION

Blessed are those who are persecuted in
the cause of right: theirs is the kingdom of heaven.

Matthew 5: 10

So that was a good life! We have all of course had many good lives even if they are not always the ones that raise their heads most easily. Trauma often surfaces more readily for the simple reason that it still needs dealing with. It is nice when we can use healing talents to benefit society and have our work acknowledged, but persecution of healers has been endemic throughout the ages. Many regression therapists of my acquaintance have persecution as one of their own themes. Burning at the stake, for instance, is indeed a common scenario in workshops!

As a Catholic I had at one time in my life had some success in encouraging anti-racism to be incorporated more firmly into the Justice and Peace scene. So, when I first became convinced about reincarnation, I started off with a sense of mission in the Church. I realised that, like the Cathars, my Christianity was now more in line with that of the pre-553 Christians – like the beliefs of Jesus himself in fact, who had after all stated very clearly that John the Baptist was Elijah (quite apart from

3. These are two of the previous lives of Jesus mentioned in the Edgar Cayce readings. See 'Lives of the Masters,'Glenn Sanderfur, ARE Press, USA.

other things he may well have said on that topic which were cut out of the New Testament after the Council of Constantinople in 553 AD). This mission might have seemed almost realistic the first time that I went to Sai Baba's ashram in India, where I met so many fellow Christians, but I had by then come round to the view of my friends who had always claimed that it would be a hopeless task. I still went to mass regularly because the parish where I lived was a real, vibrant community which did a lot of worth while things and, besides my good friend Cynthia, who founded our local Baba group, I in due course uncovered a couple of other "clandestine reincarnationists". After qualifying as a regression therapist, I made no attempt to advertise my work in the parish, but the local paper once did an article on me, and of course my plaque was up outside the clinic in the centre of Hull where I practised.

When I reached the age of sixty I had quite a big birthday party, to which I invited a number of my friends in the parish. One woman, whom I had not known for very long but liked, refused the invitation "on account of my beliefs", even though I had never discussed these with her. She commented that "Jesus was the only healer". This I found puzzling in view of Jesus' own injunction to do as he did, and it was not very long after that that the parish priest, whom I had found unusually open-minded in many respects, forbade me to give out communion because of what people had been saying about me. The thought of people talking unfavourably about me behind my back hurt deeply, but fortunately I had already booked to go on another Woolger workshop shortly afterwards.

PART FOUR - THE "WITCH MIDWIFE"

The panel of judges were all glowering at me, but I tried very hard not to cower in front of them. After all, what had I really done wrong? Childbirth was a hazardous business, and I had done all in my power to save the baby. Why would I have done otherwise? I loved helping people, I loved my work as a healer, and I loved delivering babies. But, as well as glowering at me, the judges were muttering to one another. I overheard the odd phrase. "It's not only that poor baby, you know...", "Yes, poor Simpkins was only twenty-eight when he died last year, and I heard that she'd been treating him..."

The mutterings and discussion carried on for what seemed like an eternity, until eventually one particularly severe-looking man said "So what should we condemn her to? The stake? The gallows?" Still I endeavoured not to cower before them, but I knew that pleading my case would be quite useless, so I simply stood in silence, waiting. "A young woman like her isn't worth burning good wood for!" said another member of the panel. "I don't think our gallows are working properly at the moment," said a third.

"Well, while you're all thinking about it, let's just tie her up and leave her outside," said the man who seemed to be the chief judge. "We've got a lot of much more important business to be getting on with."

******

Handcuffed and tied to a post outside the court, getting steadily colder, hungrier and thirstier, my mind kept going over and over the tragic scene. "What could I have done?", I asked myself, remembering the intense pain that the mother had been in, the yellowish colour the poor baby had had, and his great difficulty in starting to breathe.... "A son!" the father had exclaimed when he had come into the room just after the delivery of the afterbirth. "I who needed a son so badly after she'd given me three daughters, and you've let him <u>die</u>! I can't believe it. How <u>dare</u> you offer your services to my family if you cannot do your job properly?"

And after that things had gone from bad to worse. There seemed to be conspiracy against me throughout our entire village. One or two of my "old faithfuls" had still called for me when they were afflicted with aches and pains or dropsy, but I could scarcely leave my little abode for a moment without someone pointing a finger at me. I had gone on and on searching my conscience, often unable to get a good night's sleep, and then finally I had been brought to this horrible court to face a panel of men who knew nothing of what they were talking about. How hard life was! Was it really worth living? I used to think it was – very much so – but now....

******

It had got dark and the panel were adjourning. One by one they gave me a kick and uttered a few more words of abuse as they passed me. "Witch!", "Useless whore!", "You deserve to burn to death!", "Witch! We'll deal with you tomorrow.", "Those herbs you gave my grandmother accelerated her death!", "What have you to say for yourself, then, just cowering there?", "Coward!", ... It seemed to be never ending. I was not dressed for a cold night, and I was hungry and thirsty as well as bruised and sore. Then suddenly one man gave me an extra strong kick and the next thing I knew....

******

I was in the arms of an angel. "It's all right. We're escorting you home now. That last kick was so hard that you fell, hit your head, and left your body. Don't worry, you don't need that body any more, and there is plenty of healing work to be done over here."

The partner who was guiding the regression asked me a few questions, one of which was "Take another look at that panel of judges. Is there anyone among them that you recognise?"

"Oh yes!" I exclaimed fairly quickly. "One of them is the woman who refused to come to my birthday party. I don't know how I know, since obviously she's a man here, but I do know, for sure."

"Well, now's your chance to tell him how you feel."

"I don't think there's any point because he'd never understand. She's a much better person now. A good person, who adheres to her beliefs just as strongly as I adhere to mine."

"So you forgive her?"

"Yes, but there's nothing to forgive really. She was only following her conscience."

Then Roger came and sat down next to my partner. "Now, just look around in the Bardo for someone that you helped," he said. Very quickly a grateful-looking young man appeared (Simpkins!), recounting how I had healed him just before he died and how it had eased his pre-destined passing. Then came another, then another, all with nice stories and nice things to say about my work.

"So you see how much good you did?" said Roger.

"Yes, but the father of that baby blames me for his death and I feel terrible about it."

"He should know that babies often die, and it was much more common in those days without all our modern technology. You obviously did the best you could in the circumstances, so don't you think you should forgive yourself?" I decided to forgive myself, and then Roger continued. "Who taught you your healing skills?"

"My grandmother," I replied without hesitation, not knowing where the answer had come from.

"And who taught her?"

"Her mother."

"And who taught her?"

"<u>Her</u> mother."

"And who taught her?"

"<u>Her</u> mother."

"So there," said Roger, "you have a long line of healers who've done a great deal of good over a long period of time and passed on their knowledge from one to the other. Now I want you to call on these ancestors. Just let them gather around you and feel their loving presence and support." I did as he said, and felt a wonderful loving warmth surrounding me.

"Right," continued Roger, "now just remember whenever you suffer criticism for what you do, you can just call on them to support you. Their help and guidance is always at hand."

PART FIVE - HEALING FOR THE HEALER!

Each religion defines God within the limits it demarcates and then claims to have grasped Him. Like the seven blind men who spoke of the elephant as a pillar, a fan, a rope or a wall, because they contacted but a part and could not comprehend the entire animal, so too, religions speak of a part and assert that its vision is full and total.

Each religion forgets that God is all Forms and all Names, all attributes and all assertions. The religion of Humanity is the sum and substance of all these partial faiths; for, there is only one Religion and that is the Religion of Love. The various limbs of the elephant that seemed separate and distinct to the eye-less seekers of its truth were all fostered and activated by one single stream of blood; the various religions and faiths that feel separate and distinct are all fostered by one single stream of love.

Sathya Sai Speaks, Volume XII

Gosh, how much better I felt after that workshop! And the next time that I went to the church I did not mind at all about feeling different. When David had retired and we moved to Shropshire, I would not bother looking for a church, but would concentrate my efforts on a Sai Baba group (Anyway, Sai Baba says that it is good to be born in a Church but not to die in one.)

EXERCISE

Do you sometimes suffer criticism because of your work or other interests? How do you react to it?

With anger? If so, remind yourself that we are all on different paths each time, and that in a previous life you might well have been the one voicing the criticism. So forgive the person concerned, and thank them for giving you the opportunity to become mentally stronger.

With self doubt? Then take a good look at what you do that arouses criticism and decide whether it is justified in any way. If it is not, congratulate yourself on the good that you do and think of yourself as being in league with vast numbers of other people, both on Earth and in the spirit world. If, on the other hand, you feel that some of the criticism is justified (e.g. one of my own faults is that I sometimes try too hard to help people who are not ready for it), then endeavour to modify your behaviour accordingly.

Does it make you feel very alone? If so, look around at the support that is available to you. Perhaps you could join some group or organisation and go to regular meetings? If there is no such group where you live, how about forming one yourself? (My friend Cynthia, who had never believed herself to have any leadership qualities whatever, prayed to Sai Baba for a whole two years for a group to be formed in the Hull area. Eventually it occurred to her that He might be wanting her to do it. Then she put an advertisement in a national Baba magazine and received several phone calls from local people who had also been wanting to belong to a group. It is now still going strong more than eight years later.)

XVI
CONTINUING ROLES

PART ONE - CHRISTOPHER AND LAWRENCE

Bringing up children is never easy, and bringing up adopted children is extra difficult on account of their subconscious feeling of having been rejected[1]. Since they do not know how to deal with these feelings because they do not understand them, it is natural and normal for such children to take them out on their adoptive mother – the symbol of the person who "rejected" them - even when (as in our own son's case) they were given up out of love. Christopher and I are extremely closely linked karmicly, one indication of this being that my sun sign is Aquarius while my rising sign is Scorpio, whereas Christopher's astrology is the reverse. From the moment I first set eyes on him (at ten days old, in the foster home), I loved my younger son deeply, and I suffered much on his account over the ensuing eighteen years. Lawrence understood the difficulties perfectly and took a great interest in Christopher, as well as giving me immense support, from the very first time that we went to see him.

While in my own case the original pretext was backache but the treatment has extended very much further, with Christopher the pretext was asthma, which started

1. See *THE PRIMAL WOUND – Understanding the Adopted Child*, Nancy Newton Verrier, Gateway Press, Baltimore, USA, 1994.

when he was seven. Lawrence, however, while treating his asthma, took his behavioural problems more seriously still and, though we saw a number of therapists who were nearer home, all of whom had a lot to be said for them, Lawrence's help was the most valuable of all. When Christopher reached the age of twelve, Lawrence supported my desire to send him to boarding school, as did the well known astrologer that I consulted. His birth chart analysis, as well as detailing every minute aspect of Christopher's very complex character, said that he needed to learn control, and that this had to come from outside the home.

The decision was a difficult one, as neither David nor Christopher himself was at all keen on the idea of boarding school, and there was also the financial aspect to consider. But we found a State school in Cumbria that took boarders, and I insisted for the sake of my own sanity, at the same time taking up some French and Spanish coaching to help pay the boarding fees. We all missed Christopher of course, but his absence during term time made Alice's life more peaceful as well as my own.

This was, however, by no means the end to the problems. Almost every time the telephone rang we feared it might be the school reporting another of Christopher's misdemeanours, and he was excluded for a week (which of course meant being sent home) on several occasions. But his amiable nature and his academic prowess endeared him to the Headmaster, who stood by him even after having been driven to the point of being forced to exclude him from the school permanently. This apparent "disaster" – initially the most worrying moment of my entire life – proved to be Christopher's eventual salvation! Firstly, the sympathetic Head persuaded the Headmaster of another State school in Cumbria that took boarders to consider him, and secondly he had just taken to playing basketball. The fact that the second Head assured him that he would be able to play basketball at the new school made Christopher feel happy about the move, and he very soon got noticed and was asked to play for Cumbria. Lawrence, to whom I still took Christopher every holiday and also every time that yet another crisis occurred at school, gave him every possible encouragement in the basketball.

Fortunately for Christopher, who was being reared in a very unsporting family, the Cumbria team coach recognised his potential and knew about the possibility of doing degrees in the United States on basketball scholarships. He made a video of Christopher's playing and sent it round to various American universities and colleges. Thanks to that, and to his obtaining all 'A' grades in his Advanced Level examinations, he was awarded a scholarship to a prestigious college in North Carolina. The American coach, however, would not rely solely on the video, but flew to England to watch Christopher play before making his decision. This gave us the opportunity to meet him and learn something of what life at that College would entail and, by the end of the day spent with this delightful man, we felt happier about our eighteen-year old son going off so far to do his degree than we would have done if he had been going to a university somewhere in England.

Christopher himself had long dreamed of going to America, and his four years there were unbelievably happy and successful. When we flew over to North Carolina for his graduation, the jubilation was tinged with sadness, as one and all – teachers and friends – were as upset about losing Christopher as he was sorry to be saying "goodbye" to them.

PART TWO - PARENTS OF A PELOTA PLAYER

Towards the end of 1981 David was invited to work for a term at one of the universities in Mexico City. I enjoyed being school ma'am for Paul and Alice for a little while, but most of all I enjoyed seeing some of Mexico. Not so much the heavily polluted city itself – a difficult place in which to spend three months with young children – but the wonderful archaeological sites. But we were limited by both time and money, and so our dream of getting to the Yucatán was not fulfilled that year. In those days the concept of having lived before could not have been further from my mind, yet I felt an immense yearning to see Chichén Itzá.

A yearning which was fulfilled exactly twenty years later! Having sorely missed having Christopher at home three Christmases in a row, we decided to spend the Christmas of 2001 in North Carolina. Before we had got round to booking our flights, David was suddenly invited to a conference in Taxco in early December. I had fallen seriously in love with Taxco on the weekend we had spent there with the children, and this seemed also to be a golden opportunity: our longed for holiday in the Yucatán could be sandwiched between David's conference and the family Christmas in North Carolina.

Taxco was busier and noisier than twenty years previously, but still enchanting. David's conference was good, but by the end of the week he felt ready for a holiday. We flew from Mexico City to Cancun so that I could satisfy a yen to swim in the sea in December, and then took the bus to Mérida. Mérida itself was interesting, the day trip to Uxmal was wonderful, but we kept the best till last. To be sure of having enough time at Chichén Itzá, we booked a hotel within walking distance and got there in time to walk to the site for the *son et lumière*. We were not disappointed, but the evening show was only a taster. Determined to follow the guide book's advice and arrive before the crowds the next morning, we got up, had breakfast and left without my having made time for my morning meditation. When I mentioned this to David, he replied "Well, the ideal place for you to meditate would be the *Cenote*, the sacred well.". I thought to myself "I wish I were like some people I know, who go to a sacred place and immediately get triggered into a past life they have had there!". Anyway, we climbed the Castillo first (just in time before it was completely swamped by the other tourists and – fortunately - before seeing the notice declaring it forbidden to the over sixties!), and then we made our way via one or two other fascinating spots, to the massive, awe-inspiring, *Cenote*, where I sat down and began to meditate. Instantly, for the first time in my life, I found myself precipitated into a previous existence....

CHAPTER ONE - THE CENOTE

It was my turn to be sacrificed. Somehow I had always known that it would have to happen one day, but resignation did little to alleviate my fear. Our beloved *Cenote* was so deep and, though it had been known even in my own short lifetime, survival was rare. It was said that the young girls who did survive communed with the gods and were subsequently endowed with gifts of prophecy. Anyway, whatever happened was in the hands of God and the Nine Mayan Spirits. It was my duty simply to accept my fate.

Being thrown into the great well was even more terrifying than I had imagined. First I plunged down deep, but then somehow or other I floated up again, and what should I see when I rose to the surface but a big brown furry creature. I soon realised that it was a bear – the animal I loved the most, shy though they always were. Without thinking, I made a huge leap with my whole body and grabbed hold of its rear end. The bear then swam to the edge of the well and I clung on with all my might. Then he began to climb out and I was able quickly to transfer my grip from its back to a sturdy rock. He then scampered up the side and disappeared into the forest, leaving me slowly to make my way to the top unaided.

When eventually I arrived, very footsore, at the top of the steep bank of the *Cenote*, there was my family and the rest of our tribe gathered in a circle awaiting me. Our H'men (the one who sees[1]), The Wise One, stepped forward and took me by the hand, enveloping me completely in his loving smile. Jaguar Girl, his beloved wife, was by his side, and on the level which was still in the twenty-first century reality I recognised them instantly as Ngawang and Silvia, Ann's friends from the Roger Woolger training[2]. "Congratulations!" said the dear H'men, "You are among the few young virgins to have survived this ordeal. It is now my duty to give you a

1. See *Sastun, My Apprenticeship with a Maya Healer*, by Rosita Arvigo, HarperSan Francisco.
2. Lama Ngawang is now French, but lives and teaches in Switzerland, and Silvia, who is German, is also a wonderful therapist and meditation teacher.

new name, and the name I am choosing is "The one who is loved by the bear". It is the right of young girls who escape from the grip of our sacred *Cenote* to choose for themselves a husband. So I now call upon all those young men who consider themselves eligible for the hand of this brave woman to step forward."

An inner circle of young men was quickly formed and, looking around them also with the eyes of twenty-first century reality, I picked out the one whom I immediately recognised as Lawrence. "Running Deer – one of our tribe's finest Pelota players - is my choice," I said. "If he will be so good as to have me.".

"I shall be honoured," he replied, blushing a little; and within a couple of weeks a great wedding feast was prepared.

CHAPTER TWO - OUR FAMILY

Running Deer and I were both overjoyed when our first child was born. It was a boy, and we named him Rising Sun because he seemed to us just like the sun coming into our lives in order to enrich it still further. As soon as I started to suckle him, however, I knew that we would not be able to keep him until we had reached old age. I knew that he was destined for greatness, but that he would die young. For that reason, dearly though I loved him, I always held something back in the relationship; I simply would not allow myself to get too attached to him. I shared this knowing that I had with no-one, not even my dear husband, and I was happy to watch a very close father/son relationship develop between the two of them.

I was fertile, and over the next few years, though we lost two babies fairly early on in the pregnancies, I gave birth to another three fine sons, interspersed with two beautiful daughters. The first baby that we lost, who would have been our third, caused me the most intense distress, and it was also frightening for both of us as I haemorrhaged a great deal. When Running Deer rushed off to look for our H'men, Jaguar Girl said that he must not be disturbed as he was journeying, but that there was no need to worry as she could make us a brew with rose leaves and red rose petals.

Caring for our children of course took up much of our time, but we both had to intersperse the tasks that entailed with other duties. Running Deer was a keen astronomer and mathematician as well as a fine Pelota player, and he liked to give as much time as possible to passing on his knowledge to others. As for me, people often came to consult me about various things. I did seem to have a gift for seeing the future, but my husband always discouraged me from telling people any more than seemed absolutely necessary. "They have to make their own future," he would say to me. "If you tell them too much they will cease to be masters of their own destiny."

The Wise One also gave me much help and support. Sometimes we would sit together under our sacred Copal tree, and he would explain to me how, as well burning incense from it at our ceremonies of purification, thanksgiving or supplication, he would use its resin for treating such spiritual diseases as envy, fright or grief[1]. Jaguar Girl, his wife and twin soul, was always his chief helper, but sometimes he would ask me too to help mix the Copal resin in preparation for the Primicia ceremony, when we gave thanks to God and the Nine Maya Spirits and prayed to them for the harvest or for sick people[1].

CHAPTER THREE - PELOTA

Yes, Running Deer was a fine sportsman and a keen *Pelota*[3] player. But the game frightened me a bit! The ball was so extraordinarily heavy and the hoops were so high that the chances of real success always seemed small. Running Deer would say to me, "and I shall teach all our sons to play with me as soon as they are old enough." Rising Sun expressed an interest almost as soon as he had learnt to run, but he had of course to wait a long time until he was strong enough to lift the ball. In the meantime my dear husband had him practise other physical skills that were useful training for the game.

Near where we lived, and near to the *Cenote* and our great temples, was the finest ball court in the whole of the Maya region. People would come from a long way around to play there, and Running Deer played a big part in selecting and training one of the finest teams.

However, one day not long after Rising Sun's twenty-fifth birthday, the disaster I had been dreading for so long suddenly struck. Our dear son failed to get himself far enough away from the ring as, unusually, a member of the opposing team succeeded in sending the ball straight through it. He was struck on the head and knocked unconscious. As he fell on to the hard rock ground I called hastily upon the brown bear and my other protective spirits, but I was too late. By the time The Wise One had been able to get to him, he was forced to pronounce Rising Sun as departed from us.

The game was suspended and the opponents stayed with us to pray and to mourn. The funeral was a truly beautiful ceremony, but nothing can console a

---

3. *Pelota* is of course the Spanish name for the Mayan ball game.

mother's heart. At least I had my dear husband and our younger children to share my grief, and we all knew that death, whenever it came, had to be accepted as a part of life.

And I have to say that from that day forth until my own death at quite an advanced age, my work really blossomed. There is no doubt that grief is one of the greatest teachers, and my personal experience helped me to have even more compassion for others. The Wise One and Jaguar Girl were both getting very old now, and ever increasing numbers of people came to me for counselling. I had also learnt quite a lot from the H'men, and was able to prescribe *Epasote* for intestinal parasites[1], *Cocolmeca* for arthritis, kidney complaints or diabetes, and I knew how to boil the red bark of the *Chaca* and use it as a bath for skin problems. When Running Deer was not too busy with his astronomy and the great Mayan Calendar, he would also give help to some of the many patients. All in all it was a very rich and fulfilled life.

PART THREE - MY REACTIONS

"Phew! Where did that come from?" I asked myself as the half hour came to an end and I was expecting David to rejoin me any minute. "The brown bear seemed a bit far fetched for a start. Surely they're mountain animals!". But it was hard to dismiss it all. For one thing it certainly explained Lawrence's great interest in Christopher's basketball, and I was quite sure that Rising Sun was the same soul as our now adopted son. For another, whenever Lawrence had commented to me about his feelings of closeness with my younger son, I had always replied "I'm sure you must have been his father in the past.". But each time I had said that it had never entered my head even for a second that I too might have had anything to do with it, and one of the criteria I have developed in my process of trusting what comes to me in regression is when it is something I would never have imagined.

When David rejoined me we made straight for a little shop which has a few shelves of books. The one on the Maya people that I opened had a section on animals, and lo and behold, to my complete amazement, it said that at the height of the great Mayan civilisation there had been brown bears inhabiting the region! Suddenly my story appeared not to be quite so far fetched after all.

It is much said that the Maya were a bloodthirsty, warring people, but that was not at all the feeling that I obtained while meditating at the *Cenote*. I felt enveloped in an immense sense of calm and, though of course I may be quite wrong, this peace seemed to me like a peace inherited from past centuries.

Another thing that I found hard to swallow was the claim that the winners of the *Pelota* game got sacrificed. At least the guide book said that that was the claim; others believed it to be the losers! How was I to know what really happened? All I had to go on was my own feelings and, while being pretty sure that Christopher had died young in that life, my feeling was that it had been an accident.

But by the time I sat down to write up this section, I had another tool at my disposal, having just done a "Way of the Shaman" weekend. I had bought myself a drumming tape and was now using it at home to practise journeying. Asking myself the question about what really happened in the Mayan ball game, the answer that came first to my head was Simon Buxton's "Journey on it!". He had taught us how to journey to the Lowerworld, to the Upperworld, how to find a power animal for ourselves and for others, how to ask a question.... So I took my question to the Upperworld, where I encountered an elderly Mayan who said that he had been my uncle when I had been married to Lawrence. He told me to trust my own feelings, and that the Maya had been far too interested in learning to want to be bloodthirsty or warring, although they had been strong and had needed to defend themselves when attacked by, for instance, the Toltecs. Well, as I say, I cannot prove it, but until anyone else does, we are all entitled to our individual view on the matter!

EXERCISE

Is there some place in the world that you are really keen to visit? What's been stopping you? Money? Time?

Has it occurred to you that the reason for your desire could be some past-life connection with the place? It may not be at all necessary for you to uncover that, but it is probably important for you to achieve your ambition of going there.

Make up your mind that you are going to go there. Buy a guide book and start looking into the various ways of getting there. Even set a date if you possibly can. Once you have a plan clearly set in your mind, all the obstacles to it should start falling away. And when you're there, relax, enjoy yourself, and take lots of photographs!

XVII DISCOVERING ONE'S LIFE PLAN

PART ONE - MY WRITING

The world is a great teacher, a constant guide and source of inspiration. That is the reason why man is placed in the world. Every bird, every animal, every tree, mountain and star and each tiny worm has a lesson for man, if he has but the thirst to learn. These make the world a veritable university for man; it is but a Gurukul (a school for spiritual learning), where he is a pupil from birth to death.

Sathya Sai Baba, Thought for the Day, 26 July 2003

The subject of discovering one's Life Plan merits a whole book, but you are going to have to wait a bit for that one!

My own story in this regard is slightly strange, since right through both school and university I was absolutely no good at all at writing. Obviously the fact of having been brainwashed into believing myself to be stupid did not help here, and it was not until I got a job in which I was passionately interested (recruiting teachers for Africa) that I finally found I could express myself on paper. However, another thirty years passed before the idea of writing as a serious occupation took hold of me.

When Christopher was ten we went to Sierra Leone for Christmas as we felt it to be important for his black identity. We had a Sierra Leonean friend who was a mature student at Hull University, and he kindly offered us the loan of the house he had built for his family in Waterloo, twenty miles from Freetown. My old friend Peter Sarpong, now Archbishop of Kumasi, also invited us to Ghana for ten days, and I was so moved by our West African experiences that I wrote a little article about it. When Lawrence read the article he said that I should write a book, but I replied that I didn't think that I had a book in me.

Then another two and a half years went by and, as a result of attending my first Edgar Cayce conference, I sent for a past life reading from Aron Abrahamsen in America. In addition to outlining five of my previous lives, he said that I had come this time "partly as a writer - to disseminate information on the spiritual life". This came as a big surprise, but within a month we happened to be on holiday in Spain, where I began to reflect on my life as a nun in that country and consequently the idea for this book was concieved.

It took me three years to do the research and write the first version of the book, and my teaching gradually dwindled of its own accord to give me the time I was needing. During this time my sister Philippa met her twin soul and in due course they managed to get together. That stimulated my interest in twinsoulship, I did a lot of research on that subject too, and in 1997, after this book had narrowly missed being accepted, *CORDS THAT CANNOT BE BROKEN – A Study of Twin Souls* was published by Regency Press, under the pseudonym of Judith Merville.

After that I returned to this book, but when it had got far too long and again been rejected, I shelved it and wrote a book about the Life Plan, which also narrowly missed getting accepted by a major American publisher early in 2003. So then that book got shelved for the time being while I sat down seriously to rewrite this book from scratch, giving it a completely new title. My disappointment of 1995 (when I had first had a very useful interview at Thorsons, and then Foulsham had wanted to publish it but not been allowed by their committee to take on as many New Age books as they had been hoping), was replaced by a feeling of relief that a book which I would no longer want to own had escaped publication. Usually our helpers on "the other side" know better than we do about timing!

PART TWO - BACK TO ATLANTIS

Aron Abrahamsen told me about a life I had had in Atlantis as a teacher of creative writing, but that seemed very remote, not only time-wise. All the attempts I had ever made at writing poetry were pathetic, and when writing prose, metaphors and so on never came to me naturally. Although we often retain abilities and talents from lifetime to lifetime, we also vary them regularly, and I gradually realised that where my talent lay this time was in logical thinking and putting things down on paper in a well ordered fashion, rather than writing, say, a novel. So I decided to look for a life that related more to that than did the Atlantean one which Abrahamsen had given me.

Nowadays I occasionally have flashbacks to previous lives, and in this case I glimpsed a completely different life in Atlantis in which I was living and working with the man that I called Giuseppe in the Ticino. I felt sure that the work I did was more in line with the type of writing that I am doing now than the Abrahamsen life was, but did not have the opportunity to go into it at a workshop.

The regression tape that Edwin Courtenay had made has served me on a number of occasions, but I have found getting to Atlantis particularly difficult. The tape helped me, however, to elaborate a little bit on my flashback and I saw some glass pyramids which appeared to be sort of hospitals.

I did not feel that I obtained enough information to be able to write about that life in my normal fashion, but neither did I feel that that mattered. I have been told that monogamy was rare in Atlantis, and the feeling I got was that, though Giuseppe and I were deeply connected and partners in both senses, we had both had previous lovers and it was not quite the same sort of "romantic" match that it was much later in the Ticino. We obviously took our work very seriously, and I felt that we were pioneering something. Giuseppe seemed to be the creative one, while I was the scientific one, who was documenting everything very methodically in a way that would make it useful for posterity. We were obviously an important partnership, while my present daughter Alice (who in her present life is an exceptionally methodical person) seemed to be a colleague.

PART THREE - MY LIFE PLAN

Training in regression therapy seemed to be the logical step following all my research and writing and, once I had decided to do it, I wondered why I had not thought of it sooner. But I am also a firm believer that things happen when the time is right. All the jobs that I have ever had – working for the Third World, editing, motherhood, language teaching – felt right for me at the time, but it was not until I had given everything else up in favour of my writing and therapy that I finally felt fully myself.

However, when books get rejected and clients fail to keep their appointments (or do not make them in the first place!), it is not always easy to keep faith that one is adhering to one's Life Plan. I solved this problem for myself by making an appointment with the *Nadi Gruha* in Bangalore in March 2002.

The *Nadi Gruha* is the present guardian of some six thousand-year old prophecies that have been handed down from generation to generation in the same family. These prophecies, which are written on palm leaves, concern people "who would be working around the avatar Sathya Sai Baba in the twentieth and twenty-first centuries" and, if you get an appointment with him, the *Nadi* finds you in them. My appointment was on 14 March and, after beginning by telling me the main astrological influences during each period of my life, he read from the relevant palm leaf "and you will be given this information at the age of sixty-two years one month and five days". Exactly right, and everything that he then told me about my present life to date was mind-bogglingly accurate. When he asked about the date of my husband's retirement and I replied "2004", he looked surprised and said "No, it should be next year.". Four months later the University of Hull announced a major financial crisis and David, to whom I had not mentioned that bit of the session, decided to retire a year early!

I did not mention my writing to the *Nadi*, but after a bit he said to me "Three books. One's published already, isn't it? Well, the next one will be published before you're sixty-five and the third before you're seventy-one." I wait and see about the Life Plan book, but the *Nadi* was right about this one, and our predicted "retirement move to the countryside" has now taken place. He also told me a tiny bit about four of my previous lives – one, for instance, as a language teacher in the Mediterranean area, which explained my interest in Mediterranean languages this time round, and one in India as an expert in Vedanta and Non-Dualist Philosophy. This latter, he explained, was the reason for my writing about different philosophies in my third book (the Life Plan one). My regression therapy was also part of the predictions, and the foretold year of my death still gives me plenty of time in which to complete all my work.

QUESTIONS

When our younger son was only about nineteen and had just begun to realise his dream by starting to do his degree in America on a basketball scholarship, he was asked in an interview for his College magazine what advice he would give to young people. His reply was very straightforward and simple "Find something to be passionate about.". Certainly the basketball was Christopher's salvation following a very fraught childhood.

Are you passionate about your work? If you are, you are probably well in touch with the Life Plan that you made before you came in this time.

If you find your work tedious and are only doing it to earn a living, have you a spare time activity about which you are passionate? If so, have you ever thought of making it your livelihood? Would it be feasible? It might be worth exploring! And don't be put off by apparent obstacles. Obstacles and challenges help us to develop and grow.

Are you quite content with your life as it is just now? If not, have a really good look at what you would like to change and then do something about it. There are always things we can do for ourselves, and equally there is always help and advice available. So just ask!

Do you feel you are realising your full potential? If not, and if you feel unsure about what you might be good at (or even if there is anything that you are good at!), keep trying different things. There is sure to be some hidden talent inside, and you may surprise yourself. Although they can both be useful, you do not need a clairvoyant reading or a past life regression to uncover your latent gifts; just follow your inclinations and practice listening to your inner voice, and then (particularly important) learn to trust it.

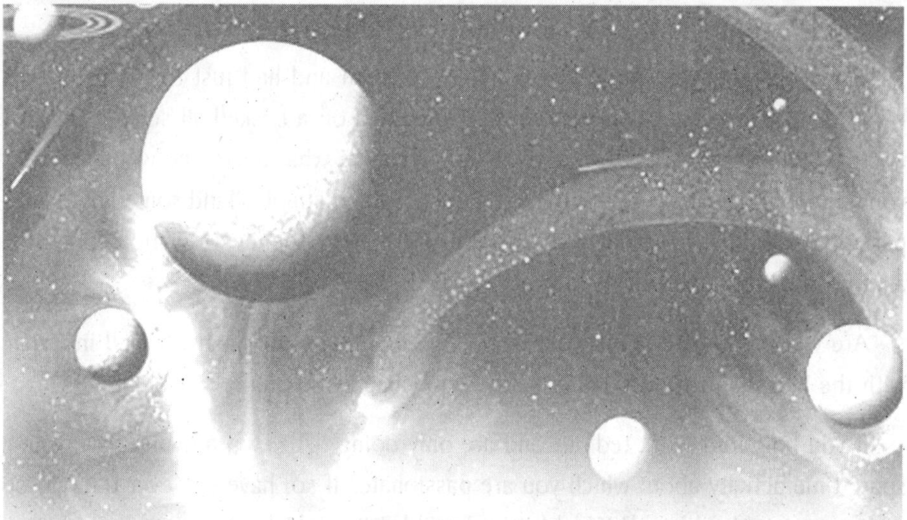

XVIII NOTHING THAT WE DO IS EVER WASTED

PART ONE - MARCH 2003

Yet another rejection from a publisher, but by now I was already used to disappointment. On the other hand, no longer did it make me feel "The book's no good. I'm no good. All that work is for nothing." So many people had seen the book's outline, read one or more of the chapters, and confirmed my own feeling that it was bringing through some worth while information. In any case the publisher's email had been an encouraging one, urging me not to give up. So this time I moved quite quickly through the initial reaction of "How am I ever going to do it?" and reminded myself that another two books were part of the Life Plan read for me the previous year by the *Nadi Gruha.*

It so happened that the following weekend we were holding a meeting of the Integral Regression Network, and a slot was allotted for those wanting to swap regressions. My dear friend Katarina also had an issue which seemed to need dealing with quickly, so the two of us paired up eagerly. With the skill developed through her Woolger training, combined with great sensitivity to the body given her by T'ai Chi and Qui Gong teaching, Katarina soon had me lying down on the mat. "Where's the charge around all this writing business?", she asked me. "What are you feeling?... What are the words that come?...."

"What a waste! My life's work lost!". Words that seemed to come not from me, but through me, as though from elsewhere.

"And when those words come, where in your body do you feel them?"

I pointed immediately to my chest, and almost instantly the feeling of heaviness in my chest went straight through to my back and became that pain – that chronic pain between my shoulder blades for which I had for so long been seeking a cure.....

PART TWO - ASTRONOMER ROYAL

CHAPER ONE - THE BULLY

"My back, my back. Oh, the pain in my back!" I realised immediately that, when that brute pushed me, I had landed on a jagged rock, which was now digging right through the flesh next to my left shoulder blade. Blood must be seeping through my clothes, I reflected, and I had no clean ones to put on. Father would be angry. He would think I had provoked Vincent to a fight, but in fact I had done nothing of the sort. It was just that he was jealous of me. Jealous of my brain, which was better than his. If "better" was really the right word to use. I wasn't at all sure that it was. Just different. I was different. Not different simply because Mother had died when I was six and I had no-one but Father to care for me, but because I had never been interested in the usual boyish games and pranks. "Look at Jules. He's just staring at the stars again!" the other boys of our village would say to one another. "What's so fascinating about the stars, Jules?"

"I want to understand them," I would reply.

"Understand? What is there to understand? They're just there. God put them there when he made the world, to light us at night. The moon isn't as bright as the sun, so we need the stars too. That's all there is to it."

"No, that's not all there is to it," I would reply. "They move, you know. I want to understand what makes them move, and whether there's a pattern to it. I want to know...." But the other boys would run off without waiting to hear about everything I wanted to know. They ran off laughing at my idiocy. Now and again, however, I would overhear one of them say "He's not really an idiot, you know. He can do sums. Big, complicated sums. Not just adding up six and three like my father taught me."

"And he's persuaded Father Damien to teach him to write," added another.

But red-faced, burly Vincent had had it in for me ever since that day when I had corrected his grammar. Of course, it had been silly of me, but it offended my ears to hear our beautiful language massacred. And even now, four or five years later, he didn't speak any better. "T'es un beau imbécile!" he had yelled as he, threw me backwards on to this sharp rock, and tore my slate from my hand. That treasured slate on which I had been plotting the course of an unusual star which seemed to have a reddish tinge. "He should know that "beau" changes to "bel" when it's in front of a vowel."[1]

CHAPTER TWO - PROPER TUITION

I'd done it! Thanks to Father Damien's recognition of my special ability at reading and writing, and to his sympathy for my desire to understand something about the stars, a benefactor had been found for me, and now I seemed to be truly on my way to realising my dream. Father had been a bit reluctant at first. He had always assumed that I would just follow him into being a shepherd. He couldn't imagine any other way of living. He never talked very much – the pain of losing both Mother and my baby sister in childbirth obviously still affected him so deeply, and the sheep never needed many words – but he had always led me to understand that I should follow in his footsteps. Of course it was from Father that I had first formed the habit of gazing at the stars. When I was little he never liked to leave me alone in the cottage if he was still at work after dark, and the sheep never ragged me like the other boys in the village did.

"But how could I ever pay for him to travel to the town? And anyway a teacher would need paying too," Father had protested to Father Damien. So Father Damien had made enquiries about a benefactor. "And later," he had explained to Father, "when he's a bit older, he could go to Paris and study at the Sorbonne. That would enable him to get a well paid job one day and support you in your old age." That was the thought that had triggered Father's agreement . He loved the sheep dearly, but I had always suspected that he had a secred fear of one day being too old or too

1. Vincent would obviously not have been speaking twenty-first century French, but I have put his remark into a modern idiom since my mediaeval French is a bit rusty!

sick to care for them. "Yes," I thought to myself, "if I learnt so much at the Sorbonne that I could eventually earn a living from it, taking care of Father would always be a priority for me."

Monsieur du Val was old. Over forty, I believe. He wore a black cap and black spats and a severe expression, but underneath that he had a heart of gold. He taught other little classes of boys as well, but they were all older than me and he thought I might not fit in with them. So instead he took me under his wing, even giving me his attic room to sleep in. I missed Father of course, and the sheep, and Father Damien, but I was so eager to learn that none of that seemed important. Or anyway I cut myself off from it. Whenever little feelings of homesickness came to me, I just pushed them away and absorbed my mind in Monsiur du Val's last lesson.

My first big surprise had been the discovery that there <u>were</u> men who had studied the stars. Men who even <u>understood</u> something about their movements! No longer did I have to struggle on my own to discover whether there was some sort of pattern. Now I could stop wondering if everything that happened was quite random and begin to learn about the patterns. I would even be taught about the stars' relationship to us – how they affected our characters, our moods and so on. Amazing!

But there were other things to be learnt too. My new teacher soon explained to me that, if I was to go on to study at the Sorbonne, I would firstly have to master Latin, which everybody spoke there, and secondly gain a really good grasp of Mathematics, learn to write poetry and study the music of the Troubadours. For Theology he sent me to the Friars a few streets away.

Monsieur du Val lived alone. "It would have been difficult," he commented, "to support a wife and children on a teacher's wages, and anyway it might not have left me enough time for my own studies." So before too long he and I became almost like a little family. At home, while the other boys ragged me for being "different", I had sometimes envied their positions in large families. My father's parents had died soon after I was born and he was an only child, and my mother's family lived too far away to visit us, so I was at least used to being an only child with nothing but a father.

Monsieur du Val was a hard taskmaster, but I was eager to learn and he was nearly always satisfied with my efforts. Sometimes I found things very hard to understand, but he assured me that it was wasn't my fault, that these facts were complicated even for those much older than myself. The most exciting part of all the lessons was when we went out after dark to the Green, carrying my teacher's measuring instrument. We looked at the sky with it and then noted down our findings and compared them with those of the previous expedition. This instrument was Monsieur du Val's pride and joy. Gradually I learnt, with the aid of this instrument, which were the stars that most influenced our characters and so on. They were the ones which I had already noticed at home in my village seemed to move the most, and they were known as "wanderers" on account of their strange movements.

My teacher had a housekeeper, who came in regularly, swept the floors, cooked wonderful soups and casseroles, and baked bread for us. Never before had I been so well fed. But she scolded me if the few belongings I kept in my attic room were not carefully folded or stacked, or if there were crumbs on the floor from the left over crust of delicious bread that I had sneaked upstairs with me. "Mice!" she would scream. "You'll attract the mice!"

CHAPTER THREE - CAREER

The Sorbonne! What could be further removed from the village in which I had always been regarded as an oddity than this great seat of learning where so many people had some of the same interests as I had? Though younger than most of them, I had even made one or two friends who were near me in age, and, when I wasn't seeking odd jobs to pay for my board and lodging, we would have truly fascinating discussions. Monsieur du Val told me that he had persuaded the University authorities to let me study there *gratis*, but I sometimes wondered whether in reality he was secretly paying for it himself. Anyway, whatever happened, I would not let him down. He would be proud of me when the day eventually came for the award of my *Licence.*

To the subjects in which my dear teacher had so diligently versed me were now added further disciplines. Ancient Greek was important for my continued studies of Theology. But no subject interested me half as much as my studies of the stars, and in that I soon became known as the student with the most profound knowledge.

Before my journey to Paris, my benefactor had paid for me to travel home to spend a brief spell with Father. It was wonderful to see him again, but it grieved me to notice how he had aged. Within a year of my becoming a student at the Sorbonne, news was brought to me of my father's death. This was a terrible blow, as I had always imagined myself in due course bringing him to live with me. But I could not allow grief to spoil my studies. Instead I threw myself into them with increased fervour. My benefactor had also died recently, and the little town where Monsieur du Val lived was too far away to visit regularly. So now – apart from my fellow students – I was completely on my own. Often I had to work far into the night because the end of the afternoon, when classes were over, was the time to seek work to pay for my room.

Degree day in due course came, and with it a cherished visit from Monsieur du Val. How proud he was! "Well, it's all thanks to you," I said, but he simply shrugged his shoulders and patted me on the back affectionately. "Now you can earn yourself a living as, say, astrologer to a noble family. In the Loire Valley perhaps?"

******

A wonderful life? My dear teacher's words rang in my ears. Yes, it was wonderful in many ways. I had comfort and security in beautiful surroundings, but so much about château life bored me. The wine was good, certainly, but I had to be careful not to drink so much that it would cloud my thinking. Also, it wasn't always easy to find enough time for the thinking and writing. So much of each day was taken up by ladies who wanted their birth charts composing. Ladies who weren't at all interested in understanding the subtle influences of the stars that they were under, but who simply wanted to know whether their current lover was really compatible with them, or whether a good husband lay in their future. Sometimes I would try to explain to one of these good ladies that, for instance, Uranus, her ruler, had just moved out of her sign and into Pisces, and that she could consequently really trust and flow with her intuition, but she simply would not want to hear that. Instead she would go on insisting that her lover knew best and she must obey his every command or suggestion. It got more than a little tedious at times!

My own research had to be done in snatches at often too long intervals. It was also difficult to find time to write down all the results of my studies, which was a pity as I had long since come to regard this as my life's work. At least my salary was fairly handsome. Consequently I could always hang on in the back of my mind to the idea of being able to save enough to take early "retirement". It would not be a proper retirement of course. It would simply enable me to devote all my days to what I had come to regard as my real work – the work that I could leave for posterity.

CHAPER FOUR - THE LOSS

It was nearly finished. I was getting on in years, my sight was failing (my precious sight!), and I was becoming very hard of hearing. But none of that really mattered, for I had finally almost achieved my ambition. My luxurious château days on the banks of the tranquil Loire river seemed very distant now, and I had made a home of the little garret room which had proved to be a perfect refuge for the pursuit of my studies. The title that the King had so kindly bestowed on me gave me status rather than duties, but that very status made it necessary for me to avoid the public eye if I was to have the time and space for my work.

It had taken many years for me to solve the puzzles that had begun to pose themselves to me as soon as I had first begun to get seriously involved in these enthralling studies. Not that it would ever be possible for one man to solve all the puzzles. I had had to be selective. I had decided to concentrate all my efforts on the movements of Saturn and to leave study of the other planets and constellations to colleagues. Now at last I had completed my research and had only to finish writing it all up before depositing the document in the Sorbonne library.

******

It was done! With my eyes straining in the dim light, I gave the work a final read through before rolling up the scroll carefully and tenderly. My next step was to walk the comparatively short distance to the Sorbonne library. I was not particularly interested in fame, but it was rewarding to think that the fruits of my many years of work could now benefit future generations of students of the subject so very dear to my heart. Slowly and gingerly I descended the stairs. Out in the street I turned in the direction of my beloved library. That library in which during my student years I had spent so many long hours. Dusk was drawing near, the light was slowly fading. My hearing was not as good as it used to be, but nevertheless I suddenly heard a shriek of delight as a young lad streaked past me on the right. He shouted to some friends, who all came running, and then I noticed them gather round to look at something that the first boy was holding in his left hand. "Oh no! It cannot be. It is. It's my scroll. My precious treatise. My life's work!" My right hand went to my right pocket, and sure enough it was empty. I yelled at the top of my voice "You can't take that. It has to be deposited in the library." But I was too late. They laughed, ran on a few more yards, then stopped. They unrolled the precious treatise, passed it between them for perusal, laughed again, and then began to tear it into little pieces. I screamed louder still and tried to run, but it is impossible for an old man like me to run. By the time I reached the spot where they had stopped, they had rounded a corner. Pieces of parchment were lying on the ground, some were floating in a dirty puddle. I turned the corner as fast as I could, desperately hoping to salvage a tiny part of my work, but the lads were already completely out of sight. Still more pieces of the treatise were lying on the ground. I stooped to pick them up, but the pain in my legs and back as I did so was almost as acute as the pain in my heart. "Too late," I said to myself. "It's lost. My entire life's work is wasted." In grief too profound for tears I turned and walked slowly home.

******

The staff in the hospital were quite a kindly bunch, but it was nevertheless a cheerless place. Only a few months had passed since the loss of my scroll, but I had nothing left to live for. My lungs had already been weak, and now they were getting even weaker. The nurses were unable to tempt me with food, the doctor felt my pulse and turned away. Now I was free to go. Free to leave this poor tired body for ever. Gently, painlessly, I floated out of it. There was a sort of tunnel and I could see a light at the end of it. The next thing I knew I was being whooshed through the tunnel, and who was there to greet me when I come out into that marvellous light but my first teacher. My beloved Monsieur du Val, his now young looking face wreathed in smiles and exuding the love which on Earth he had never really expressed openly. "I've let you down," I sobbed. "The treatise got lost all through some young ignorant lads' silly pranks. My entire life's work is wasted."

"No work is ever wasted," replied my dear teacher. "Let me take you straight to the Akashic Library." Instantly we were there. The librarian was already prepared. The moment we arrived, he took a book from the shelf. A book beautifully bound in dark red leather. He handed it to me and I opened it. I could not believe my eyes. It was my scroll, my precious treatise! Tears rolled down my cheeks, but through them I could just make out the lettering, the numbers.... and all of it appeared not in my own spidery scrawl, but in the most beautiful handwriting imaginable. As for the pages, rather than being dull parchment, they were shining white and illumined with pictures of beautiful bright stars and planets. It was too good to be true. "You see," said my dear teacher again, "no worth while work that we do is ever wasted. Here in this etheric library your book is preserved for ever. And now that you're back here with us, you might want to write and study some more, as well as give classes in astronomy and astrology."

My joy was indescribable. "Study and teach? Can I really do that in Paradise?"

"Of course you can. Gradually you'll remember about the sort of things we get up to over here. But now it's time to look at some of the other aspects of this life of yours that has just ended. Let the librarian return your book to the shelf for the time being and come along with me..... Right. So how are you feeling now?"

"Well, happy of course, now that I've seen that beautiful book, but the pain in my back is troubling me again. It was first caused by a wound when I was a boy."

"Show me exactly where it is.... Ah, that's your heart chakra area. Are you aware that you closed down your heart when your mother died? It's a natural response, when pain is intense, to cut ourselves off from it; but doing that does not really serve us in the long run. If you look back over that whole life, you will see that every time something sad happened to you, you coped with it by retreating into your head. Your good brain and your passion for astronomy were simultaneously your salvation and your downfall. You see, feeling is one of our greatest teachers. Only by feeling grief as well as joy can we learn compassion, and compassion is the best tool we have for helping others. Can you think now of any lives you have lived in which compassion figured highly in your make-up? Can you remember how it enabled you to do good?"

"Yes, yes, I can. There must have been many. It's just that this time I don't think my work would have gone so well if I had allowed myself to wallow in grief. But I see what you mean.... Feeling grief isn't quite the same as wallowing in it uncontrolledly."

"Well done – you've got the idea! Now that you've seen the two sides of the coin, we can proceed to the three beings of light who can help you with your Life Review, and then think about where you can move on to next."

******

"Phew!" I said to Katarina, the tears still flowing. "No wonder, when my books get rejected, that I have such strong feelings about my work being wasted. But wasn't that lovely? The confirmation about all work being worth while anyway."

"It was. It was beautiful! So what do you think you have to learn now, as Ann, from that character's experiences?"

"Well, it seems obvious that in this life I've had to learn to open my heart and let myself really feel pain."

"But have you? Have you really done that, or is there something still protecting this area here?"

"Maybe......"

"So what colour is it, this pain just here?"

"It's dark red."

"Right. So let's talk to it then, this dark red pain? What is it that you're protecting

Ann from?..... What are you preventing her from feeling?......." And so Katarina carried on with her questions, until in due course the dark red "thing" changed into a little black demon. Then I could see that I no longer needed a demon's protection, that it was time to let go of it.

Also, I resolved from now on to take more seriously Sai Baba's constant exhortation to work without attachment to the fruits. He had taken from my hand the letter in which I had asked Him to help me to remember that I had handed over all the details of my life to Him, yet again and again since then that little ego had crept back in. I did not think that the French astronomer had had an ego problem – his only reason for wanting to deposit his work in the Sorbonne library before he died was to hand on the fruits of his research to future students – but I needed to question myself on my real reasons now for seeking acceptance from a publisher. Was it purely so as to help others through my books, or was it to prove myself to, for instance, my father? A bit of both no doubt! So I obviously still needed to show that I really meant what I had said in that letter to Baba.

PART THREE - CONNECTING WITH MY FATHER

A couple of months had passed since the regression which had made me feel so much better about my writing, and Lawrence, who had been learning the skill of divination with the great African shaman Malidoma Patrice Somé, was keen to try and find out what was causing the blockage to publication. He had already asked on my behalf and been given the answer that my books still needed more work doing on them. This seemed to me to make a lot of sense, and so I decided to shelve the Life Plan, which clairvoyants had told me was going to be THE book, for the time being and embark on a complete rewrite of my first book. Now I asked Lawrence to do another divination in my presence, and I found the experience completely fascinating.

To Lawrence's first question, the answer that came was "No blockage, but the next step should be to make a connection with your father, who is now coming in as a guide and wanting to help you with your work." Hard for me to believe, since I had always imagined to myself how much my father would have disapproved of everything I was doing! However, a whole three years earlier my friend Marie had also told me in a palm reading that my father was coming in as one of my guides. At that time the fear with which I still remembered him had made me unwilling to take the idea on board, and I had consequently pushed the information right to the back of my mind.

But now the instructions came through Lawrence very clearly: I was to go my parents' grave, put some *vibhuti* there, dig up a little bit of soil from nearby, mix it with water and get someone to anoint my back with it, particularly in the heart chakra area where I get most of the pain. How good the spirits are at organising one's life for one! My parents were buried in a London cemetery, and the very next weekend I had already booked a train there in order to spend two nights with Alice prior to setting off for France for a workshop with some fellow Woolger graduates. This would give me the opportunity to go to the graveyard, and clearly there could be no more perfect an environment than Le Moulin for a little healing ceremony of that nature. I also knew that my friends would be among the best equipped people to help me to turn around the false image that I had held of my father for over sixty years. False because, until we become enlightened, we are unable while on Earth to be our true selves – to let the *atma* (our true being – our soul, which is part of the universal soul) shine out fully for all to see. Obviously my father was now doing that in the spirit world.

My dear brother John knew which London cemetery our parents' grave was in, and he gave me directions as to its whereabouts to the best of his ability. I thought to myself "Well, if Daddy wants me to bring *vibhuti*, he must be in league with Sai Baba, and surely between the two of them I'll be guided to the grave." But no! I asked and asked, I wandered and wandered, checking every gravestone that looked as though it might conceivably be of the right age; I sat down and put myself into meditation mode waiting for a sign.... Eventually I gave up. My frustration was alleviated by a voice in my head saying "It doesn't matter. At least you've tried." So I made for an inviting horse chestnut tree, dug a small hole for my *vibhuti*, and came slowly away with my little pot of soil, a strong sense of angelic presences, and a deep feeling of peace.

The flight to Toulouse with my friends who were gathering for the workshop at Le Moulin, Kris and Steve's wonderful guest house, was pleasant. It was the third year in succession that we were meeting there, and so now it felt like coming home. And what a powerful week it was! My friends were all excellent therapists and, when a little group has studied together and come to understand and trust one another, the most profound things can happen. Though only Kris had been consciously seeking it, this turned out to be an entire week of spirit releasement. Mine were of course the young soldier and his friends (of Section III) who were all still waiting to hear that the War had ended.

But a few days before that session I had the opportunity to tell my friends about

Lawrence's divination and my need to change my view of and feelings towards my father. They understood my difficulties perfectly, and I started there and then trying to visualise him not with the severe expression so familiar to me, but looking calm and happy with a loving smile on his face. It was far from easy, however, on account of my negative memories. At one point I expressed a desire to look for a clairvoyant artist to paint me a picture of him, but then I remembered my resolution to give up relying on clairvoyants; and on my return home Lawrence echoed my friends' reminders that we all have latent clairvoyant ability.

After five days of very intense work we needed a weekend of holiday, and this year the spot chosen was the charming cliff-built village of Rocamadour in the Dordogne – a pilgrimage centre on account of its particularly beautiful Black Madonna. (This statue itself is twelfth century, but, though most Christians are probably unaware of it, the concept of the Black Madonna actually pre-dates Christianity.) We stopped en route for a picnic on the banks of the river Lot and, though it was still only May – some of us felt warm enough (or mad enough) to swim. What bliss! The next day, after paying the Black Madonna our respects and exploring Rocamadour, we descended into the Gouffre de Padirac and had a one-kilometre boat ride on the fifteen-kilometre underground river. We were all equally moved by the majestic "palaces" and the clarity and purity of the river water. Esmeralda had the presence of mind to refill her empty water bottle in this magical river, and it was with some of that "nectar" that I later mixed the soil for my little healing ceremony. Had my father been with us in his physical body, he would have had to stay in the café with Grace, who was awaiting a hip replacement, and Justina, who was pregnant, rather than following the rest of us down and up all those slippery steps. So it was nice now to think of him no longer being restricted in his physical activities, and I again invited him to join me.

The return journey to Le Moulin the next day was also enjoyable, but in St. Cirq Lapopie, the enchanting village where we stopped for a coffee, we learnt that the French were continuing their recently adopted habit of striking on Tuesdays. This meant that our plane would not be departing the next day, so alternative arrangements had hastily to be made. Phone calls to the airport revealed a choice of either staying an extra day or leaving that very evening. Since many of us had a number of client appointments and I had Christopher arrived home from France and a wonderful concert in York to go to, a decision was reluctantly made, and somehow or other we managed not to let the change of plan mar the closing of the workshop. Time was short, yet into it we fitted our packing, another of Steve's delicious dinners, and a final sharing.

Since she had both released my attached soldier spirits and provided the very special water for making my graveyard mud, I asked Esmeralda, when my turn had come, to spread the mixture (to which I added some *vibhuti*) on my back. She afterwards invited the whole group to join in giving me healing. Never have I felt more tenderly wrapped in all-embracing love. As I lay there comfortably basking in the strong energy coming through my dear friends' hands, I reflected that my father must surely be pleased to see me now receiving what he – through no real fault of his own – had been unable to give me during his lifetime. I further reflected that, even if my backache was never cured, it was a minor affliction compared with the inconvenience and discomfort he had suffered for forty-seven years following the polio which had almost taken his life during his first year at Cambridge.

A few weeks later I went to London again – this time for my first shamanic workshop, which (believe it or not!) took place only two tube stops from the family cemetery. My efficient daughter gave me the telephone number of Brent Council, who were able immediately to give me all the details about the grave, and I went straight there after the workshop finished. I still had to hunt for quite a while, as the graves did not appear to be in any order, but having the plot number made all the difference. When I finally located the grave, I was not at all surprised at having missed it before. Both the upright cross which had been erected in memory of one-month old Mary Merivale in 1893, and the flat stone inscribed with my parents' names, had broken in half, and much of the writing was covered up by a bush. But finding it made me feel much more able to make the connection with my father.

So I asked whether he approved of my having just done the shamanic workshop and received a very positive answer and encouragement to do more of such studies. I then asked whether we should do anything about the broken cross and stone, and the voice in my head replied "Don't worry about it. All material things perish in due course. That's the way of the world." I then dug a little hole and put some *vibhuti* into the grave itself, bringing the soil I had removed back with me, together with a little branch from the bush for myself and one for each of my siblings.

A few months later two things happened. Firstly, I was afflicted one day with a migraine and rested until it was better. I was by now trying to make a regular habit of tuning in to my father, and as I was lying in bed the name Abdul flashed into my head apparently from nowhere. I had just finished reading the autobiography of the great spiritual teacher John Bennett, who spent a lot of time in Turkey and learnt that language well, and almost simultaneously with the name coming into my mind

I got a very clear picture of a delightful turbaned man with twinkly eyes and a grey beard. I asked whether, now that he was my guide, my father wanted to appear to me not as Stephen with the severe expression that had so scared me in my childhood, but rather as the personality of one of his previous incarnations. The reply to that question was a very clear "Yes".

Secondly, the next time that I saw Lawrence and he performed some treatment on my back, he noticed a real change. Loving as he does to tease me, he said "I'm sorry Ann – since you never want change – to have to inform you of a definite improvement..." We then discussed the fact that it is often much easier to recognise in others than in oneself a resistance to being healed. Reasons for this can be many: a wife who fears that her husband will cease to care for her once she is well, the desire of someone who was undervalued in childhood to prove himself "cleverer than the therapist".... Certainly, I reflected, I had frequently observed in my clients an unwillingness to get better, but, as I explained to Lawrence, whenever I had asked myself why I might not want deep down to get better, no satisfactory answer had ever been forthcoming. Maybe we human beings tend too much to request answers, and Sai Baba says that if we were completely happy all the time we would have no need to call upon God. Since the spine is all about support – the thing that my father failed to give me when I was a child – Lawrence is sure that the improvement coincided with my new relationship with him as a now more enlightened spirit.

QUESTIONS

1. Do you have experience of doing something that you subsequently felt was a waste of time and effort? What did you learn from it? Keep looking until you have found something. Now can you appreciate that everything happens for a reason? However, we do not necessarily always understand the reason straight away. Go outside and look all around you. Think about how much you can see. Now imagine yourself as a bird flying overhead and compare its view with your own. See the difference? Down here we can only see a tiny part of the overall pattern, but trust that eventually you will get a view that is at least as good as the bird's, and probably better.

2. Do you give up easily when you fail to achieve something, or do you believe in perseverance? Think about the achievements that have given you the most satisfaction in your life. Were they the ones that more or less landed in your lap, or the ones for which you worked really hard?

Now can you think of something that you really wanted at one point in your life but in fact had to wait for? Can you see a reason why it was better that it came later? Does that help you appreciate that there is a right timing for everything? And that our guides have a better view of the overall picture and so can be of help in getting the timing right?

XIX
COMPENSATING FOR PAST LIFE TRAUMA

PART ONE - "ANN, YOU'RE NEVER HERE!"

"Ann, *you're* never here!" commented two different friends independently when I announced my departure for our first workshop at Kris' guest house in France in May 2001, about a month after obtaining my Woolger diploma. It was true, I had been travelling a great deal, both with David when he was invited to work in Geneva and when we went to visit Christopher in America, and on my own when I went off on pilgrimages to Sai Baba's ashram or on one-week workshops with Roger Woolger. In fact we had travelled considerably as a family throughout our married life. Astrologers had told me that, though none of the five of us was a Sagittarian, we did as a family have a lot of Sagittarius in our charts.

The graduate weekend at which I was awarded my Woolger diploma was held at Hazelwood House in Devon. David had travelled down with me to Devon and we were able to share a room and walk the dog in the large grounds during the breaks. The hilly countryside in that part of Devon is dramatic, and I saw it as beautiful objectively, yet I found myself unable to appreciate it in the way that I appreciated Dartmoor. When I tried to analyse my feelings, just one word came into my head: claustrophobia. I talked about it to David, but he did not share this feeling at all.

Then I suddenly remembered a previous visit to the very same area a few years previously. On that occasion David and I had been with a group of people who were looking for a property that would be suitable for a spiritual community – a sort of alternative retirement home. There was at the time an old farmhouse for sale near Kingsbridge and, when we all went to have a look, though I could see that the place had a lot going for it, I found myself overcome by this very same, inexplicable feeling of claustrophobia and could not imagine myself being comfortable living there.

By the time of the visit to Hazelwood, of course I knew enough about reincarnation to understand that there was an explanation for my feeling claustrophobic in that particular part of Devon. Since I no longer had the remotest intention of ever going to live in that part of the world, I did not know whether I needed to access the relevant past life, whether I could access it if I tried, or whether it would surface of its own accord.

PART TWO - A DEVONSHIRE LADY

CHAPTER ONE - THE WEDDING

My wedding day had come, and I was too excited and nervous to eat the breakfast put before me, despite my mother's remonstrations. I had of course tried on the dress when it was in the final stages of stitching, but now I could not wait to put it on and make sure yet again that it was perfect. My younger sister Camilla, who as bridesmaid was to be dressed in a beautiful shade of rose pink, and Mary our servant, helped with the fastenings and then did up my ringlets with ribbons. I surveyed my tall slim figure in the mirror and was unable to suppress a smile of self-satisfaction. To compensate for my snow-white skin my mother had chosen a brocade of a rich cream colour, and I could see now that the choice was perfect. Camilla and I kissed to indicate how proud we were of each other's appearance, and then young Jonathan came in to show off his page boy's costume. What a wedding it would be!

My betrothed was Lord of the largest manor in the whole of our area. He was only seven years older than myself, rich, handsome and reputed for his archery. My parents could not have been more delighted with the match, and I felt very privileged. I would miss my family – it was not an easy journey from the large manor to our smaller one – and I would miss my spinet, but my father said it should go to Camilla now, since my husband could buy me a new one. I had not mentioned that subject to him – partly because we had as yet had little opportunity for conversation, since the wedding arrangements were naturally made entirely by my parents. So I resolved to make my request as soon as I was properly installed in my new home.

******

What a day it had been! Mr. Jenkins, now my husband, had seemed more than satisfied with my appearance, and relatives, friends and acquaintances had travelled from all over the county for the occasion. The wine had flowed freely (not that I was particularly partial to that, but Mr. Jenkins must certainly have drunk my share as well as his own), and as for the food, I had never seen such an abundance of tempting delicacies. Eventually, with a few tears in my eyes, I kissed everyone "goodbye" and Mr. Jenkins proudly helped me into the carriage to make the journey to the Manor. Our arrival in the dark made the drive through the grounds seem longer than ever, and fumbling our way through the dimly lit passages of the house made my butterflies resume their vigour, but I supposed that I would get accustomed to it all in due course.

"Right, Daisy. This is Mrs. Jenkins. Show her to her chamber. Anne, I will come and find you there in half an hour, so make yourself ready.". My husband's voice had a sharpness I had not observed before and that I did not all together like. I had been told little about the intimate details of matrimony, but I knew that there was a physical side which involved rather more than the kiss on the hand with which my betrothed had always bade me "farewell" at the end of his brief visits. Was I now about to find out?

The room to which Daisy showed me was to my liking, though I could not at this hour tell whether it had a good view over the garden. It was spacious, and the large four-poster looked inviting to my weary body. Its olive green drapes were not the colour I would have chosen, but no doubt that was something I could get rectified in due course. The butler followed close behind us with my trunk, and so I began forthwith to hang some of my frocks in the wardrobe and to search for my night clothes. I was not yet done when my husband appeared.

"What! You are not undressed yet? I told you to be ready for me."

"I have just been hanging my clothes and looking for my night attire."

"You do not need any night attire right now. Off with that dress and let us have a good look at you." My hands trembled so with the fastenings that Mr. Jenkins rapidly took over. He then, to my intense embarrassment, removed both my corset and my underskirt, turning me round as he did so with his eyes roving all over my body. "Hmm. A bit skinny. You should have stopped growing upwards and started growing outwards instead."

"I grew as God intended me to grow," I replied stiffly. "You should not have needed to see me naked in order to observe that my build was tall and slender. Had you wanted someone shorter and plumper, you could have waited for Camilla to be of an age for matrimony."

"No, I could not have waited for your sister since I am myself already more than old enough to be a father. And regarding that matter, we might as well proceed without further ado, so on to that bed with you. Oh, and by the way, Mrs. Jenkins, it is not seemly for the wife of a man of my status to reply to her husband in that way."

"I was only being logical."

"I am not interested in logic, only in obedience," he replied, leaping on top of me and then completely ignoring my shrieks of shock and pain.

After he had left me for his own room and I had washed my private parts as thoroughly as I could with the small jug of water on the dressing table, I lost little time in falling asleep, so weary was I. By the time I awoke the sun was well risen, but I made no move, preferring to lie for a while and reflect upon what had happened. "It is rather far from anything I had imagined," I said to myself, "but maybe it will be less painful next time, and no doubt I will soon get used to this new life. I must ask Mr. Jenkins about the spinet today, lest my playing suffers for lack of practice."

In due course I arose and went to the window. I found to my disappointment that there was no view, only thick dark trees which cut out much light to the room. I looked around again and suddenly the room seemed less attractive than it had the night before. "Ah well," I said to myself, "if I can get the drapes on the bed changed to a pretty shade of blue and the walls redone in a much lighter colour, it will make a big improvement." Then Daisy knocked at the door with a jug of clean water for my morning ablutions. I asked her kindly to come back in fifteen minutes in order to show me the way down for breakfast.

Mr. Jenkins was nowhere to be seen when I went down, so I breakfasted alone. There was a copious spread on the table of bread, ham and fruit, but I had little appetite. The cook came in and introduced herself, saying "The master told me to feed you well since you could do with putting on some weight."

"You can try," I replied with a smile, "but my own family's attempts to do that were never successful. Where is the master this morning?"

"He said that he would be back for lunch at 1.0, and that in the meantime you could familiarise yourself with the house and make an inventory of the contents of the larder."

The morning passed not too slowly and the lunch was again copious, but I had eaten well at the wedding feast the day before. "This evening we shall be alone," my husband said, "but tomorrow I have invited some dozen people, so you must spend this afternoon planning an impressive menu.". My heart sank, as at home that had always been my mother's province, but I reflected that no doubt the cook could help me. I remembered my resolution and determined not to tarry. "My spinet has been left at home for Camilla, but my father said that you would surely obtain a new one for me."

"He made no such suggestion to me," was the reply. "I have no ear for music and have no wish to see my wife idling away her time with such activities."

"It would not be an idle activity. Playing the keyboard is a skill that requires many years of practice. I shall need something to do when I am not planning menus or stitching clothes for the baby you are desirous that I conceive for you."

"I am the master of this house and I shall be the one to decide how my wife will spend her time." Obviously a repetition of my request would have to await a more opportune moment.

CHAPER TWO - THE FULL TRUTH DAWNS

Two years had passed. I had lost one child in the early weeks of pregnancy and there was still no sign of another conception. That grieved me, as the companionship of a son or daughter would have filled my often empty days. I had become quite adept at planning menus for my husband's regular, lavish, dinner parties, but there was little else to keep me occupied, and my pleas for a spinet always fell on deaf ears. Nor would Mr. Jenkins even permit me to take walks in the manor's extensive grounds. The doors were firmly locked day and night and the butler, who was guardian of the keys, was under strict instructions not to allow me access to them. What, I wondered, would Mr. Jenkins think I would do if I went outside? Run off home and arrange with my father to have the spinet brought over? It was too far to walk, and anyway I would not know the way. Ask the gardener to cut down the trees outside my window to improve the view? Elope with one of our many dinner party guests, such as Mr. Sanderson?

Elope with Mr. Sanderson, now that did have some attraction! He seemed to be a really kind, gentle, man as well as handsome – the complete opposite of Mr. Jenkins in character – and the last time he was here I could not help noticing him eyeing me in a certain way. Of course there would be no chance really of anything remotely like an affair, but if only I could just make friends with him, perhaps I could at least talk to him a bit about my plight. Perhaps he would be sympathetic and be able secretly to get a letter to my family for me. My husband censored all the letters I sent to them, as well as those I received, and during their rare visits here he never left me alone with them for a single moment. On their last visit I said that I wanted to take Camilla to my room to see what she thought of the colour, but he said that he was planning to have it redone, to be more in accordance with my taste, and so we should wait; and my parents supported this argument. My dear parents, if only they knew what a lie this was! When I had said that olive green was not really to my liking and that I would prefer the décor to be blue, Mr. Jenkins had cursed me for complaining and threatened me with a whipping if I "complained" again. So yes, perhaps if I smiled more sweetly at Mr. Sanderson the next time that he was here, we could gradually become friends and I could somehow find an opportunity to confide in him. More than that I would have no desire for anyway. My physical relations with Mr. Jenkins were less excruciatingly painful now than they had been on that hateful wedding night, but sexual intercourse was not something I could imagine myself ever doing for pleasure.

******

How painful it was sitting at this dinner table for what seemed like hours on end! The corset into which Mr. Jenkins now locked me each morning dug into my back, and the intense feeling of restriction decreased my appetite. How absurd to deem a chastity belt necessary for a poor prisoner like me. All it had taken to arouse Mr. Jenkins' jealousy was one little smile directed at Mr. Sanderson when I felt that he was trying to speak to me somewhat affectionately. After that evening he was not invited again for several weeks, and when his name did finally reappear on the list of guests, he was made to sit right at the far end of the table.

******

"No, no, no! Even though I am married to you, you have no right to force me when I do not wish it." I might be slender, but I was strong, and the last time he had come into my room late at night having had a bit too much to drink, I had kicked him so hard that he had shrieked with pain and then beaten me angrily. Now he was binding my legs together to make me unable to kick, having already tied my wrists to the bed posts. Still I fought, however. He had no right to humiliate me in this way, and I would go on fighting until my dying day. Oh, if only that day would come soon now! I could see no other way out of this dreadful prison. But I was still young and I was strong, so death looked unlikely to come in a hurry. Ah well, at least I would never let him have his pleasure easily.

I had consumption. The doctor was quite sure about it, but said that he had known people who were young like myself to survive it and that, since my health had always been good up till now, I had every chance of making a good recovery. Mr. Jenkins said that I must survive because it was still not too late for me to bear him a son and that, if he were widowed, it would be troublesome to find another young woman to marry and train her to perform all the duties of Mrs. Jenkins as efficiently as I did.

I of course had no wish to survive the consumption. It was my only means of escape from this prison. I lay in my bed and prayed to God to take me.

******

"And take you he finally did, though it was quite a struggle for that soul of yours to free itself from a strong body with so much zest for life and attachment to the worth while things of Earth!"

"Yes, but all the worth while things were deprived me from the moment of my unfortunate marriage to Mr. Jenkins."

"So what do you think you have learnt from that very difficult life?" continued my guide, who had been waiting to greet me in the Bardo.

"Well, I suppose I learnt to be strong and always to fight adversity."

"Yes. Death is sometimes the result of people giving up the struggle, but in this case you fought for death to come and rescue you since you had no other means of escaping from your cruel husband. This painful experience will serve you well for the future."

"That's right. I'll make sure not to marry a brute like that again!"

"So can you forgive him, since he has taught you a valuable lesson?"

"Oh yes. Now that I am back Home I feel more sorry for him than vindictive. Inflicting pain on another only causes still greater suffering to oneself."

PART THREE - COMPENSATION

That life did not surface at all easily. On a practice weekend at Jen's, when a few of us had been getting some of the supervision that we needed as one of the qualifications for the Woolger diploma, Grace had been helping me to overcome my difficulty in working from the body. The first thing that came, under her skilled guidance, was a strong feeling of my legs being bound, but initially I was unable to work out the reason for that. Gradually it became apparent that I had had a cruel husband who was something of a sexual pervert, but his reason for binding my legs, which would surely make intercourse more difficult for him as well as for me, did not come clear on that occasion. Nor, when I went to Devon a couple of moths later, did it occur to me to make a link between the feeling of claustrophobia that I had there and the marital rape with my legs bound.

When, however, we were on the workshop in France a couple of months later, Grace picked me to demonstrate on after we had each done a picture of a first scene. Mine was of a tall slender woman seated at a huge dining table in a huge house and screaming inwardly "Oh the pain!" on account of the corset digging so sharply into her back. As Grace took me through the life with my friends all watching and supporting me, I gradually got to the painful rape scenes, and suddenly I was able to make the connection both with the leg binding and with the claustrophobia. Somehow I just <u>knew</u> that it had all taken place in that very same part of Devon which made me feel claustrophobic, but neither the reason for my legs being bound nor the chief lesson of the life came through in that regression, useful though it was.

I left it to brew for a couple of years until the time came to write up the life for the book. Then, being on my own, I used Edwin's tape to help me go back into it a third time, and suddenly I saw why that brute of a husband had found it necessary to bind my legs. I was so determined not to let him rape me, and caused him so much pain with my kicks, that the poor man had no alternative! It also came clear then that he had had to tie up my hands as well.

What had been really useful when I did the regression in France was all my friends' support, without which I would have had difficulty in facing up to the cause of the problems around sexuality that I have had in my present life and not really wanted to admit to. With their help I was finally able to let go of all that. Also, of course, that life of imprisonment in a big house in Devon explained my desire always to be a free spirit now. "Ann, you're never here!" my friends would exclaim, and now I could see what I had been reacting against and was compensating for.

And I had chosen the right husband for a free spirit. Aquarians never like to be tied down, and I had never responded well to 9.0-5.0 office hours. At certain times in the past I had had little choice in that particular matter, but even when I was working in an office, I had only ever been comfortable when I could be my own boss. Now, fortunately, offices were a thing of the past for me, and my good, gentle, husband firstly enjoyed travel too, and secondly was always happy to let me do my own thing. I have recently been compensating with a vengeance for my imprisonment in Devon!

EXERCISE

Where you live is important, both for your general well being and for your work. Of course many of us do have restrictions. (My daughter had no great desire to live in London, but almost all the jobs in her field are there.) Never pooh-pooh your feelings about a place; there is sure to be something perfectly rational behind them. If you are not fully content where you are, think about where you would really like to live. Perhaps you could at least make it a long-term aim, if not a short-term one? Perhaps you could go there for weekends/holidays on a regular basis?

Although I have not to date found a past life there, the place where I feel the most at home is Geneva, and my husband loves it too. We both find it very good for working. I have done a large percentage of my writing there in recent years, and David finds the River Arve (where he always has his picnic lunch when he is invited to do research at the University in the summer) conducive to thought. It would not be possible for us to retire there for financial reasons, but we have appreciated being able to return so many times during the thirty years of our marriage. When I first moved to the Hull area shortly after my marriage, it was with some reluctance. I missed the mountains dreadfully, and I never imagined that we would stay there for very long. Cottingham, on the outskirts of Hull, which was our home for twenty-nine years, is actually quite a pleasant place to live, yet I never felt able to put down roots there. For a while we thought of retiring to Spain, but when it came to the crunch there were many arguments against that. In Shropshire, on the other hand, we both felt comfortable and at home from the first time that we went to look at it. Although it is not mountainous like Switzerland, we love its gentle hills, and I suspect that we have both had pleasant past lives there. I therefore anticipate being content to spend the whole of the rest of my life here.

So good luck in your search for the perfect place to live!

XX
SATHYA SAI BABA

PART ONE - PUTTAPARTHI

Men cannot comprehend the Formless and the Attributeless Absolute. Avatars appear in human form to enable humanity to experience the Formless in a form which is accessible to them and helpful to them. An Avatar assumes the form that is beneficial to and within the reach of human beings. An effort must be made to understand the nature of divinity. It is only when God comes in human form that human beings can have the full opportunity to experience and enjoy the Divine.

Sai Baba's Thought for the Day, 20 October 2003

At last, here we all were aboard the taxis and travelling the dusty, bumpy road to Prasanthi Nilayam. Only a few more hours now till we would actually be seeing with our very own eyes the physical form of this amazing being about whom we had read, talked and dreamt so much! Sathya Sai Baba - the Universal Messiah, partly for whom we knew we had chosen to incarnate in the present century. The decision (in July 1997) to join this particular pilgrimage had been a hasty one but, having made it, the time until February Ist had seemed to drag. And the nearer the date came, the more unreal did the trip seem to me. David and I had often talked of visiting India as something for the distant future ("when we're retired"). More recently Cynthia and I had talked frequently of visiting Baba's ashram as something for the less distant future, but certainly not as soon as 1998, "because we can't afford it while we've still got children at university."

But then suddenly the decision was more or less made for me. Mary, the member of our Sai Baba group who was wheelchair-bound by MS, had decided to join Janet and Frank Talty's pilgrimage group, and her wonderful husband Gordon had agreed to accompany her there, although himself not a devotee. Gordon could take care of Mary most of the time at the ashram but, in view of the separate entrances for men and women both to the Sai Kulwant Hall and to the canteens, someone else would be needed to push her wheelchair to *darshan*[1] and meals. A friend had volunteered for this, but then her mother had become very ill and so she had had to withdraw. So Mary had phoned Cynthia and suggested that she join the three of them "since you say you want to go to India some time anyway." Cynthia, however, was very loyal: "Yes, but I said I would go with Ann, and anyway I don't know that either of us can afford it yet." So she had in turn phoned me and, when she mentioned the cost, I realised that it was the exact sum I had put aside "for emergencies" from money that I had inherited from my mother. Was this an "emergency?" I asked myself as I put down the phone. Was this a call from Baba Himself? It was said that no-one went to Puttaparthi except by His will, and that when He sent out His call it was unmistakable. Only a very few days were needed for me to make up my mind. I knew in my heart that the time was right. I would miss David's birthday, but he would understand, and anyway how wonderful to have my own (the following day) in the ashram!

The nearer we came to February, the more we read about Sai Baba and I was also busy both with my Regression Therapy training and working at my writing. Poor Mary, however, got so ill before Christmas and had to spend so long in hospital that there were fears of her being unable to join us after all. "But if Baba intends her to get there," Cynthia and I concluded to one another, "she'll get there". And get there they did, even if, as the long flight and seemingly interminable middle-of-the-night wait at Mumbai airport took its toll on Mary, Gordon wondered to himself at times whether they had been foolhardy.

1. *Darshan* means "seeing and beholding the Lord and receiving His blessing". Sai Baba comes out and walks among the devotees twice daily.

The travelling was taking its toll on me too just now, I reflected, as I gazed in a bemused fashion through the window of the rickety taxi. Through the fog in my head flittered images of cows wandering tranquilly along the middle of the road, totally unperturbed by the tumultuous traffic, women in dazzlingly beautiful saris - such a riot of varying colours as one could scarcely have imagined possible this side of Heaven – rickety rickshaws and, as we drew further away from Bangalore and more into the open country, red anthills so reminiscent of West Africa despite being of less imposing stature. (I already knew that Puttaparthi meant 'anthill.') Yes, I was unbelievably tired, but what did it really matter? We were here, in India, the home of so many of the world's greatest spiritual leaders, the country to which Jesus had travelled in order to study and prepare himself for his mission....[2] (I thought too about the great Mahatma Gandhi's reply when he was asked what he thought about Western civilisation: "I think it would be a very good idea."!) And yesterday in Bangalore had been such a wonderful day! After settling into the comfortable hotel well after 4 a.m., Cynthia had woken me up when we were already too late for breakfast.

The taxi driver had waited so patiently as we had hummed and hahed over the punjabi suits in the two clothes shops of Mahatma Gandhi Street. The prices were higher[3] than we had been quoted by our group leaders, and we wanted to be sure of the most suitable colours as well as the cheapest suits. Eventually, however, the "big decisions" had been made and, content with our packages under our arms and realising that we still had a whole half day at our disposal, we had asked the obliging taxi driver to "show us Bangalore". What a fascinating city, and what a perfect climate! An invigorating sort of heat, and besides we had our sun cream and our sun hats with us. We wandered in leisurely fashion through tranquil parks, photographing a little "Bull Temple", communing with monkeys eager to show off their tricks just above our heads, and with a group of charming young Muslim boys, more or less the only people we met throughout the whole trip who were not totally convinced of Baba's divinity.

"So what was your first impression?", Janet, our group leader, asked me as we came out of the Hall after our first *darshan*. I thought hard and eventually replied that, having at last seen Baba in the flesh, I found it even more difficult to believe

2. See *The Lost Years of Jesus – Documentary Evidence of Jesus' 17-year journey to the East*, Elizabeth Clare Prophet, Summit University Press, USA, 1993. It is also widely believed that Jesus survived the crucifixion, returned to India, where he lived to a great age, and was buried in Kashmir. The tomb alleged to be his can be visited to this day.

3. To anyone thinking of visiting Puttaparthi for the first time I would recommend waiting until you get there to buy your punjabi suits etc. The prices there (particularly in the ashram shop) are much lower than in Bangalore.

in His divinity "because He looks so ordinary". I was also surprised that He looked even smaller than I had anticipated[4], and because His features, as well as His hair, looked to me more African than Indian. Reactions to their first sight of the avatar are as varied as are people themselves, and I wondered initially whether I was going to be disappointed. Gradually, however, as the three weeks wore on, something began to get to me. I could not even try to explain it – either to myself or to anyone else – but I just knew deep inside that what I was beholding was PURE LOVE walking on two feet, and that somehow or other my life would change radically from that moment on. I also before very long saw Him from very close up materialising *vibhuti* for people, and I witnessed Him manifest a gold chain for a young man who had just performed at a concert. I knew for sure that these were no conjuring tricks, and that no ordinary human being could do anything comparable.

So what, I kept wondering to myself, had I done to deserve this call to India, when others whom I regarded as much more spiritual than myself had not even heard of Baba? And why when, the following year, Cynthia and I and a couple of other friends flew over to Germany to see Mother Meera, did I find the experience moving but not one that I felt any compulsion to repeat? Gradually I learnt, both from the many excellent lectures I heard at Prashanti Nilayam[5] and from my further reading, that God's grace was not restricted to the most deserving. I also came to believe that my good friend John was quite right when he said that the extent to which one felt drawn to any particular Master depended entirely on the previous links one had with Him or Her. (I was later very happy to be present at a session with the "hugging avatar", Amma, on one of her visits to London, but again that is an experience I feel no need to repeat.)

Since February 1998 I have made – much to my initial surprise, as I had imagined the first to be a "once in a lifetime" occurrence – six further pilgrimages to Sai Baba's ashram. Each has been totally different, each has been totally wonderful. I have never yet had an interview with Him, yet, following each of the trips I can name something very specific that He did for me, and on each occasion it was something that I would not have even thought of asking for.

After returning the first time I felt depressed (Janet told me on the phone that that was normal after having had to leave Baba's physical presence, but it has never happened to me since), and at the same time I felt that He was forcing me to do the "inner child" work that I knew I still needed to do, but had been putting off and putting off. (Why? Because I was "too busy". Do you ever make that excuse too?!)

---

4. He is five feet two inches tall and very slim.
5. Prashanti Nilayam is the name of the Puttaparthi ashram. It means *Abode of the Highest Peace*.

Each day during the ensuing weeks, I put aside an hour to attend to the needs of the little Ann who had been a neglected child. I started from birth and gradually worked my way up, giving her at each stage the love of which she had been deprived.

Also each day I tuned into my body in the way that Lawrence had taught me to do, noting down the physical sensations that I became aware of. One day I felt an intense pressure on my head. It started as a tight band around my forehead, and then increased and increased until I felt as though I was suffocating. Then suddenly I realised that I had once been buried alive.

PART TWO - SAI BABA OF SHIRDI

He is the wisest who seeks God. He is the most successful who has found God.

Paramahansa Yogananda

I heard a sudden slither of rocks and soil just above my head. Oh no! Some of it was beginning to fall into the hole by which I had entered the site. Had Maria been right in trying to dissuade me from coming out here to check on things so late in the day? Now here it came: my head was getting covered. Never mind; I was strong; I could fight my way through. But no. I heard a noise much louder than the first one, and instantly realised that a real landslide was taking place up there above my head. I knew that more, larger rocks were tumbling down, and now the pressure on my head was unbearable. I wanted to shout "Help! I can't breathe.", but it was impossible to open my mouth, for my whole head and body were now buried in soil and rubble. I made a desperate attempt to push myself free, but my arms simply would not move. "So this is the end," I thought to myself. "What an uncomfortable way to go! How on earth shall I be able to bear suffocating to death?"

No sooner had the words come into my head than it was all over. What a relief! What bliss to be free!" Ah yes, but it won't be bliss for Maria," I reflected ruefully, "when she finds out that she hasn't got a husband any more. Or for the children. Of course they're all grown up now and can fend for themselves, but they'll miss me. I know that old body won't be fit to inhabit any more, even if they do manage to dig it out tomorrow. Not that I need it of course," I added, looking down admiringly at this new, much less cumbersome, body which with I now found myself adorned. "Quite an improvement!" I said aloud to anyone who might be able to hear. "Fifty-four years on that old one were beginning to show. Fifty-four years of pretty hard work one way and another.

Now I was suddenly filled with a wonderful new energy such as I couldn't remember feeling in years. Dying was so easy, I reflected, and being dead was really exciting. I'd forgotten what it was like, being so engrossed all those years in my work, my family… but now it was gradually all coming back to me. I remembered that being dead meant that I could GO HOME; and I knew that I would be able to go wherever I wanted just by wishing myself there. But I must not go home straight away because Maria would be getting worried. "What should I do?" I asked myself. Well the answer was simple: "I'd better just go back to the house and tell her."

******

How frustrating it was! I walked into our house to tell Maria I was dead and not to worry because I was fine, and that the children would take care of her, but she didn't see me. She was just sitting by the fire looking anxious and, though I shouted as loud as I could, she didn't react at all. Ah well, I suppose I should have known really. I suddenly remembered having been taught in previous interlives that communication between realms was usually difficult without training. So I just carried on watching Maria, sending her my love and praying that she would feel it. After a while she got up out of the wooden chair and walked round to the Foreman's house at the other end of our village.

"Kavanja, I'm sorry to disturb you at this time, but I'm worried. Julius went to check on the site two or three hours ago and he hasn't come home yet. I fear he may have had an accident."

"Oh dear!" said Kavanja. "We'd better go and see. Just wait there a moment while I fetch a lamp."

I followed them both as they walked along the dirt track road and then took the little path leading up to the site we were currently working on. Kavanja held the lamp high with one hand and Maria's hand by the other, fearing she might slip. I told him not to worry as I had her tightly by the arm, but of course he didn't hear me. Nor did she, judging from her anxious breathing, have any idea that I was looking after her. It seemed a long climb, and I had to slow down to their pace when it would have been so easy for me to soar ahead, but eventually the path levelled off and the site of the excavations came into view. At least, it came into my view, but I realised that Kavanja and Maria could see no further than a few feet in front of them, no further than the end of the lamp's beam. We had been getting on so well digging out the wonderful remains of those ancient buildings left by our ancestors. How proud I was to be Kenyan, and how fortunate I had been in my career!

Suddenly I recalled my difficult childhood, when mother and father had had to struggle so to feed us all. Difficult, yes, but happy. We had been content with so little in those days, and we had never suffered from lack of either love or laughter. Then how pleased my parents had been when, as still a young lad, I had been offered the job as a digger on the nearby archæological site. It had been hard work, but my meagre wages had helped to buy food and the occasional piece of cloth for some member of the family. A couple of times in recent years I had managed to make the journey back to my native village to see some of my relatives. My parents were long since dead of course, but some of my brothers and sisters were still there, and they were all so proud of me. "We always knew you'd go far," they would say. "You always were the most enterprising and intelligent of all of us." And I would reply modestly that it was all thanks to the support I had been given, and then I would give out little presents, some of which were treasures I had brought back with me from India.

Now we were only a few feet from the site. "Oh no!" said Kavanja. "The entrance hole seems to have got filled with rubble. There must have been a landslide."

"Julius, Julius!" Maria screamed desperately.

They walked round and round, climbing carefully over the little walls, Kavanja holding the lamp closer to the ground to make sure that they didn't put their foot into a hole or trip against a small boulder. Eventually Kavanja said "I'm afraid there's nothing for it but to wait till morning. If he's underneath that rubble there'll be little hope for him."

"How can we wait?" asked Maria. "Shouldn't we be digging?"

"But it's so difficult and dangerous in the dark," replied Kavanja, "and anyway we haven't got any proper equipment with us."

"Oh Julius, my poor Julius," wept Maria.

"I'm so sorry," said Kavanja gently, "but we mustn't give up hope yet. Now let me take you home to bed. In the morning all the men will come and we'll be able to search properly."

"No, I can't go to bed. Let me just wait here."

"You can't do that. It's already getting cold. At least you could go to your daughter's."

I followed them back to the village to Shivu's house, which she shared with her husband and two children. Shivu was our second daughter. Our eldest daughter, Wamboi, had married a man from a neighbouring village and moved there, while Ngina, the third one, was working in Nairobi, where Ng'anga, the youngest, was practising as a clergyman. We loved all our children dearly, but Shivu was special because we had once very nearly lost her. Lost her to that dreadful dengue fever so rampant in India, where I had been sent for a couple of years as an archæological advisor. She had been healed by a holy man, the great Sai Baba of Shirdi. How incredibly fortunate were we to have met him! He would look after Maria now if I couldn't. I had recently heard that he had passed away only about a year ago.

Passed away? Now that I was dead, that meant that I should be able to see Him again. How wonderful! It seemed so long now since I had had to return to Kenya from India. We were now just outside Shivu's house, but I looked up. What should I see but Sai Baba's loving face and tall gaunt figure. He was smiling affectionately at me. I ran and knelt at his feet. He put his hand on my head and said "Bless you, Julius."

"So you remember my name after all these years!" I exclaimed. "How wonderful to see you again! It seems so long since we left India."

"I was with you all the time," He replied. I never desert my followers."

"Oh, I know!" Tears of joy were streaming down my face, but then they turned once more to sadness.

"What shall I do about Maria and the children?" I asked him. "Tomorrow they will dig up that rubble and find my body buried under it. They won't understand that I'm really not dead at all and that I've come back to You. And just at the moment my poor wife is so worried."

"You underestimate your good wife," Baba replied gently. "You know that she is a very evolved soul. Don't you remember how, when you were fretting about how you could reconcile being a follower of Jesus with being one of my disciples, she explained to you that we - Jesus, Buddha, Krishna, Allah.... - were all one? She will grieve of course over your body when they dig it up, but then her tears will dry and she will know that you are better off, here with me, and that she will join you herself in good time."

Of course, Baba was right. How well I remembered! We had only been in India a few months when little Shivu had fallen sick. "Take her to Shirdi," the neighbours had said. "It's not so very far, and the holy man Sai Baba heals so many people daily."

Well, I had been a Christian ever since soon after the good Mortimer, under whom I worked at the site near my home village, had taught me to read and write and then given me so much archæological education. I had learnt fast - I found it so enthralling - and it had been entirely thanks to his encouragement and support that

I had eventually risen to a position normally held only by a white man. His devout Christianity had impressed me too and, after accompanying him to church for a number of weeks, I had requested baptism. Maria had supported me all the way through my conversion, and had not objected to the children being baptised as well, but she herself had preferred to remain an outsider. "Of course," she had said, "I can see that Jesus was as perfect as any man could be, and the world would be a much better place if only everyone were to follow his example, but I do find some of your church people a bit limited in their beliefs. How can they say that theirs is the only way when there are so many obviously good people who do not know about Jesus? And how can they say that we all have only one life? I know full well that my sister's first child, who died, returned to her when the second one was born...."

And so it had been Maria who had persuaded me that we should pack a small bag and travel to Shirdi with Shivu. (The kind neighbours had taken charge of the other three children until our return.) I said when the suggestion was put to us "But I'm praying hard to Jesus. He is the one and only healer and saviour..." After a few days, however, I had become desperate and, as they said, Shirdi was not impossibly far. We had nothing to lose, and Shivu already looked lost anyway. The road to Shirdi had seemed long; so dusty and bumpy. But then what an amazing miracle had occurred at the end of it all!

There was nothing particularly remarkable about the little town of Shirdi itself, but somehow as we got nearer and nearer to Sai Baba's abode, the atmosphere seemed to change in a way that was palpable yet indefinable. Outside his dwelling was a long, long queue of people, and all we could do was join on to the end of it patiently. Poor Maria was exhausted, and Oh so anxious, and as for little Shivu, I kept checking every few moments to make sure that her soul was still with us. She had been hæmorrhaging badly, and been tossing and turning with fever, but now she seemed to have slipped into a coma. Several people in the crowd turned and looked at us sympathetically, and one kind elderly woman insisted on giving Maria her quite comfortable seat on a large boulder. She took it gratefully and cradled Shivu on her knee, while I stood behind with my hands firmly on Maria's shoulders. Though I found it difficult to let my gaze wander from my little daughter's face, now and again I glanced at some of the Indians around us. What a noble people they were! How full of serenity were their beautiful faces, however haggard, and however ragged their clothes. "Maria is right," I thought to myself. "God dwells here just as much as he does in our little church back at home."

And then He had appeared! The crowd, already quiet, had suddenly hushed completely. All eyes were fixed on this turbaned man in the white robe as He wended

His way slowly past all of them, stopping here and there to bestow a blessing, accept an offering or a letter, or utter a few words of evident wisdom. Eventually it was our turn. I still cannot find words to describe the feeling. He looked at Shivu in such a loving way, then He gazed into Maria's eyes, then mine, then He placed His hand on the little head. "Fear not," He said. "She will live. Then he waved his hand and said "Take this *udhi*". I held a clean kerchief out underneath his hand and into it He put some black ash. "Anoint her forehead, throat and heart with it," He said, "and as soon as she awakes and can drink, give her a little of it mixed in water. Continue to do this daily until she is fully recovered, and then return to see Me again." Then, having placed His hand on her head once more for a moment, He moved on to the people next to us.

Maria turned and looked at me. All she could say was "I'm so thirsty!"

"We must find somewhere to spend the night," I said. "We won't be fit to travel again until tomorrow."

An Indian gentleman, who could not possibly have understood our tongue, took me by the arm and signalled to us to follow him. We pointed to our oxen cart and he gestured to us to get into it, and then he gently led the ox to a small back street. After a little while he brought it to a halt outside a simple dwelling. Motioning to us not to move, he went inside, and we overheard him talking with a woman. His wife then came out and, with a beaming smile, she beckoned us to follow her to a water trough. Having no vessels, we drank eagerly from cupped hands; then the good man and his wife took us inside their little home and indicated a place on the floor where we could spend the night. The woman spread out a mat. We sat down and immediately began to anoint Shivu with the ash as we had been instructed. Her breathing now seemed to have changed - it was less erratic and more peaceful - and the Indian couple smiled first at each other and then at us, and we heard them utter the name "Sai Baba" with obvious awe. The wife then set about preparing food, and before long wonderful dishes of rice and curried vegetables were set before us. It had not occurred to us that we were hungry before the delicious smell reached our nostrils, but it was only minutes before all the dishes were empty.

We all slept well for a few hours, but I woke early and, after checking on Shivu, who still appeared to be breathing peacefully, I lay awake thinking and thinking about the man Sai Baba. "Who is he?" I asked myself. "It couldn't be Jesus returned again. If it were, we should surely have heard about it even in Africa."

"Why worry about who He is?" asked Maria, who woke not much long after. "He is so obviously the embodiment of Love, and He said that Shivu would live. Look, her mouth is open. Let us quickly give her water mixed with some of that ash."

The Indian lady was soon up and cooking once more for us, although we tried to signal to her that it wasn't necessary. When we had eaten more than we really needed, we turned and looked at Shivu and suddenly her eyes opened. What a sight, those eyes! No longer did they look troubled and wracked with pain. In fact her whole, dear little face was a picture of tranquillity. The good Indian lady offered her rice, and she ate a little bit willingly.

"I must go back and thank him," I said to Maria. "I couldn't bear to return without seeing Him once more."

"But it's a long journey, and the other children will be anxiously awaiting our return," she protested.

"They can wait just a little bit longer," I insisted. "Let us thank these good people and be on our way."

"Sai Baba?" I said to the gentleman.

He turned to his wife and they talked for a moment. Then he led us outside and installed us in our oxen cart. His wife smiled and waved, and he again took hold of the harness and led us back the way we had come the previous day. Before long we were once more in the queue outside Sai Baba's dwelling....

******

"And when you came to say "Thank you" for Shivu's healing was really only the beginning, wasn't it?" Sai Baba was laughing up there above Shivu and her husband's house.

"Yes," I replied. "That was only the beginning. How many more times during my two years in India did I travel to see you? I can't remember! The only thing I do remember is that the visits seemed to be over too quickly. Then my work called me back to Kenya."

"And you thought that was the end?" asked Sai Baba with his little wry smile.

"Well yes, I did in a sense, but on the other hand I knew that I would never be the same again after having known You."

"And you weren't and won't be! That "end", when you left India "for good", was in fact only the beginning."

"How do you mean?" I asked in astonishment.

"There is plenty of time for me to explain. Come back after you've seen to Maria and your daughter, and after the funeral is over. It is always important to attend one's own funeral."

******

The funeral went on for hours and hours. We Africans know so well how to celebrate death! I had always appreciated the music and the dancing at other funerals I had attended, but for this one - my own - I was in a much better position for getting an overall view. It was hard saying "Goodbye" to all my dear ones, friends and colleagues - especially since they could not see or hear me. It would have been easier, I suppose, if the death had not been so sudden, but on the other hand how fortunate I was to be have been spared old age. Now I was looking forward to moving on. That was one of the many things that were so good about my people: their readiness to accept death when it comes, and their willingness to let go of the person concerned. They never hung on so that souls got trapped in the lower astral realms, as I knew sometimes happened in places such as Europe.

The worst bit of course had been the unearthing of my body. The shock for my family and everyone else had been terrible, even though they had been preparing themselves for it. All the family arrived in good time to lend support at the funeral, and now they were all a great comfort to Maria and to each other.

"He'd had a good life," they said, "and he'd come very close to retirement anyway. Just think how difficult it would have been for you if he had fallen ill and you'd had to nurse him through old age."

"Yes," she replied, "I know I've been spared a great deal, and I shall have many good memories to treasure through my last years...."

******

"So what do you think was your chief lesson from that life?" asked Sai Baba. I had now moved right away from the lower astral realms and, in the company of my guides and Gadrasiel, my guardian angel, had travelled on to a place that was just FULL of light and indescribably beautiful. I thought hard and then replied "I think I needed to learn about God...."

"Ye-e-e-s?" said Sai Baba.

"You see, when I first became a Christian, I was so excited. I thought that I now had all the answers; that Christianity was superior to all other religions; that indigenous African beliefs were rather naïve and simplistic.... I suppose I thought that God was somehow locked up safe inside that little church I used to go to every Sunday...."

"And then?" asked Sai Baba.

"Well, then I went to India, and I found You.... And You seemed to be as great as Jesus, even though I couldn't understand exactly who You were, and You were a Muslim by birth and I'd been taught that it was better to be Christian than Muslim.... And then I noticed more and more how spiritual most of the Indians I met were, whether they were Muslim, Hindu or Christian, and I began to feel that God must belong to everyone equally, and that perhaps it didn't matter at all what religion one was...."

"Which is what Maria said all along."

"Which is exactly what Maria had always told me.... But now I can see that YOU'RE God. Why didn't you tell me that when I used to go and see You at Shirdi?"

"It's no good telling people things that they're not ready for. Have you heard that old joke: that when God first made people He wondered where to hide Himself, and so He decided to put Himself inside them because that was the last place anyone would ever think to look for Him?"

"So are you saying that not only are you God, but that you're also inside everyone?"

"I'm saying more than that. I'm saying that you are just as much God as I am. It's just that you've forgotten."

Suddenly, in a flash, it all came back to me. Now memories of countless earlier lives were flashing through my memory. I was going back and back in my mind, back and back to even before Lemuria, the first civilisation on Earth.... Back and back till I saw my Self (and my twin soul) as one with the Source and, with that amazing memory, the most incredible feeling of ecstasy came over me.....

After what might have been seconds, minutes or hours, I asked Sai Baba "What did You mean when you said before my funeral that my meeting You at Shirdi was only the beginning?"

"Well," He began to explain, "you've heard of Raama and Krishna?"

"Ye-e-e-s," I replied, slightly hesitantly.

"They were both avatars. The word *avatar* literally means *descent*. Since the beginning of its history things have gone badly wrong in the world many times, haven't they?"

"Oh yes!" I exclaimed.

"Well, when things go badly wrong, the Lord has to step in Himself to put them right again. So I "descended" as Raama, then later as Krishna, to remove the poison. Hindus still worship me in those forms, though of course the main essence of God is formless. It is only for limited, human eyes that I need to don a human form...."

"Yes..."

"Then were was the man known as the Buddha, who achieved Enlightenment, and who still serves as a source of inspiration to many. Then, not so long after that in Earthly terms, I sent another man - Jesus - who, unlike most of you, had never strayed very far from me, and who remembered that he was God. He came to set an example of perfection and to show people the way back, and he also took a lot of the world's karma upon himself through his suffering. This did a tremendous amount of good, and during the last two thousand years there have been many people who have genuinely followed him, but also there has been much distortion of what he said, and too many people have been completely ignoring it. That's why it was time for another descent, but now, since things are worse than ever, I decided that it would have to be triple."

"How do you mean?"

"Well, as you know, I incarnated in Shirdi, where many came to know of Me besides yourself, and, before My *samadhi*[6] last year, I told my disciples that I would return eight years later."

"You'll be back on Earth in only seven years' time? But I won't be able to see You there, since I'll presumably still be dead then."

"You weren't thinking that you'd had your last life, were you?"

"Well no. I fully appreciate that I'm still a long way from self-realisation."

"How far away will be up to you, my dear Julius. What I <u>can</u> tell you now, however, is that before very long you will have a brief life as a Jewish boy, in which you will experience the horrors of a forthcoming Holocaust, and that soon after that you will have a much longer life - a life in which you will again see Sai Baba."

"Really?"

"Yes, really. I shall declare myself as Sai Baba in 1940, when I shall be just fourteen years of age. You might well choose that very year to incarnate yet again. It would be appropriate."

"So would I incarnate in India that time?"

---

6. *Samadhi*, which in Sanskrit means state of union with God, very deep meditation, is also used for "death" in the case of great Masters.

"That would not be necessary. The next Sai Baba will be the most powerful avatar of all, and there will be no corner of the globe where He will not be known. It will be a long lifetime – ninety-six years. You might well choose to incarnate in Europe - a continent with which you are already very familiar."

"Indeed I am!" I exclaimed, recalling several lifetimes passed there as nuns, another in which I had again been husband to Maria....

"In Europe it will be particularly important for there to be people who know Me because, sadly, so many people there have completely forgotten God."

"But how shall I get to know You again if I am in Europe and You in far away India?""

"I just said that My fame will spread to every corner of the globe. There will be innumerable books written about Me. People will flock from every country of the world to Puttaparthi. You will be among them. You might even be among those who will write books. Remember your latent talent for writing?" My thoughts flashed back to Atlantis....

"Maybe you will not be able to speak to Me in the flesh. There will be so many thousands of people at Puttaparthi all the time that they will not all be able to have private interviews. I shall have to select those whose needs are greatest, and those who have particular merit from their previous incarnations. You will have to learn to meet Me in your heart, remember that I have been there all along, and you will have to seek "inner view" rather than interview."

"In that case it would not be necessary to travel all the way to India."

"You are right. But I know you! You will be one of those who feel that you <u>must</u> see with your own eyes. You will want to witness my miracles at first hand. Indeed, I will give you personal experience of one or two of my little *leelas*[7] .... All that you experience will give you the desire to belong to a Sai group in your own country, to spread my message among those who are reluctant to hear...."

"And what will that message be?"

"Quite simply what it has always been: Love and Service. Nothing else. Nothing else is needed. You will also be interested in healing. Remember that that is another of your latent talents?"

"You mentioned a triple incarnation."

---

7. A *leela* is a "divine joke" or "playful miracle". The ones that I have experienced are described in the next section.

"Yes indeed. Eight years after I have reached the end of the long life as Sathya Sai Baba (Sathya means Truth, by the way. This incarnation is prophesied in the Book of Revelations[8]....")

"And Sai Baba?"

"Sai Baba means Divine Mother and Father."

"So, eight years after the end of Sathya Sai Baba's life, I shall incarnate a third time as Prema Sai."

"And what does Prema mean?"

"Prema means Love. By then the world will once again be ready for Love. But now it is time for you to go and find out what work is going to be asked of you here in these realms. I think you might be wanted as a guide for one of your grandchildren...."

PART THREE - GIFTS FROM BABA

Sometimes upon this path of life, we meet someone we know.
From times gone by? Within our dreams? Maybe so long ago we met somewhere;
we passed some time, or shared our lives as one.
And so it is we meet again. I listen to your song,
yet somewhere, way down deep inside, there's something that's unknown.
Our past has brought us back to Earth, maybe to share alone
some moments of our lives again – enjoy and celebrate.
The memories of our hidden past reveal how we relate.
Though our paths, within this life, cross but for a short while,
the memories of our sojourn here remain within your smile.
And so it is, our lives reveal the mysteries of the past.
May God be with you on your way, 'til you reach home at last.

Nick Nicholls[9]

---

8. *And now I saw heaven open, and a white horse appear; its rider was called Faithful and True; he is* a judge with integrity, *a warrior for justice. His eyes were flames of fire, and his head was crowned with many coronets; the name written on him was known only to himself,* his cloak was soaked in blood. *He is known by the name The Word of God. Behind him, dressed in linen of dazzling white, rode the armies of heaven on white horses. From his mouth came a sharp sword to strike the pagans with; he is the one who will rule them with an iron sceptre, and tread out the wine of Almighty God's fierce anger. On his cloak and on his thigh there was a name written: The King of Kings and the Lord of lords.* (Revelations19: 11-16)

The name Sathya means *Truth.* The "many coronets" are said to refer to Baba's extraordinary hair, and the "cloak soaked in blood" to the orange or red robes that He normally wears. The "white horses" are the white cars that are used at the ashram, and the men who work around Him all dress in white.

9. Nick Nicholls is a friend of mine from the Integral Regression Network.

I had to wait until my fifth visit to Puttaparthi for my first look from Baba. This was fine: I had read so many books written by people very close to Him but whom He had ignored – sometimes even for years. Firstly, just a few days before our departure, I found on my bookshelf – lying horizontally on top of the other books, so that there was no way I could have missed it beforehand – Volume I of Sathya Sai Speaks, which had been inside the briefcase that I had had stolen on a train to London the previous June. "Knocked for six" is a gross understatement of the reaction of someone who firmly believed that His miracles were things that could only happen to other people, but I took it as His acknowledgement of my impending departure for India.

Then, during the stay, I felt my presence to be acknowledged when my long woolly socks, which had fallen out of my folded seat/bag the previous day, were returned to it during my early morning pre-*darshan* meditation. What, you may well ask, was I doing with long woolly socks in India? The answer is simple. One afternoon an alarm was raised by some of my friends who had burnt their feet badly when they were made to enter the Sai Kulwant Hall for *darshan* via the hot dais rather than the usual passageway protected by wet cardboard. So the next day I put into my seat/bag my one and only pair of socks (which I needed for the journey home from London in February) in case the same thing happened again, which it didn't. On noticing the loss of my socks at the end of *darshan*, I searched in vain high and low. The next morning it was my turn to wheel Mary in for *darshan*, and while waiting to go in I liked to do my early morning meditation sitting on the steps at the back of the Mandir (temple). As I finished that, I said to Baba "OK, I accept that there are worse things one can suffer from than cold feet". Then I opened my eyes, looked down into the bag at my feet, and lo and behold there were the socks!

It is not uncommon for Baba to grace people with little miracles such as these in order to make them believe in Him, but after that to leave them to work at sustaining their faith on their own. No doubt the fact that I had been a disciple when He was Sai Baba of Shirdi helped me to come to Him fairly easily this time round, but my conversion was nevertheless less speedy than many people's. My friend Cynthia only needed to read two books about Him in order to be immediately convinced of His divinity. When she lent them to me, I was intrigued, but the Christian brainwashing about there only being "one divine incarnation ever" made me more cautious to start with, and I have met very many Christians at the ashram whose tale is similar to my own. The book that influenced me the most initially was *A Catholic Priest Meets Sai Baba*[10]. The now deceased Mazzoleni, who was alas excommunicated

10. *A Catholic Priest Meets Sai Baba*, Mario Mazzoleni, Sri Sathya Sai Publications Trust, India.

by the Vatican for writing the book, drew to my attention the obvious question "Is it logical to believe that God can only incarnate once?" "Of course," I replied to myself, "if God is truly omnipotent....", and gradually as I experienced more and more, I realised our extraordinary good fortune in having the Lord Himself incarnate on Earth HERE AND NOW.

Soon after my return from India that first time, our son Christopher was awarded the basketball scholarship to do his degree in America, and the coach from his College flew over to watch him play before making his decision. We picked him up at Manchester airport and then drove them both up to Cumbria for the match that had been organised specially. Oh the tension! And during the game a chunk of the cheap but solid Baba ring that had been on my finger ever since my trip suddenly fell out. I took it as a sign from Baba that Christopher was being looked after, and so was not surprised when the basketball coach announced his favourable decision. But after that the *leelas* stopped; I had been hooked, and from now on it was all up to me.

Sai Baba has a great sense of humour and is a tremendous tease. Also, though He does give us what we want, He first gives us what we need, and I needed to deal with my "thing" about being ignored. In February 1998 I had my birthday at the ashram and so, though I did not expect it, I yearned particularly on that day for a look from Baba. Of course I did not get it. On my third visit, in November 2000, He took a letter from my hand for the first time. The letter contained several requests (one of which was for a job for Alice and she got one very soon after), but the main request was for a look from Him. So many people had been raving to me about the looks He had given them, and there was nothing I desired more at that moment. Well, He took the letter from me standing sideways and looking very firmly in the other direction. Being so close to Him physically even for a split second leaves one feeling churned up inside, but I had to laugh too. "I simply wouldn't be capable," I said to myself, "of taking a letter from someone like that."

So after that I stopped even hoping for a look and just tried to carry on with my *sadhana* (spiritual discipline). My fourth visit must wait till the final chapter, but my fifth visit was in January 2003, when the threat of war in Iraq was so imminent. I wrote a little letter to Baba imploring Him to stop Bush and Blair, and I took it in with me to *darshan* after *darshan*. One day I had the good fortune to be in the second row, and He stopped right in front of me. I held out the letter and He looked at it as though He was reading it. Then He raised His gaze from my hand to my eyes, looked directly into them and gave me <u>such</u> a smile. It was a smile that said "I know. I understand. Don't worry. Everything's OK.", and I promptly understood why everyone said "When He looks at you, you know that it's you He's looking at.". My friend Therese, who was sitting right next to me, said afterwards "He gave you a wonderful smile!". And of course He didn't take the letter because it seems that that war was inevitable.

My friend Cynthia had started the Hull Sai Baba group in April 1996, and we had met without fail ever since, first monthly then fortnightly. It was a great support to me throughout my last years in the Hull area, but the fluctuating numbers never grew beyond about nine members. However, another of Baba's gifts to me has been David's frequent work invitations back to Geneva. In the summer of 1999 we were once more on a two-month visit there and, thanks to the internet, I found out shortly beforehand about the Sai Baba group, which met without fail every single Thursday and also on all the Indian festival days. When I attended the first meeting, I found out to my great surprise that the group had been going for thirty years, and secondly that it had over fifty members. Also at that first meeting my eyes fell upon 'Giuseppe' – yet another gift from Baba, to whom I had been praying to let me meet one or two of my companion soulmates. As soon as this man walked into the room I knew that I knew him, I knew that we had been together many times, and I suspected that we were companion soulmates.

At the Geneva Baba group meetings they sing bhajans (devotional songs) for an hour and sometimes have discussions on spiritual subjects, but there is normally little opportunity for socialising. That year Giuseppe and I exchanged scarcely so much as a glance, but during either the second or third summer during which I was able to attend the meetings, we started occasionally to exchange smiles. The first smile he gave me let me know that the recognition was mutual, even if it was subconscious on his part, and by the fourth summer we had started to exchange the occasional odd word. Only after that did I find him in the regression to the Ticino.

According to Edgar Cayce we all have anything up to about twenty companion soulmates. These tend on the whole to be more comfortable relationships than those of twin souls. Companion soulmates are people who have shared many lives, either in sexual or in other types of family relationship, and consequently know and understand one another very well indeed. Edwin Courtenay had told me quite some time ago that one of my companion soulmates was Maria, who had been my wife and a woman of letters when I worked with Dr. John Dee during the Elizabethan era, and was now my writing guide. (It was later that I myself recognised her as my wife again in the lifetime when I knew Sai Baba of Shirdi.) I call upon her for advice and chat with her when I remember, but, unless one is very clairvoyant, it is difficult for that to seem as good as a physical presence. When later on I had a chance to participate in one or two social gatherings of the Geneva Baba group, I got to know Giuseppe a little bit and found that we had read all the same spiritual books and spoke exactly the same "language". We both have our own families and we live in different countries, but I find it nevertheless very pleasant, on the rare occasions that we meet, to feel a bond of friendship and understanding. We have done the comfortable, contented lives together, and so now we are no doubt both here to work on bigger challenges.

EXERCISES

> *By meditation we connect the little joy of the soul with the vast joy of the Spirit. Meditation should not be confused with ordinary concentration. Concentration consists in freeing the attention from distractions and focusing it on any thought in which one may be interested. Meditation is that special form of concentration in which the attention has been liberated from restlessness and is focused on God. Meditation, therefore, is concentration used to know God.*
>
> ***Paramahansa Yogananda – SRF Lessons***

1. How have you been getting on with the meditation since Section XIII? Do you sometimes keep it up for a few days and then let it lapse again? Never mind: you are in good company. But it really is worth persevering until it has become so much of a habit that your day won't feel quite right until you have started it off that way. Is it hard to find the time? Is it too much of an effort to get up any earlier? In that case your life is obviously too full, partly of the wrong things. So take a long hard look until you find something you can throw out – at least for the time being, until you have got into the habit of starting (or ending if you really prefer – both are better still!) the day with at least half an hour of meditation.

2. Do you find, if you are feeling low, that taking time off to be quiet makes you feel worse? Again, you are not alone! There is no easy way, but keeping busy in order to avoid feeling some of our pain pushes it deeper and is detrimental in the long run. Try sitting for a short time – just ten-fifteen minutes will do to start with – and really feel the pain. Let everything come to the surface: anger, frustration, grief... whatever. If tears flow, feel pleased with yourself. Then, whenever you feel ready – either straight away, or after a few days, or even a few weeks – gradually start to detach yourself. Imagine your brain being divided in half, and let one half feel the pain while the other is the observer. The real you is an eternal spark of the divine which cannot be touched by grief or pain; the mind and body are temporary clothing that you have chosen to put on for your learning. Watch what is going on in your mind and body, be thankful for what you will have learnt from it and for the karma

you will have paid through it, and let the observing bit of you open itself to the divine light. Keep repeating this exercise daily, keeping yourself conscious of the two sides of the coin. Balance the coin so that it cannot fall over on to its divine side and allow only the mind/body or Earthly side to show. Make no attempt to suppress the Earthly side and – above all – do not blame or criticise it, but over the next days, weeks, months… let the divine side pour its light on to it at the same time as observing it. If in due course you find that the coin actually wants to fall over on to its Earthly side, allowing its divine side to shine brightly, then by all means allow it to do so!

Remember that the more we persevere, the greater will be the reward.

3. Remember that keeping yourself in the presence of God does not have to be confined to your periods of meditation. You can "tune in" at any time without stopping what you are doing.

XXI
CONCLUSION

PART ONE - WHAT AM I UP TO?

Seek the wisdom that will untie your knot
seek the path that demands your whole being.
Leave that which is not, but appears to be
Seek that which is, but is not apparent.

– *Rumi*

Well, there are between twenty and thirty other lives – some satisfactory, others much less so – that I have either found or been told about, but those I have narrated here are surely enough for one volume! Reflecting on them all, and on how far back they go – the earliest, according to the well known clairvoyant Edwin Courtenay, in Lemuria, the very first civilisation on Earth - the question that comes into my mind is "What on earth am I doing still being here?" Especially if the three independent people who gave me a life as an Indian guru-type figure are right! (Two of these were on different Woolger workshops, doing what Roger calls his "10p psychic" exercise, the other was the *Nadi Gruha* in Bangalore, who guards the ancient prophecies concerning people working around Sathya Sai Baba.) How can I have gone such a long way backwards in more recent centuries? If I cannot answer this question, at least there are two things I can do: firstly give thanks for the information with which I have been graced in this lifetime, and secondly make a firm resolution never to go backwards again. Now that I have become aware that past, present and future are entirely up to me, and that the circumstances of my present life are not, as my Christian upbringing had had me believe, "the luck of the draw", I can take control and resolve finally to escape *samsara* (the cycle of worldly existence).

And perhaps you too, who have been following my story – presumably with interest or I take it that you would not have got this far – will want to make a similar resolution. Very likely you are way ahead of me anyway. But whether we start early or late like myself is unimportant – just so long as we do start. Equally unimportant is the method we use. Past life therapy and following Sai Baba happen to be the way which has suited me, but there are as many paths up the spiritual mountain as there are people to climb it.

In a moving talk at the 2003 Justice and Peace conference, the Benedictine theologian Thomas Cullinan made the point that we need to appreciate that slugs are just as much a part of God's story as are all the nice things. So do not look negatively either at the slugs in the world or at your own shadow side. Rather, recognise your shadow (go back to the exercises in Section XIV if necessary), embrace it and then shine your light on it. That special, unique and wonderful light that is the real you – the *atma* that is part of the *Paramatma*, the Supreme Soul, the Universal Self – God. Remember: Sai Baba says that the only difference between Him and us is that He knows that He is God whereas we have forgotten that we are.

Is it difficult to understand the reason why our characters can be so complex once we have got an inkling of our complex backgrounds? So many different personalities now fused into one; so many silver and gold threads woven into a tapestry of sombre colours. Or should we, rather, say "so many sombre threads woven into a background of silver and gold"? For that "place" (for want of a better word) whence we came and to which we must now aim to return is composed only of light. What is the devil but human negativity? (That is something I was very glad to learn from Sai Baba after my Christian upbringing had given me a real problem regarding the nature of "Satan"!) Would we appreciate the light so much if we had not experienced darkness? Are pain and grief not the key with which to begin the search for eternal happiness and *ananda* (bliss)?

Primo Levi, in the extraordinary book in which he recounts his experiences of the Holocaust[1], says:

---

1. *If This is a Man*, Primo Levi, translated by Stuart Woolf, Abacus, London, 1987.

For human nature is such that grief and pain – even suffered simultaneously – do not add up as a whole in our consciousness, but hide, the lesser behind the greater, according to a definite law of perspective... And this is the reason why so often in free life one hears it said than man is never content. In fact it is not a question of a human incapacity for a state of absolute happiness, but of an ever-insufficient knowledge of the complex nature of the state of unhappiness; so that the single name of a major cause is given to all its causes, which are composite and set out in an order of urgency. And if the most immediate cause of stress comes to an end, you are grievously amazed to see that another one lies behind; and in reality a whole series of others.

So that as soon as the cold, which throughout the winter had seemed our only enemy, had ceased, we became aware of our hunger; and repeating the same error, we now say "If it was not for the hunger...!"

This peeling away of the onion is observed too in past life therapy. On each workshop, or in each session with a therapist, one can lay bare another cause of the anguish. The process can be painful – in fact it can be very painful indeed – but if we carry on slumbering, repressing our pain, we will not find an escape route from *samsara.* The onion stings; it brings tears to the eyes. But oh how good it tastes when it has been roasted!

But is this the whole answer? Enlightenment, God/self-realisation, *moksha*, or Liberation (whatever you care to call it) sounds incredibly hard to achieve, and I personally cannot imagine myself being anywhere remotely near it at the moment. Is there another means of escape?

PART TWO - THE LINGAM

It was March 2002, and I was on my fourth visit to Puttaparthi, but this time I had come on my own. Two possible companions had backed out for different reasons, and I had been quite nervous about making the trip alone, but as soon as I had met a room mate at Frankfurt airport, where I changed planes, I knew for sure that the cosmic avatar was organising everything for me. To "prove" it Caroline and I found out as soon as we got talking that we were booked on the very same return flight! Could that be coincidence? (If indeed there were such a thing.) Caroline was a German doctor and homœopath, but her mother was from the French-speaking part of Belgium, so we had no difficulty in communicating. I even did my first regression in French with her one day during the month's stay. Arriving at the ashram in a pair greatly reduces the chance of being housed in a dormitory or (worse!) a shed. My friend Marion and I had survived six nights in a shed shared by about sixty women when we went for Sai Baba's seventy-fifth birthday, but it was not an experience I was madly keen to repeat. This was Caroline's first visit to Puttaparthi, and she was as happy to meet someone who could show her the ropes as I was to find a room mate in advance.

My reason for choosing mid-February to mid-March this time was to be present for the major festival of Mahashivaratri and give myself a "once in a lifetime" chance of seeing the lingam emerge. Shivaratri is the night in each month when the moon is at its thinnest, and is regarded as the best time for meditation, since the moon has control over the mind. *Maha* means "great" (hence Mahatma Gandhi – great soul), and so Mahashivaratri denotes the night in the year when the moon is at its thinnest of all. The date of this varies, but it is always in either February or March. In 2002 it was on March 12th, which is quite late and getting towards the hottest time of the year in Puttaparthi, but for some reason I was determined not to wait for another year.

Mahashivaratri being the most auspicious night of the year for turning the mind towards God, it is the custom in Hindu India to fast and stay up all night. At Baba's ashram people sit up in the Hall singing bhajans, and Baba always gives a discourse. The egg-shaped lingam is the symbol of creation – a perfect shape, it symbolises the merging of the form into the formless and vice versa – and on Mahashivaratri lingams form inside Baba's body, which He brings up through his æsophagus and eventually through His mouth. (A very painful process of course, and agonising to watch.) He says that people present who see the lingam emerge are among those who will not need to be reborn. For about twenty years He stopped manifesting lingams in public on account of the pandemonium it aroused, but in 1999 He suddenly, unexpectedly, started to do it again. Hence my great desire to put up with the crowds and attend this great festival just once.

The chances of seeing the lingam emerge seemed very remote indeed, and in any case I found it impossible to imagine myself being anywhere near to God-realisation. Finding one's Self was the first step, and I had perhaps come near to doing that now, thanks to getting to know myself through exploring some of my previous lives and appreciating that we are not the body, but the next step was for the *atma* to escape *samsara* and merge with the *Paramatma* – to achieve Enlightenment as the Buddha did, and how many million miles ahead of me was he? On the other hand, I had friends who had seen the lingam emerge, and I knew that Baba was here partly to help us all to get off the world, so there seemed to be no harm in giving myself a chance and hoping.

A vain hope perhaps? Firstly, the fact that Baba had manifested the lingam in public the three previous years was no guarantee that He would do so a fourth year in a row. Secondly, there was no knowing exactly when the event would occur if it did; sometimes it had been at the time of the evening discourse, others years it had been the following morning. Thirdly, the crowds were so immense that there was no guarantee of getting into the Hall at all, and to do so would necessitate sitting in a queue outside for hours and hours. And fourthly, even if one did secure a place, one's chances of seeing the amazing sight would depend entirely on which way the heads in front of one were leaning at that particular moment.

As March 12th approached, the crowds of people arriving at the ashram grew daily. Each time that Caroline and I went to the accommodation office with our rent we were allowed to pay for two or three more nights, "and then you will have to move into a shed". The meal queues grew longer and longer, the helpings of fruit salad on which I loved to gorge myself for breakfast, grew small and smaller. My friend Agnes from Geneva, who had witnessed the emergence of the lingam both the previous years but was leaving before Shivaratri this time because she so hated the crowds, strongly advised me against even trying to get into the Hall. (Her own view had been from a standing position outside.)

Caroline, my room mate – we had by Baba's grace been permitted after all to stay in the room until our departure - was planning to get up at about 2.0 a.m. for the morning *darshan* and then queue again all morning for the afternoon one; but she was seventeen years younger than me and I probably never had her stamina anyway. And my new friend Valerie, the mother of Jon, one of the architects of the Puttaparthi hospital, was equally resigned to not seeing it, since her chair in the "patients' row" was situated immediately behind a pillar. (The "patients" are all those who are physically unable to sit on the floor.) Since, however, Valerie was busy finishing the book that Baba had asked her to write, I could not imagine the pillar posing a serious problem for her view! I was later proved right.

During the night of March 11th I woke up with a sore throat, feeling sure that I was starting a bad cold. I took some Aconite and slept a little more, then woke up again feeling even worse. When Caroline, who had asked me to pick up her white punjabi suit from the *dhobi* (washerwoman), left the room, I was just about aware of it, but later I abandoned all idea of attempting to join the *darshan* lines. I saw this cold I was getting as a sign that I was not meant to see the lingam, but that was OK since I accepted anyway that I was not ready to get off the world. I would just have to go on working at my spiritual exercises and hope to achieve a life of greater spirituality next time round.

******

It was midday, and here I was sitting bang in the middle of the Sai Kulwant Hall! Baba says "Learn to love my uncertainty", and working on this is a constant challenge for His devotees. "But my sitting here now is the most unexpected thing of all," I thought to myself, now that I at last had time to think. Because of feeling so unwell, I had got up at 7.0 - a good couple of hours later than usual – and had made no attempt to join the queue, but had simply wandered around the ashram marvelling at the vast numbers of people it now contained. I chose the route which goes past Baba's house and garden simply because both are so beautiful, and lo and behold I happened to walk past at the precise moment when He walked out of His front door (somewhat later than usual) to go towards the Hall for *darshan.* A moving sight that I had never seen before because I had hitherto always been sitting inside awaiting His appearance. Gift number one.

Then the *darshan* music started up, and oh how beautiful it was! Quite different from anything I had ever heard before (Vedic, I learnt later). I continued my wandering, absorbed in the music and almost forgetting about my sore throat. Gift number two. In due course I reached the entrance at the very back of the Hall, where a long line of women were queuing to squeeze in. These were the ones who had not made it into the *darshan* lines, where numbers are drawn for order of admittance. I stood just outside the gate for a moment, looking at them, still absorbed in the music, and then suddenly an Egyptian woman whom I had never seen before (or since!) stepped back and beckoned me to step in front of her. Like an automaton I did so and, to the justified protests of those nearby, my new friend (or rather probably old friend!) replied "She's with me.". And so I got into the Hall for the bhajans without even trying! Although I was right at the very back, I had an excellent view of Baba. Gift number three.

The Western Canteen does not open for breakfast on big festival days, so when the bhajans were over, I returned to the room for a cup of tea and some fruit, picking up Caroline's white punjabi suit on my way. Then I went to the Indian Airlines office in a vain attempt to collect our tickets, which had been taken to Bangalore to confirm our flight a couple of days later. Linda and Renny, with whom I had just made friends, had a room right next to the office, so I then called on them to get their address in London. I was greeted by an excited Linda saying "I've got you a yellow ribbon!". This was a total mystery to me, but it turned out to be gift number four. Linda soon explained that Baba had decided to give three hundred good places in the Hall to Westerners. A group of Latin Americans had taken charge of this, and had purchased yellow ribbons for the lucky three hundred to wear round their necks as "badges". Further instructions were that everyone in the group should dress entirely in white, and that they should assemble outside the temple at the back of the Hall at eleven o'clock. I told Linda that I did not have anything white to wear apart from Caroline's punjabi suit, and we agreed that Caroline would not mind my borrowing it. Gift number five. There remained the question of a white shawl[2], but Linda was sure I had time to get one in the ashram shop. So I rushed off there as fast I could, and fortunately they had some in stock. Gift number six. I then decided that I still just had time to return to the room and eat the two samosas I had purchased in the Northern Indian Canteen the previous day in case I did not feel up to joining the very long lunch queue. This was gift number seven because we were supposed to fast from midday, which I would have found difficult after my simple breakfast of fruit.

All that done, I joined the large group of white-robed, yellow-ribboned women outside the mandir. They were trying to sort everyone into countries and, as I was the only English woman there, I kept getting pushed to the back. Since I speak Spanish, it was quite a big temptation to pretend to be Latin American, but I told myself that it was no good trying to get in to the see the lingam by dishonest means! One by one each national group was let through into the Hall, and when finally there were only a handful of us left, the *Seva Dals* (service people) suddenly put up a rope saying that they were not sure that there was any room left and we should wait. I told myself that I was in Baba's hands and, since I had never expected to get in anyway, there was no reason for disappointment. Then suddenly, however, the rope was dropped and the last few of us there allowed through. Gift number eight.

Once one has secured a place in the Hall by putting one's seat down, it is possible to come and go. This is not a thing to be greatly recommended among such huge crowds, but since I was starting what developed after I had got home into a massive chest infection, I was better off lying on the bed in my room than sitting on the floor. I made sure, however, to be safely back in my seat before the start of the evening bhajans and discourse.

The first speaker mentioned in his speech that Baba said that those who saw the lingam emerge from His mouth would not need to be reborn. So it seemed that this did not, as my friend Valerie had been fearing, apply only to those who had seen the lingam in 1999. "But how small," I said to myself, "are the chances among this great sea of people – especially when one is this far back. Anyway, no-one knows for sure whether He will do it again this year. And if He does, there's no knowing when it might be. It could be within the next hour or so, or it could be early tomorrow

---

2. All the women in the ashram who are not dressed in saris are obliged to wear shawls for *darshan*.

morning before I've managed to get up. Besides, whatever chance could there be of my seeing it? I can't possibly be ready to get off the world. Of course they do say that God's grace is always there for the asking.... But what have I done to deserve such a huge gift as that? Nothing! It would be wonderful to be able to help from the other side after this life of mine is over, but surely I haven't paid nearly all my debts yet. Ah well, never mind, it's still a wonderful experience to be inside this Hall on such as auspicious occasion – especially after not even trying to get in. I can hardly ask for gift number nine when I've already been given so much today!"

Finally Baba began His discourse. Sometimes it was just possible to move my head in such a way as to be able to see Him; at other times it was quite impossible. In any case several of the women around me were becoming more and more unruly. One was used to the Indian peasants who came in from the nearby villages for the big festivals behaving in a most unladylike way, but now it was Westerners too – many of them, that is – who were being extraordinarily selfish. Everyone knows that standing or even kneeling in the Hall is strictly forbidden, yet now the poor *Seva Dals* had an impossible task trying to control everybody. "It's no use," I said to myself, "trying to see the lingam by being selfish. Anyway, would it work? Surely not! One has to be pretty saintly to get off the world!" I looked one by one at the faces around me. Some were peaceful and serene, some were agitated, some were positively aggressive. I felt that it was easy to guess which were the women who deserved to see the amazing sight should it happen.

Baba finished His discourse and sat down. Now it was even more difficult to see Him. The bhajans started; the excitement and agitation grew still further. Suddenly Baba took a sip of water and put His hand to his throat. Then a whole bunch of women on my right suddenly shot across in front of me, pushing themselves aggressively into position and forming a solid wall of heads through which it was impossible to glimpse a single thing. "Never mind. I always knew the chances were incredibly remote," I consoled myself. "Acceptance of what IS. That's my big lesson. That's what I must remember." Then, equally suddenly, a German woman just in front of me who had an exceptionally sweet face moved across into the space that had just been made by the aggressive group. Instinctively I followed her. Now there was a pillar blocking my view of Baba, but sometimes by leaning my head one way or the other I could just catch a glimpse. But by now no-one seemed able any more to remain seated. Against my will I found myself too bobbing up and down. "It's no good trying to see the lingam emerge by being selfish," I again reminded myself, forcing myself down, but again repeatedly bobbing up just for a second. "Will I see it? Won't I see it? IT DOESN'T MATTER. He is the doer. Only His Will matters.

Fifteen months ago He took from my hand a letter in which I surrendered my life to Him. I MUST REMEMBER THAT!"......

EXERCISES

Do you ever think about whether you want to finish your incarnations on Earth? Perhaps you are less selfish than I am and want to keep coming back to help others. Whatever is the case, perhaps now would be a good moment to take stock of your life. (However young you are, it is never too soon!)

1. Do you feel that you have found your chief purpose for this lifetime? We generally have one main purpose and several secondary ones, and we differ greatly in the length of time we take to discover our purpose. If you are not a hundred per cent sure yet why you are here, do not worry about it, but just remain open to any signs/ suggestions that might come your way. (It took two and a half years for Lawrence's suggestion that I write a book to sink in fully, and after he had urged me to study the question of reincarnation in greater depth, it took a further five years before I decided to train in regression therapy.)

2. Are you aware of having been paying certain debts in your lifetime? These could be financial (do you always find it hard to make ends meet?), or they could be in relationships. Have you ever been badly hurt by someone in a manner which you felt to be totally unfair and unjustified? Try to appreciate that nothing ever happens without a reason, and that if you are now prepared to say "Yes" rather than "No" to what happened, you are thereby cancelling a karmic debt that you had either to that person him or herself or to somebody else (possibly someone not at present known to you).

3. Look back now over your life and think about anything that you would like to be able to rectify. If there is someone with whom it is not possible for some reason to rectify things, don't worry about it. Just tell them mentally that you are sorry about what happened and then FORGIVE YOURSELF. That is often the hardest thing to do, but keep working at it! You may well be able to pay your debt by helping someone else. There is always so much we can do. For instance, if you feel bad about saying "No" to a beggar ("because he/she would only go and spend it on drink or drugs"), give a little something to a charity that is dear to your heart. And may the Lord be with you as He/She always is, whether you are aware of it or not.

